# POLAND'S INTERNATIONAL AFFAIRS 1919-1960

# POLAND'S

# INTERNATIONAL

# AFFAIRS 1919-1960

A Calendar of Treaties, Agreements, Conventions, and Other International Acts, with Annotations, References, and Selections from Documents and Texts of Treaties

## by STEPHAN HORAK

INDIANA UNIVERSITY PUBLICATIONS
RUSSIAN AND EAST EUROPEAN SERIES
VOLUME 31

*Published by*
Indiana University · Bloomington
1964

Russian and East European Series
Russian and East European Institute
Indiana University
Volume 31

All orders should be addressed to the

Indiana University Press
10th and Morton Streets
Bloomington, Indiana

Library of Congress Catalog Card Number: 64-63009
Printed in the United States of America

CONTENTS

Documents Issued, 1945

# INTRODUCTION

With the growing interest in studies of East and Central Europe, the need has arisen for an increasing number of publications, especially basic reference materials, that may serve existing study programs and assist further research in this field. The purpose of this volume is to help students of international affairs and of Polish affairs identify the international agreements in which Poland participated. Historians, specialists on international law, and economists may also find this Calendar of Treaties very helpful in their writings and teaching.

This book contains almost a complete list of bilateral treaties and a selection of multilateral treaties which have been important for the existence and activity of the Polish state on the international scene. The period evaluated includes inter-war Poland as well as the People's Republic of Poland (1945-1960). This coverage makes possible a comparison of the activity of the Polish state in two different world political systems, that of free European states (1919-1939) and that of Soviet-American rivalry (1945- ).

To assist the reader in the use of this Calendar, a brief explanation of the principles by which agreements were compiled and listed may be useful. In some cases, it was necessary to include a series of agreements in order to indicate the future fate of given treaties. Thus, the individual treaties are arranged chronologically, for the most part.

The main body of each entry consists of the following: (1) Name of the country-partner; (2) Title of the given treaty; (3) Date of signature (S); (4) Date of ratification or exchange of ratification documents (R); (5) Duration of treaty (D); (6) Annulment (A); (7) Abbreviated sources or other secondary material; (8) Annotations. In some cases names of signatories are given. Secondary sources which do not give a complete text are placed in brackets. A key to abbreviations of the literature is given directly before Part I. Besides treaties, this Calendar also presents the more important declarations, communiqués, and other forms of state activity, especially for the period, 1945-1960.

IX

      This work is analogous to that of R. M. Slusser and J. F.
Triska, A Calendar of Soviet Treaties, 1917-1957, (Stanford,
1959), and is based in part on the list of Poland's treaties which
I originally compiled as part of Osteuropa-Handbuch Polen(Köln,
1959), edited by Werner Markert. However, that list is very
selected and incomplete.

      The basic sources used in this volume are the following:
Dziennik Ustaw Rzeczypospolitej Polskiej; League of Nations,
Treaty Series; United Nations, Treaty Series; and Nouveau
Recueil (NRGT).

      Part II of this volume presents selections from the texts
of the most significant treaties for both periods of the history
of modern Poland. Except for the Warsaw Pact, all agreements
quoted are bilateral. Since the scope of this work made it im-
possible to present excerpts from all of Poland's treaties, I
attempted to select those that seemed to me of greatest significance.

      Selections from the most important documents dealing
with the re-emergence of the Polish state at the time of World
War I and following World War II are to be found in Part III of
this volume. Many of them have never before been  translated
into English; therefore, they may be of value to scholars who
do not command Polish.

      Finally, I wish to express my sincere thanks to all who
have shown interest in the progress of this work, notably to
Professors Piotr S. Wandycz, Vaclav L. Benes, and W. J. Wag-
ner of Indiana University, who kindly read the manuscript and
offered critical comments and recommendations for improvement of this collection and to Miss Merikay Wiley for the editing
of the manuscript. I am also deeply indebted to Professor John
M. Thompson, Director of the Russian and East European Institute at Indiana University, who greatly encouraged me in the decisive stage of preparing the manuscript for publication by the
Indiana University Press.

      A grant-in-aid of research from Indiana University pro-
vided the funds necessary for completion of this work.

August 1963                                     S. H.

# BIBLIOGRAPHY AND KEY TO ABBREVIATIONS

AFR      Documents on American Foreign Relations. Boston, Mass. World Peace Foundation. vols. 1-12. 1939-1950.

AHE      Aussenhandelserlasse. Frankfurt/M. (Beilage zu:) Nachrichten für den Aussenhandel. Hrsg. Deutscher Wirtschaftsdienst Köln, Jg. 12 1949 ff.

American J.      American Journal of International Law. Washington, D.C.

AÖ      Aussenhandelsdienst der Handelskammer Niederösterreich. Wien, 1950 ff.

Arch. VR      Archiv des Völkerrechts. Tübingen vol. 1. 1948/49 ff.

BAZ      Bundesanzeiger. Ed. by the Ministry of Justice. Köln, 1949-.

BCB      Bulletin Commercial Belge. Bruxelles.

British S.P.      British and Foreign State Papers. London.

BGRO      Bundesgesetzblatt der Republik Österreich. Wien.

BNS      Bulgarian News Summary. Edited by the Bulgarian National Committee. Washington, D.C., 1945 ff.

BOT      Board of Trade Journal. London.

BSE, 1958      Ezhegodnik Bolshoi Sovetskoi Entsiklopedii, 1958.

BT      Bulletin trimestriel. Banque Centrale de la Republique de la Turquie. Ankara.

Ciechanowski      Ciechanowski, Jan, Defeat in Victory. New York, 1947.

Czechoslovak Sources     Czechoslovak Sources and Documents:
                         No. 2, Struggle for Freedom. New
                         York, 1943.

DCW                      Destiny Can Wait. The Polish Air Force
                         in the Second World War. London, 1949.

DDR                      Dokumente zur Aussenpolitik der Regie-
                         rung der Deutschen Demokratischen
                         Republik. vol. 1. Berlin, 1954.

Degras                   Degras, Jane. Soviet Documents on
                         Foreign Policy, 1917-1941. 3 vols.
                         New York, 1951-53.

Dewar                    Dewar, M.: Soviet Trade with Eastern
                         Europe 1945-1949. London, 1951.

DG                       Danzieger Gesetzblatt. Danzig, 1920- .

DIA                      Documents on International Affairs.
                         London, Oxford University Press.

Documents                Documents on Polish-Soviet Relations,
                         1939-1945. General Sikorski Historical
                         Institute. London, 1961.

Dokumenty                Dokumenty Československe. zahranični
                         polityky, 1945-1960. Praha, 1960.

DpA                      Der Polnische Aussenhandel. Warsaw.

D. S. Bull.              The Department of State Bulletin. Wash-
                         ington.

DURP                     Dziennik Ustaw Rzeczypospolitej Polskiej.
                         Warsaw, 1919-1939, 1945-1960.

L'Echo                   L'Echo de l'Industrie. Luxemburg.

EGS                      Eidgenössische Gesetzessammlung.
                         Bern.

ETA                      Economic Treaties and Agreements of
                         the Soviet Bloc in Eastern Europe 1945-
                         1951. Mid-European Studies Center.
                         New York, 1952.

Eur. Arch.               Europa-Archiv. Frankfurt/M. Jg. 1.
                         1946/47- .

FDN                      Frau Department och Namnder. Stock-
                         holm.

Financial Times.     London.

Freund     Freund, Heinrich: Russlands Friedens-
und Handelsverträge 1918-1923. Berlin,
1924.

FS     Forex Service. Zurich.

Handelsblatt.     Deutsche Wirtschafts-zeitung. Düssel-
dorf.

Heike     Heike, O. Das Deutschtum in Polen,
1918-1939. Bonn, 1955.

Hoetzsch     Dokumente zur Weltpolitik der Nach-
kriegszeit. In Gemeinschaft mit W.
Bertram herausgegeben von Otto Hoetzsch.
Heft 6: Der Europäische Osten. Leipzig-
Bln. 1933.

IC     Supplément aux Informations Commerciales Belge. Brussels, 1955- .

Inf.     Informazioni per il Commerio Estere.
Roma.

IW     Internationale Wirtschaft. Wien.

Izvestiia     Izvestiia. U. S. S. R. Government. Moscow.

Jaworski     Jaworski, Kazimierz and K. Blaszczyński. Zmartwychstanie Polski w. świetle
dokumentów. Poznań, 1928.

JCEA     Journal of Central European Affairs.
Edited by S. Harrison Thomson. University of Colorado 1 (1941) ff.

Jóźwiak     Jóźwiak, Franciszek: Polska Partja
Robotnicza w walce o wyzwolenie na-
rodowe i spoleczne. Warsaw, 1952.

Keesing's CA     Keesing's Contemporary Archives; Week-
ly Diary of Important World Events.
London.

Kliuchnikov     Kliuchnikov, J. i A. Sabanin: Mezhdu-
narodnaia politika noveishego vremeni
v dogovorakh, notakh i deklaratsiiakh.
Moscow, 1925-1929. 3 vols.

Komarnicki     Komarnicki, Titus. Rebirth of the

Polish Republic: A Study in the Diplomatic History of Europe 1914-1920. London, 1957.

Korolenko      Korolenko, A. S.: Torgovye dogovory i soglasheniia SSSR s inostrannymi gosudarstvami. Moscow, 1953.

LB      Livre blanc sur les procédés agressifs des gouvernements de l'URSS, de Pologne, de Tchechoslovaquie, de Hongrie, de Roumanie, de Bulgarie et de l'Albanie envers la Yougoslavie. Belgrade, 1951.

LKD      Lovtidende for Koneriget Danmark. Kobenhavn.

LNTS      League of Nations, Treaty Series. Geneva.

Makowski      Makowski, Julian, Zobowiazania między-narodowe Polski, 1919-1929. Warsaw, 1929.

Meissner      Meissner, Boris: Das Ostpakt-System. Dokumentensammlung, T. 1. Das Sowjetische Paktsystem in Europa. Hamburg, 1951.

MELP      Mid-European Law Project: Economic Treaties and Agreements of the Soviet Bloc in Eastern Europe, 1945-1951, 2nd ed. New York, 1952, pp. 87-89.

MO      Moniteur Officiel du Commerce et de l'Industrie. Paris, vol. 63. 1945- .

MoHeAPol      Monatshefte für auswärtige Politik. Hamburg-Berlin, Jg. 1-10 1934-1943.

ND      Neues Deutschland. Berlin.

NfA      Neue Nachrichten für Aussenhandel. Berlin.

NRGT      Nouveau Recueil Général des Traités et autres actes relatifs aux rapports de droit international. Continuation du Grand Recueil de G. Fr. de Martens par Heinrich Triepel. 3. Serie Göttingen 1909-1944.  41 vols.

NT — New Times. Moscow.

NU — Norges Utenrikshandel.  Oslo.

NZZ — Neue Zurcher Zeitung.  Zürich.  Jg. 166. 1945 ff.

Official Documents — Official Documents Concerning Polish-German and Polish-Soviet Relations, 1933-1939.  The Polish White Book. London, n. d.

PDB — Pressedienst.  Herausgegeben von der Presseabteilung der Militar-Mission der Volksrepublik Polen beim Alliierten Kontrollrat in Deutschland.  Berlin, 1945 ff.

Pravda — Pravda.  Communist Party of the S. U. Moscow.

Press Release — Polish Embassy, Press Office.  Washington D. C.

PV — Politische Verträge.  Eine Sammlung von Urkunden.  Hrsg. von V. Bruns. Bearb. von Georg von Gretschaninov. Berlin, 1936-1942. 3 vols.

QuPV — Quellen für Politik und Völkerrecht. Hrsg. von W. Cornides und E. Menzel. Oberursel vol. 1, 1948.

Reshetar — Reshetar, J. N.: The Ukrainian Revolution.  Princeton, 1952.

RGBl — Reichsgesetzblatt.  Teil 2, Berlin 1919-1939.

Ronnefart — Konferenzen und Verträge.  Vertrags-Ploetz.  Ein Handbuch geschichtlich bedeutender Zusammenkunfte, Vereinbarungen, Manifeste und Memoranden. Teil 2: Bielefeld, 1953.

Sbornik (SDD) — Sbornik deistvuiushchikh dogovorov, soglashenii i konventsii zakliuchennykh RSFSR s inostrannymi gosudarstvami. Vyp. 1-5, Moscow, 1921-23; Vyp 1-7,

|  |  |
|---|---|
|  | Moscow, 1924-1933. |
| SBZ | Sbirka zakonu ........ Prague, 1920- . |
| Shelukhyn | Shelukhyn, S.: Varshavskii dohovir mizh poliakamy i Petliuroiu. Praha, 1926. |
| SFP | Soviet Foreign Policy During the Patriotic War. London, n. d., 2 vols. |
| SGBO | Sammlung der Gesetze des Bundesstaates Österreich. Wien, 1919. |
| SGVCS | Sammlung der Gesetze und Verordnungen des Tschechoslowakischen Staates. Prague, 1920-1938. |
| Sluzbene Novine | Sluzbene Novine Kraljevine Jugoslavije. Journal Officiel du Royaume de Yougoslavie. Belgrad, 1929-1941. |
| Sobranie | Sobranie zakonov i razporiazhenii pravitel'stva SSSR. Moscow, 1933-1940. |

Sprawy Międzynarodowe. Warsaw, 1947- .

| Times | The London Times. London. |
|---|---|
| Taracouzio | Taracouzio T.A.: List of Treaties entered into by the Soviets. In: The Soviet Union and International Law. New York, 1935. S. 450-80. |
| Trybuna Ludu | Trybuna Ludu. Polish Communist Party. Warsaw. |
| UNTS | United Nations, Treaty Series. New York, 1946- . |
| Ust. Gosp. | Ustawodawstwo Gospodarcze, Warsaw, 1945 ff. |
| Vilna | Question de Vilna. Documents diplomatiques de conflict Polono-Lithuanienne 1918-1921. Kaunas, 1924. |
| VPSS | Vneshniaia politika Sovetskogo Soiuza. Dokumenty i materialy. Moscow, 1949-1953. |
| VPSS (V) | Vneshniaia politika Sovetskogo Soiuza |

|                   |                                                                                                                                                                                                |
|-------------------|------------------------------------------------------------------------------------------------------------------------------------------------------------------------------------------------|
|                   | vo vremia Velikoi Otechestvennoi Voiny. Moscow, 1944-45.                                                                                                                                        |
| VVS               | Vedomosti Verkhovnogo Soveta SSSR. Moscow.                                                                                                                                                      |
| VWD               | Vereinigte Wirtschaftsdienste. Frankfurt/M.                                                                                                                                                     |
| VT                | Vneshniaia Torgovlia. Moscow.                                                                                                                                                                   |
| Wandycz           | Wandycz, Piotr S., France and Her Eastern Allies 1919-1925; French-Czechoslovak-Polish Relations from the Paris Conference to Locarno. Minneapolis, 1962.                                       |
| Wandycz (II)      | _____, Czechoslovak-Polish Confederation and the Great Powers, 1940-43. Indiana University Press, 1956.                                                                                  |
| WD                | Wissenschaftlicher Dienst Südosteuropa. Quellen und Berichte über Staat, Verwaltung, Recht, Bevölkerung, Wirtschaft, Wissenschaft und Veröffentiichungen in Südosteuropa. Südost-Institut München. Jg. 1.1952. |
| WPA               | War and Peace Aims of the United Nations. Boston, Mass. vol. 1 (1939-42). 1943, vol. 2 (1943/45). 1948.                                                                                         |
| Zbiór dok         | Zbiór dokumentów. Warsaw, 1948.                                                                                                                                                                 |
| Zbiór traktatów   | Zbiór traktatów handlowych Rzeczypospolitej Polskiej. Warsaw, 1924.                                                                                                                             |
| Zbiór Umów        | Zbiór umów międzynarodowych PRL za lata 1957-58. Warsaw, 1959                                                                                                                                   |
| Zbiór Umów        | Zbiór umów międzynarodowych PRL 1960. Warsaw, 1962.                                                                                                                                             |
| ZOR               | Zeitschrift für Ostrecht. In Gemeinschaft mit der Deutschen Gesellschaft zum Studium Osteuropas, herausgegeben von Osteuropa-Institut in Breslau. Berlin 1 (1926)- .                            |
| ZTKH              | Zbiór traktatów i konwencyj handlowych zawartych przez Polskę. Recueil des                                                                                                                      |

traites et conventions commerciales
condues par la Pologne.   Warsaw, 1921- .

Żyzie Warszawy.        Warsaw.

# POLAND'S INTERNATIONAL AFFAIRS 1919-1960

# Part I

# CALENDAR OF TREATIES

POLISH REPUBLIC, 1919-1939

(Rzeczpospolita Polska)

The Polish Republic was formed on November 14, 1918,
after the surrender of the state's supreme power to Józef Pilsudski by the Regency Council.  In a memorandum of November 16,
1918, Pilsudski, as Provisional Head of the State, notified the
European governments of the foundation of the Polish State.

-1919-

FRANCE, GREAT BRITAIN, ITALY, JAPAN, USA.
Treaty Concerning the Recognition of the Independence of
Poland and the Protection of Minorities.
S:    June 28, 1919, Versailles.
R:    January 10, 1920, Versailles.
      DURP, 1920, No. 110, p. 1933; NRGT, vol. 13, p. 504.

At the same time, the agreement provided foundations
for future trade, customs, consular, and transport agreements.
The Minorities Treaty provides:  Art. 2:  Poland undertakes to
assure complete protection of life and liberty to all inhabitants
of Poland without distinction of birth, nationality, language, race,
or color.  All inhabitants of Poland shall be entitled to the free
exercise, either public or private, of any creed, religion, or
belief whose practices are not inconsistent with public order or
public morals.  Art. 7:  All Polish nationals shall be equal before the law and enjoy the same civil and political rights without discrimination of race, language, or religion.  Differences
of religion, creed, or confession shall not prejudice any Polish
national on matters relating to the enjoyment of civil or political
rights, such as, admission to public employment, functions, and
honors, or the exercise of professions and industries.  No restriction shall be imposed on the free use of any language by any
Polish national in private intercourse, in commerce, in religion,
in the press, in publications of any kind, or in public meetings.
Notwithstanding the establishment of an official language by the
Polish government, adequate facilities shall be given to Polish
nationals of non-Polish speech for the use of their language, either

orally or in writing, before the courts.   Arts.  8 and 9 guarantee
equal educational opportunities in the public  minorities' schools.

On September 13, 1934, the Polish Foreign Minister,
Józef Beck, on the forum of the League of Nations, announced
Poland's refusal to collaborate with the league under the articles of the Minorities Treaty and asked, at the same time, for
establishment of a unified system of international protection of
minorities' rights.

PRINCIPAL ALLIED, ASSOCIATED POWERS AND GERMANY.
Peace Treaty.
S:     June 28, 1919, Versailles.
R:     By Poland, September 1, 1919.
       DURP, 1920, No. 35; RGB1, 1919, No. 140; NRGT, vol.
       11, p. 323.

PRINCIPAL ALLIED, ASSOCIATED POWERS AND AUSTRIA.
Peace Treaty.
S:     September 10, 1919, Saint Germain.
R:     By Poland, August 28, 1924.
Became effective:   July 16, 1920.
       DURP, 1925, No. 17, p. 114; SGBO, 1920, No. 90, p. 995;
       NRGT, vol. 11, p. 691.

PRINCIPAL ALLIED, ASSOCIATED POWERS AND STATES
WHICH SUCCEEDED THE FORMER AUSTRIA-HUNGARY.
Agreement Concerning the Payment of "Liberation Tax" by the
States Which Succeeded the Former Austria-Hungary.
S:     September 10, 1919.
       NRGT, vol. 14, p. 40.

Also Declaration of December 8, 1919, concerning the
realization of the Agreement.

AUSTRIA.
Trade Protocol.
S:     September 24, 1919, Warsaw.
       Hereto:
Trade Agreement.
S:     March 17, 1920, Warsaw;
Additional Protocol to the Agreement.
S:     January 8, 1921, Warsaw.
       Makowski, p. 10; LNTS, vol. 7, p. 182.

GERMANY.
Treaty Concerning the Release of Imprisoned Persons and
Securing the Amnesty (Amnesty Treaty).
S:   October 1, 1919, Berlin.
R:   October 23, 1919, Warsaw.
     DURP, 1922, No. 11, p. 179; RGBl, 1919, No. 205; NRGT,
     vol. 16, p. 330.
Supplement Protocol
S:   November 23, 1920.
     NRGT, vol. 16, p. 407.
     Hereto:
Supplement Treaty.
S:   February 12, 1921, Berlin.
R:   December 5, 1921, Warsaw, with exchange of notes on
     April 4 and May 10, 1921.
     DURP, 1922, No. 11; RGBl, No. 75; NRGT,  vol. 16,
     p. 333.

GERMANY.
Agreement Concerning the Military Evacuation of the Ceded
Territories and the Surrender of Civil Administration, with
Two Protocols to the Agreement (January 8, 1920; January 9,
1920).
S:   November 25, 1919, Berlin.
     NRGT, Vol. 16, p. 346; Makowski, pp. 141-143.
     Hereto:
Agreement Concerning Evacuation by Germany and the Pro-
visional Establishment by Poland of the Demarcation Line.
S:   January 11, 1920, Paris.
     NRGT, vol. 16, p. 387; Makowski, p. 144.

PRINCIPAL ALLIED, ASSOCIATED POWERS AND BULGARIA.
Peace Treaty.
S:   November 27, 1919, Neuilly-sur-Seine.
R:   By Poland, December 9, 1920.
     NRGT, vol. 12, p. 323.

-1920-

AUSTRIA.
Agreement Concerning the Problem of Taxes for Properties
Located in Both Countries and Owned by Their Citizens.
S:   January 9, 1920, Vienna.
     LNTS, vol. 7, p. 164; Makowski, p. 11.

UKRAINIAN NATIONAL REPUBLIC (PETLIURA).
Political Convention; Military Convention.
S:     April 21, 1920, Warsaw.
         Shelukhyn, pp. 10, 28; (Reshetar, pp. 301, 307).

         Both conventions were annulled by the Peace Treaty of
Riga, March 18, 1921.


PRINCIPAL ALLIED, ASSOCIATED POWERS AND HUNGARY.
Peace Treaty.
S:     June 4, 1920, Trianon.
R:     By Poland, July 26, 1921.
         NRGT, vol. 12, p. 423.
         Hereto:
Agreement Concerning the Liquidation of the Austro-Hungarian
Bank (In Accordance with Article 206 of this Peace Treaty).
S:     March 14, 1922, Vienna.
         Makowski, p. 11.


FRANCE, GREAT BRITAIN, ITALY, JAPAN, USA, CZECHO-
SLOVAKIA.
Decision of the Conference of Ambassadors Concerning Teschen,
Spiš, and Orava.
S:     July 28, 1920, Paris.
         NRGT, vol. 15, p. 100.
         The Principal Allied and Associated Powers had re-
solved in a decision of September 27, 1919, to fix the political status of the former Duchy of Teschen and the territories
of Orava and Spiš through a popular expression of opinion.
The Plebiscite was, however, abandoned. Accordingly, in
virtue of the convention of July 10, 1920, the Principal Allied,
acting as the Conference of Ambassadors, formulated a decision on July 28 and issued a decree on August 5, 1920, which
fixed the frontier lines in the districts of Teschen, Orava, and
Spiš. On December 2, 1921, the Conference of Ambassadors
decided to proceed to set a line, which was contested by the
parties. The Permanent Court of International Justice ruled
that the decision concerning the Jaworzina boundary of July
28, 1920, was to be treated as definitive. The consequent
protocol, drawn at Cracow on May 6, 1924, and approved by
the Conference of Ambassadors, September 5, carried out
the Council's recommendations.

PRINCIPAL ALLIED, ASSOCIATED POWERS AND TURKEY.
Peace Treaty.
S:    August 10, 1920, Sevres.
       NRGT, vol. 12, p. 667.
              Treaty was never ratified.

FRANCE, GREAT BRITAIN, ITALY, JAPAN, USA, YUGO-
SLAVIA, RUMANIA, CZECHOSLOVAKIA.
Agreement Concerning the Boundaries of the States Which
Succeeded the Former Austria-Hungary.
S:    August 10, 1920, Sevres.
R:    Only by Great Britain.
       NRGT, vol. 12, p. 815.

GERMANY.
Agreement Concerning the Transfer of Legal Responsibilities.
S:    September 20, 1920, Poznan.
R:    November 30, 1920, Berlin.
       DURP, 1920, No. 120, p. 2112; RGB1, 1920, No. 235,
       p. 2043; NRGT, vol. 16, p. 389.

LITHUANIA
Provisional Cease-fire Agreement.
S:    October 1, 1920, Suwalki.
       NRGT, vol. 24, p. 52.

LITHUANIA.
Agreement Concerning the Demarcation Line, Exchange of
Prisoners.
S:    October 7, 1920, Suwalki.
       LNTS, vol. 8, p. 174.

              The agreement ceased to exist on October 9, 1920,
because of the occupation of Vilna by Polish troops under General Żeligowski.

RUSSIAN SFSR, UKRAINIAN SSR, BELORUSSIAN SSR (REPRE-
SENTED BY RSFSR).
Preliminary Treaty and Protocol.  Peace and Armistice Con-
ditions.
S:    October 12, 1920, Riga.
R:    November 2, 1920, Libau.
       DURP, 1921, No. 28, p. 331; Sbornik 1 (1921), No. 14,
       p. 63; NRGT, vol. 13, p. 120; LNTS, vol. 4, p. 8.

Also: Supplementing Protocol Concerning the Carrying Out of Article 1 of the Protocol Regarding the Extension of Armistice. Repatriation Agreement.
S:     February 24, 1921, Riga.
       Sbornik 2 (1921), No. 54, p. 63; NRGT, vol. 13, p. 129; LNTS, vol. 4, p. 177.

FREE CITY OF DANZIG (GDAŃSK).
Agreement Concerning General Relations.
S:     November 9, 1920.
       DURP, 1922, No. 13, p. 218; NRGT, vol. 14, p. 45; LNTS, vol. 6, p. 189 and vol. 107, p. 459.

       This Agreement verified, according to Article 40, paragraph 2, the establishment of the Free City of Danzig by the decision of the Ambassadors' Conferences on October 27, 1920, and November 15, 1920.
       Hereto:
Agreement Concerning the Execution and Supplementing of the Agreement.
S:     October 24, 1921, Warsaw.
R:     December 31, 1921, Gdańsk.
       LNTS, vol. 116, p. 5.
Arrangement for the Execution of Article 61 of the Agreement of October 24, 1921.
S:     February 14, 1924, Gdańsk.
R:     February 4, 1925, Gdańsk.
       DURP, 1925, No. 41, Annex.

LITHUANIA.
Armistice Protocol.
S:     November 29, 1920, Kaunas.
       LNTS, vol. 9, p. 64; Makowski, pp. 105-106.

       Creation of the neutral zone between Poland and Lithuania.

GERMANY.
Agreement Concerning Restitution of German Ships.
S:     November 2, 1920, Bromberg.
       LNTS, vol. 2, pt. 4, p. 278.

GERMANY.
Protocol Concerning Exchange of Prisoners.

S:    November 23, 1920, Berlin.
D:    Six months.
      LNTS, vol. 2, pt. 4, p. 296.

-1921-

GERMANY.
Agreement Concerning the Preparation of Plebiscite of the
Inhabitants of Upper Silesia.
S:    January 20, 1921, Opole.
      RGB1, 1921, No. 12; NRGT, vol. 16, p. 409.

FRANCE.
Agreement on Political Relations.
S:    February 19, 1921, Paris.
R:    June 27, 1922, Paris.
      DURP, 1922, No. 63, p. 1115; NRGT, vol. 12, p. 880;
      LNTS, vol. 18, p. 11.

      For text of Military Convention see:  Wandycz, Piotr
S., France and Her Eastern Allies, 1919-1925, pp. 394-395.

RSFSR, UKRAINIAN SSR.
Convention Concerning Repatriation.
S:    February 24, 1921, Riga.
      LNTS, vol. 4, p. 177.

RUMANIA.
Defense Alliance.
S:    March 3, 1921, Bucharest.
R:    July 25, 1921, Bucharest.
      DURP, 1921, No. 81, p. 1472; NRGT, vol. 12, p. 881;
      LNTS, vol. 7, p. 78.

RSFSR, UKRAINIAN SSR, BELORUSSIAN SSR.
Peace Treaty.
S:    March 18, 1921, Riga.
R:    April 30, 1921, Minsk.
      DURP, 1921, No. 49, p. 813; Sbornik 1 (1924), No. 20,
      p. 121; NRGT, vol. 13, p. 141; LNTS, vol. 6, p. 52.
      Hereto:
Protocol and Instructions for the Armistice Commission to
Settle the Border Incidents.
S:    June 1, 1921.

Supplementing Protocol.
S:    January 24, 1922, Warsaw.
      Sbornik 2 (1925), No. 55.

        An attempt by the RSFSR to conclude at the Disarmament
Conference in Moscow (December, 1922) a Non-Aggression Pact
and Arbitration Agreement with the countries of Poland, Estonia,
Finland, and Latvia has failed.  Text of the Soviet Russian
Draft Treaty of December 8, 1922:
      Kliuchnikov, vol 3, No. 1, p. 211; PV, vol. 1, p. 119.

GERMANY, FREE CITY OF DANZIG.
Transit Agreement.
S:    April 21, 1921, Paris.
R:    April 27, 1921, Paris.
      DURP, 1922, No. 61, p. 1036; RGBl, 1921, No. 83, p. 95;
      NRGT, vol. 16, p. 414; LNTS, vol. 12, p. 62.

AUSTRIA.
Agreements Concerning Seasonal Workers.
S:    June 24, 1921, Cracow.
R:    March 16, 1922, Vienna.
      Makowski, p. 11.

RUMANIA.
Trade Treaty with Postal Agreement.
S:    July 1, 1921, Bucharest.
R:    November 15, 1922, Warsaw.
D:    One year with automatic extension.
      DURP, 1922, No. 103, p. 1716; NRGT, vol. 20, p. 519.

      Denounced by Rumania:  May 31, 1930.

GERMANY.
Arbitration Agreement.
S:    September 29, 1921, Geneva.
      DURP, 1921, No. 90, p. 1665; RGBl, 1921, No. 116, and
      1923, No. 22, NRGT, vol. 17, p. 751.
      Hereto:
Liquidation Agreement in Connection with the Young Plan.
S:    October 31, 1929, Warsaw.
R:    April 21, 1931, Warsaw.
      DURP, 1931, No. 90; RGBl, 1930, No. 8.
Agreement Concerning the Annulment of German-Polish Arbi-
tration Agreement.

S:    December 1, 1931, Paris
R:    August 24, 1933, Berlin.
      DURP, 1933, No. 69; RGB1, 1933, No. 41.


GERMANY, DENMARK, ESTONIA, FINLAND, FRANCE,
GREAT BRITAIN, ITALY, LATVIA, SWEDEN.
Agreement Concerning the Neutralization and Non-fortification
of Öland Island.
S:    October 20, 1921, Geneva.
R:    April 6, 1922, Geneva.
      DURP, 1922, No. 88, p. 1499; NRGT, vol. 12, p. 65;
      LNTS, vol. 15, p. 310.


CZECHOSLOVAKIA
Political Agreement, with Annex.
S:    November 6, 1921, Prague.
      Wandycz, 395-97.

      Czechoslovakia declares her disinterest in Eastern
Galicia and assures Poland that she will prohibit Ukrainian
activity in Czechoslovakia directed against Poland. Both governments will support the formation of a military and economical alliance to be formed by Rumania, Yugoslavia and Czechoslovakia.


FRANCE.
Trade Agreement.
S:    February 6, 1922, Paris.
R:    August 2, 1923, Paris.
D:    One year with automatic extension.
      DURP, 1924, No. 50, p. 835; ZTKH, vol. 1, p. 53; LNTS,
      vol. 43, p. 399.
      Substituted by the Trade Agreement of December 9, 1924.


FRANCE.
Treaty Concerning the Regulation of Judicial and Economic
Interests (Bilateral Convention; Agreement on Oil Exploitation).
S:    February 6, 1922, Paris.
R:    August 2, 1923, Paris.
      DURP, 1924, No. 16, p. 166; Makowski, pp. 71-73; LNTS,
      vol. 43, p. 415.


ESTONIA, LATVIA, FINLAND.
Political Agreement.

S:    March 17, 1922, Warsaw.
R:    October 7, 1922, Warsaw.
      LNTS, vol. 11, p. 168.

ITALY.
Trade Convention.
S:    May 12, 1922, Genoa.
R.    March 15, 1923, Rome.
D:    One year with automatic extension.
      DURP, 1923, No. 29, p. 291; ZNKH, vol. 1, p. 96; LNTS,
      vol. 49, p. 293.

GERMANY.
Convention on Upper Silesia.
S:    May 15, 1922, Geneva.
R:    June 3, 1922, Opole.
      DURP, 1922, No. 44, p. 370; RGBl, 1922, No. 10, p. 27,
      and 1923, No. 25, p. 42; NRGT, vol. 16, p. 645; LNTS,
      vol. 9, p. 466.

      The Convention consists of 606 articles divided into 7
parts.
(1)   General Regulations
(2)   Nationality and Residence
(3)   Protection and Minorities
(4)   Social Problems
(5)   Economic Problems
(6)   Mixed Commission and Arbitrary Tribunal of Upper Silesia
(7)   Final Protocol
Two organizations were charged with the supervision of the
implementations of the Agreement: the Mixed Commission and
the Arbitral Tribunal, consisting of two Germans, two Poles,
and a president to be appointed by the League of Nations. Decisions of the Arbitral Tribunal were not subject to revision by
other bodies. The Convention was signed for a period of 15
years;

      Hereto:
Protocol.
S:    December 8, 1922, Dresden.
Declaration.
S:    June 3, 1922, Opole.
R:    July 7, 1922, Berlin.
Declaration and Protocol) Supplement Concerning Extension.
S:    May 2, 1923, Dresden.
R:    October 25, 1923.

DURP, 1924, No. 5, p. 58.
S:     June 14, 1923, Berlin.
        RGBl, 1923, No. 25; NRGT, vol. 16, p. 295.
Agreement Concerning the Regulation of Some Problems Aris-
ing from the Agreement Concerning Upper Silesia.
S:     January 11, 1924, Katowice.
        DURP, 1927, No. 63, p. 833; RGBl, 1924, No. 25; NRGT,
        vol. 22, p. 152.


GERMANY.
Treaty Concerning the Mines in Upper Silesia.
S:     June 23, 1922, Opole.
R:     March 9, 1923, Berlin.
        DURP, 1923, No. 45, p. 496; RGBl, 1923, No. 10, p. 37;
        NRGT, vol. 20, p. 574; LNTS, vol. 22, p. 26.
        Hereto:
Exchange of Notes Concerning the Application of this Agreement.
S:     December 15, 1932, Warsaw.
R:     September 30, 1933, Warsaw.
        DURP, 1933, No. 88.


SWITZERLAND.
Trade Agreement.
S:     June 26, 1922, Warsaw.
R:     August 5, 1922, Warsaw.
D:     One year with the right for subsequent extension.
        DURP, 1922, No. 83, p. 1441; RLF, 1922, No. 25; NRGT,
        vol. 16, p. 626; LNTS, vol. 12, p. 306.


LATVIA
Sanitary Convention.
S:     July 7, 1922, Warsaw.
R:     April 7, 1925, Warsaw.
        LNTS, vol. 37, p. 318.


AUSTRIA.
Trade Convention.
S:     September 25, 1922, Warsaw.
R:     January 5, 1923, Warsaw.
D:     One year with the right for subsequent extension.
        DURP, 1923, No. 4, p. 32; NRGT, vol. 21, p. 620; ZTKH,
        vol. 1, p. 136; OBGB, 1923, pp. 32-33.

        Replaces the Agreement Concerning the Exchange of
Goods from January 8, 1921.

Acceded by the Free City of Danzig on October 15, 1925.
    DURP, 1926, No. 127, p. 751; DG, 1926, No. 2, p. 3;
    RGB1, 1925, p. 423.

YUGOSLAVIA.
Commercial Convention.
S:    October 23, 1922, Warsaw.
R:    April 5, 1924, Warsaw.
D:    One year with the right for subsequent extension.
      DURP, 1924, No. 35, p. 530; NRGT, vol. 17, p. 107;
      LNTS, vol. 49, p. 265.
      Hereto:
Supplement Protocol.
S:    August 31, 1930, Warsaw.
      DURP, 1931, No. 57, p. 894; NRGT, vol. 33, p. 881.

GERMANY.
Agreement Concerning the Order of Procedure for the Mixed
Commission for Upper Silesia.
S:    December 5, 1922, Katowice.
      RGB1, 1923, No. 7, p. 16; NRGT, vol. 20, p. 684; LNTS,
      vol. 107, p. 484.

JAPAN.
Commerce and Navigation Agreement.
S:    December 7, 1922, Warsaw.
R:    January 8, 1925, Warsaw.
      DURP, 1925, No. 5, p. 36; NRGT, vol. 18, p. 814; LNTS,
      vol. 32, p. 62.

GERMANY.
Sanitary Convention.
S:    December 18, 1922, Dresden.
D:    Two years.
      LNTS, vol. 34, p. 302.

RUMANIA.
Sanitary Convention.
S:    December 20, 1922, Warsaw.
R:    July 11, 1923, Bucharest.
      LNTS, vol. 18, p. 104.

BELGIUM, LUXEMBURG.
Trade Agreement.
S:    December 30, 1922, Brussels.
R:    September 20, 1923, Brussels.
D:    One year with the right for subsequent extension.
      DURP, 1923, No. 106, p. 1274; LNTS, vol. 21, p. 184.
      Hereto:
Supplement Agreement.
S:    June 10, 1933.
      DURP, 1934, No. 78, p. 1445.
Supplement Agreement.
S:    March 2, 1936.
Additional Protocol.
S:    January 7, 1937, Brussels.
      LNTS, vol. 197, p. 359.

-1923-

ITALY.
Agreement Concerning the Oil Exploitation in Poland.
S:    January 31, 1923, Warsaw.
R:    May 16, 1923, Warsaw.
D:    Thirty years.
      DURP, 1923, No. 55, pp. 388-389.

      Granting of special privileges to Italian capital.

RUSSIAN SFSR, UKRAINIAN SSR, BELORUSSIAN SSR.
Sanitation Agreement.
S:    February 7, 1923, Warsaw.
R:    January 8, 1924, Warsaw.
      DURP, 1923, No. 9, p. 111; Sbornik 2 (1925), No. 128,
      p. 118; LNTS, vol. 49, p. 285.

GERMANY.
Treaty Concerning the Procedure of the Court of Arbitration
for Upper Silesia.
S:    March 9, 1923, Bytom (Beuthen).
      RGBl, 1923, No. 15; NRGT, vol. 20, p. 747.
      Hereto:
Alteration Concerning the Procedure.
S:    March 28, 1933, Bytom.
      RGBl, 1933, No. 33; NRGT, vol. 28, p. 85.

Alteration of the Procedure for the Purpose of Liquidation.
S:   July 14, 1937, Bytom
     RGB1, 1937, No. 29; NRGT, vol. 36, p. 346.


FRANCE, GREAT BRITAIN, ITALY, JAPAN, USA.
Decision of the Conference of Ambassadors Concerning Polish
Eastern Frontiers.
S:   March 15, 1923, Paris.
     DURP, 1923, No. 49, p. 556; NRGT, vol. 15, p. 259;
     LNTS, vol. 15, p. 260.


FRANCE, GREAT BRITAIN, ITALY, FREE CITY OF DANZIG.
Treaty Concerning the Transportation of Goods in the Port of
Danzig.
S:   May 3, 1923, Gdańsk.
     NRGT, vol. 17, p. 236.


YUGOSLAVIA.
Convention Concerning Legal Relations.
S:   May 4, 1923, Belgrade.
R:   November 27, Warsaw.
     LNTS, vol. 85, p. 455.


RUSSIAN SFSR, UKRAINIAN SSR, BELORUSSIAN SSR.
Convention Concerning Postal and Telegraphic Communications.
S:   May 24, 1923, Moscow.
R:   March 2, 1925, Warsaw.
D:   Unlimited.
     DURP, 1925, No. 26, Appendix; Sbornik 4 (1928), No. 182,
     p. 141; LNTS, vol. 50, p. 341.

     Denounced by the USSR on November 8, 1930.


TURKEY.
Friendship Treaty; Settlement and Emigration Agreement.
S:   July 23, 1923, Lausanne.
R:   March 17, 1924, Bern.
     DURP, 1924, No. 39, pp. 407-408, 411-412; NRGT, vol.
     15, p. 456; LNTS, vol. 49, p. 323.

     Establishment of diplomatic relations.


TURKEY.
Commercial Convention.

S:    July 23, 1923, Lausanne.
R:    March 17, 1924, Bern.
D:    One year with the right for subsequent extension.
      DURP, 1924, No. 39, pp. 409-410 NRGT, vol. 15, p. 450;
      LNTS, vol. 49, p. 329.
      Hereto:
Consular Convention.
S:    March 25, 1927, Ankara.
      Makowski, p. 225.


AUSTRIA.
Telegraph-Telephone Agreement; Post Agreement.
S:    September 28, 1923, Warsaw.
      Makowski, p. 14.


FINLAND.
Commerce and Navigation Agreement.
S:    November 10, 1923, Warsaw.
R:    September 3, 1924, Warsaw.
D:    Six months with automatic extension.
      DURP, 1924, No. 81, p. 1229; ZTKH, vol. 1, p. 309;
      LNTS, vol. 29, p. 230.


AUSTRIA.
Arbitration Agreement.
S:    November 12, 1923, Warsaw.
R:    February 26, 1925, Warsaw.
D:    Three years.
      DURP, 1925, No. 47, p. 650; LNTS, vol. 34, p. 400.
Substituted by new Arbitration Agreement.
S:    April 16, 1926, Vienna.
R:    April 2, 1927, Warsaw.
D:    Three years.
      DURP, 1927, No. 40; NRGT, vol. 17, p. 44.


GREAT BRITAIN.
Commerce and Navigation Agreement.
S:    November 26, 1923, Warsaw.
R:    June 16, 1924, Warsaw.
D:    One year with automatic extension.
      DURP, 1924, No. 57, p. 835; NRGT, vol. 17, p. 349;
      ZTKH, vol. 1, p. 366; LNTS, vol. 35, p. 318.

-1924-

LATVIA.
Consular Convention.
S:   January 3, 1924, Riga.
R:   December 16, 1925, Warsaw.
     LNTS, vol. 42, p. 451.

ESTONIA.
Consular Convention.
S:   January 11, 1924, Tallinn.
R:   February 20, 1926, Warsaw.
     DURP, 1926, No. 26, pp. 155-156; LNTS, vol. 47, p. 129.

GERMANY.
Agreement Concerning Legal Procedure, Convention Concerning Questions of Guardianship.
S:   March 5, 1924, Warsaw.
R:   March 31, 1926, Warsaw.
     DURP, 1926, No. 36, p. 414; RGBl, 1925, No. 17,; NRGT,
     vol. 22, p. 165; LNTS, vol. 49, pp. 181, 251.

AUSTRIA.
Agreement Concerning Legal Procedure.
S:   March 19, 1924, Vienna.
R:   July 13, 1926, Warsaw.
     DURP, 1926, No. 84, pp. 467-468; BGRO, 1926, No. 47,
     p. 226; LNTS, vol. 56, p. 95.

DENMARK.
Commerce and Navigation Agreement.
S:   March 22, 1924, Warsaw.
R:   August 14, 1924, Warsaw.
     DURP, 1924, No. 74, p. 1106; NRGT, vol. 17, p. 471;
     LNTS, vol. 31, p. 14.

ICELAND.
Commerce and Navigation Agreement.
S:   March 22, 1924, Warsaw.
R:   August 13, 1924, Warsaw.
D:   One year with automatic extension.
     DURP, 1924, No. 74, p. 1101; NRGT, vol. 17, p. 467;
     ZTKH, vol. 1, p. 405; LNTS, vol. 31, p. 36.

USSR.
Convention Concerning the Transit of Goods and Passengers on the Railways.
S:   April 24, 1924, Warsaw.
R:   May 7, 1925, Warsaw.
D:   Unlimited.
     DURP, 1925, No. 50, p. 670; Sbornik 5 (1930), No. 215,
     p. 213; LNTS, vol. 37, p. 34.

     It was preceded by the previous Agreement Concerning
the Railway Traffic with the RSFSR on November 27, 1921
(Sbornik 3 [1922], No. 100) and on October 30, 1922 (Makowski,
p. 916); with the Ukrainian SSR on December 17, 1921 (Sbornik
1 [1924], No. 89) and on June 19, 1922 (Sbornik 1 [1924], No.
90).
     Hereto:
Protocol Concerning the Alteration of Some Regulations.
S:   July 26, 1934, Moscow.
R:   June 21, 1935, Warsaw.
     DURP, 1935, No. 56, p. 951; NRGT, vol. 37, p. 484.

NETHERLANDS.
Commerce and Navigation Agreement.
S:   May 30, 1924, Warsaw.
R:   May 5, 1925. Amsterdam.
D:   One year with the right for subsequent extension.
     DURP, 1925, No. 60, p. 890; NRGT, vol. 19, p. 886;
     ZTKH vol. 1, p. 457; LNTS, vol. 34, p. 10.

USSR.
Consular Convention.
S:   July 18, 1924, Moscow.
R:   April 4, 1926, Warsaw.
D:   Unlimited.
     DURP, 1926, No. 35, p. 395; Sbornik 3 (1927), No. 133,
     p. 38; LNTS, vol. 49, p. 201.

     This Convention was superseded by the Convention of
January 21, 1958.

GERMANY.
Agreement Concerning the Nationalities and the Problem of Naturalization.
S:   August 30, 1924, Vienna.
R:   January 31, 1925, Warsaw.

DURP, 1925, No. 21, p. 169; RGBl, 1925, No. 5; NRGT,
vol. 22, p. 174; LNTS, vol. 32, p. 332.

USA.
Consolidation Agreement Concerning Polish Debts.
S:   November 14, 1924, Washington.
DURP, 1926, No. 104, pp. 605-606; LNTS, vol. 58, p. 97.

SWEDEN.
Commerce and Navigation Agreement.
S:   December 2, 1924, Warsaw.
R:   June 30, 1925, Stockholm.
D:   One year with the right for subsequent extension.
DURP, 1925, No. 70, p. 1059; NRGT, vol. 17, p. 852;
ZTKH, vol. 1, p. 493; LNTS, vol. 36, p. 300.

FRANCE.
Commercial Convention.
S:   December 9, 1924, Paris.
R:   July 2, 1925, Paris.
D:   One year with automatic extension.
DURP, 1925, No. 67, p. 1009; ZTKH, vol. 1, p. 525;
LNTS, vol. 44, p. 127.

DENMARK.
Air-Navigation Agreement.
S:   December 16, 1924, Copenhagen.
R:   February 5, 1925, Copenhagen.
LNTS, vol. 32, p. 410.

GERMANY.
Agreement Concerning Facilities in Minor Frontier Traffic.
S:   December 30, 1924, Gdansk.
R:   June 22, 1926, Warsaw.
LNTS, vol. 52, p. 51.

-1925-

ESTONIA, FINLAND, LATVIA.
Settlement and Arbitration Agreement.
S:   January 17, 1925, Helsinki.
R:   By Poland, October 14, 1925.
D:   Three years.
DURP, 1925, No. 122 p. 1687; NRGT, vol. 20, p. 38;
ZOR 1 (1926), p. 241; LNTS, vol. 38, p. 358.

VATICAN.
Concordat.
S:   February 10, 1925, Rome.
R:   June 2, 1925, Warsaw.
     DURP, 1925, No. 72, p. 1083; AAS 17 (1925), p. 273;
     NRGT, vol. 20, p. 323.

USA.
Trade Agreement (Modus Vivendi Agreement).
S:   February 10, 1925, Warsaw.
R:   August 26, 1925, Warsaw.
     DURP, 1925, No. 93, pp. 654-655; ZOR 1 (1926), p. 49;
     LNTS, vol. 37, p. 142.

SWITZERLAND
Settlement and Arbitration Agreement.
S:   March 7, 1925, Bern.
R:   June 11, 1926, Warsaw.
D:   Three years with the right for subsequent extension.
     DURP, 1926, No. 66, p. 750; EGS, 1926, No. 17; NRGT,
     vol. 16, p. 64; LNTS, vol. 50, p. 261.
Superseded by Settlement and Arbitration Agreement.
S:   June 30, 1937, Bern.
R:   December 23, 1938, Warsaw.
     DURP, 1937, No. 78, p. 1418; NRGT, vol. 36, p. 840.

HUNGARY.
Trade Treaty and Agreement Concerning Transport and Traffic.
S:   March 26, 1925, Budapest.
R:   September 4, 1925, Warsaw.
D:   Fifteen months with automatic extension.
     DURP, 1925, No. 93, p. 1418; LNTS, vol. 37, p. 152.
     Hereto:
Settlement Protocol.
S:   December 2, 1928.
R:   March 27, 1930.
     DHA, 1931, pp. 786, 2484; LNTS, vol. 107, p. 416.

CZECHOSLOVAKIA.
Economic and Veterinary Agreement.
S:   April 23, 1925, Warsaw.
R:   October 22, 1926, Warsaw.
D:   One year with the right for subsequent extension.
     DURP, 1926, No. 111, p. 1228; SGVCS, 1926, No. 96;
     NRGT, vol. 22, p. 559; LNTS, vol. 56, p. 285.

Hereto:
Supplement Protocol.
A:    February 9, 1928, Prague.
      June 26, 1928, Warsaw.
      DURP, 1931, No. 55, p. 841; LNTS, vol. 107, p. 490.

CZECHOSLOVAKIA.
Arbitration Agreement.
S:    April 23, 1925, Warsaw.
R:    April 14, 1926, Prague.
      DURP, 1926, No. 47, p. 555; NRGT, vol. 16, p. 69; LNTS,
      vol. 44, p. 285.
      Hereto:
Agreement Concerning Protection of Rights.
      DURP, 1926, No. 12; NRGT, vol. 29, p. 455.
Agreement Concerning Judicial and Financial Affairs.
      DURP, 1926, No. 41; NRGT, vol. 31, p. 432; LNTS, vol.
      48, p. 287.

BULGARIA.
Provisional Commerce and Navigation Agreement.
S:    April 29, 1925, Sofia.
R:    January 12, 1927, Warsaw.
      DURP, 1927, No. 6, p. 33; LNTS, vol. 60, p. 103.

AUSTRIA.
Agreement Concerning Air Communication.
S:    May 5, 1925, Warsaw.
R:    June 28, 1925.
      DURP, 1926, No. 16, pp. 88-89; LNTS, vol. 46, p. 269.

CZECHOSLOVAKIA.
Agreement Concerning Local Frontier Traffic Facilities;
Convention Concerning Tourist Traffic.
S:    May 30, 1925, Prague.
R:    April 22, 1926, Warsaw.
      LNTS, vol. 48, p. 397; vol. 50, p. 243.

USSR.
Agreement Concerning Settlement of Border Incidents.
S:    August 3, 1925, Moscow.
R:    September 1, 1925, Warsaw.
      Sbornik 3 (1927), No. 137, p. 70; NRGT, vol. 29, p. 329.

BELGIUM.
Agreement Concerning Scientific, Literary, and Scholastic
Relations.
S:   September 1, 1925, Warsaw.
R:   June 26, 1926, Warsaw.
     LNTS, vol. 54, p. 69.

CZECHOSLOVAKIA.
Sanitary Convention.
S:   September 5, 1925, Prague.
R:   October 22, 1926, Warsaw.
     LNTS, vol. 58, p. 143.

GERMANY, BELGIUM, FRANCE, GREAT BRITAIN, ITALY,
CZECHOSLOVAKIA.
Security Treaty.
S:   October 16, 1925, Locarno.
R:   By Poland, September 14, 1926, Geneva.
     RGBl, 1925, No. 52, p. 976 and 1926, p. 42; NRGT, vol.
     16, p. 7.

GERMANY.
Arbitration Agreement.
S:   October 16, 1925, Locarno.
R:   September 14, 1926, Geneva.
     RGBl, 1925, No. 52, p. 976 and 1926, p. 42; NRGT, vol.
     16, p. 22, American J. Suppl., vol. 20 (1926) p. 31; LNTS,
     vo. 54, p. 327.

FRANCE.
Treaty of Mutual Guarantee (Locarno treaty).
S:   October 16, 1925, Locarno.
R:   September 14, 1926, Geneva.
     DURP, 1926, No. 114, p. 1299; NRGT, vol. 18, p. 655;
     LNTS, vol. 54, p. 354.

      Both parties assured each other of active support in
case of German attack.

SWEDEN.
Settlement and Arbitration Agreement.
S:   November 3, 1925, Stockholm.
R:   March 28, 1927, Warsaw.
D:   Three years.
     DURP, 1927, No. 37, p. 437; NRGT, vol. 17, p. 22; LNTS,

vol. 62, p. 263.

Denounced by Poland on June 14, 1953.

NETHERLANDS.
Provisional Convention Concerning Aerial Navigation.
S:    November 4, 1925, The Hague.
R:    October 18, 1926, Warsaw.
      LNTS, vol. 58, p. 179.

      Denounced by Netherlands effective as of April 8, 1930.

FREE CITY OF DANZIG.
Agreement Concerning the Execution of Court's Decisions.
S:    November 28, 1925, Gdańsk.
      DURP, 1927, No. 55, p. 764.

FRANCE.
Consular Convention. Convention Concerning Judicial Docu-
ments.
S:    December 30, 1925, Paris.
R:    April 21, 1928, Paris.
      DURP, 1928, No. 56, p. 1189; LNTS, vol. 48, p. 139,
      vol. 73, p. 265.
      Hereto:
Treaty Concerning Extradition.
S:    December 30, 1925, Paris.
      LNTS, vol. 95, p. 217.

-1926-

GERMANY.
Agreement Concerning Settlement of Frontier Questions.
S:    January 27, 1926, Poznan.
R:    May 19, 1927.
      DURP, 1927, No. 54, p. 722; RGB1, 1926, No. 49, p. 723;
      NRGT, vol. 26, p. 515; LNTS, vol. 64, p. 113.
      Hereto:
Supplement Agreement.
S:    July 8, 1937, Hamburg.
R:    March 24, 1938, Warsaw.
      DURP, 1938, No. 28, p. 449; RGB1, 1938, No. 16; NRGT,
      vol. 36, p. 532.

RUMANIA.
Mutual Defense Treaty.
S:    March 26, 1926, Bucharest.
R:    February 9, 1927, Warsaw.
D:    Five years.
      DURP, 1927, No. 16, p. 138; NRGT, vol. 17, p. 3; LNTS,
      vol. 60, p. 161.

      Superseded by Treaty of January 15, 1931.

GERMANY.
Agreement Concerning Railroad Traffic.
S:    March 27, 1926, Berlin.
R:    May 19, 1927, Warsaw.
      DURP, 1927, No. 48, P. 601; LNTS, vol. 64, p. 249.
      Hereto:
Supplementary Agreement.
S:    June 2, 1937, Warsaw.
      DURP, 1937, No. 76, p. 548; LNTS, vol. 78, p. 506.

CZECHOSLOVAKIA.
Agreement Concerning Air Navigation.
S:    April 15, 1926, Prague.
R:    April 2, 1957, Warsaw.
      DURP, 1927, No. 86, p. 1211; LNTS, vol. 67, p. 305.

      Denounced by Poland, December 31, 1930.

AUSTRIA.
Settlement and Arbitration Agreement.
S:    April 16, 1926, Vienna.
R:    April 2, 1927, Warsaw.
D:    Three years.
      DURP, 1927, No. 40, p. 470; LNTS, vol. 62, p. 329.

DENMARK.
Settlement and Arbitration Agreement.
S:    April 23, 1926, Copenhagen.
R:    April 4, 1927, Warsaw.
D:    Three years.
      DURP, 1927, No. 40, p. 476; NRGT, vol. 17, p. 49;
      LNTS, vol. 61, p. 245.

GERMANY.
Agreement Concerning Custom and Passport Procedure and

Railroad Traffic through Korzeniów.
S:    June 16, 1926, Berlin.
R:    July 4, 1927, Warsaw.
      DURP, 1927, No. 66, p. 859; LNTS, vol. 65, p. 379.

YUGOSLAVIA.
Treaty of Friendship and Co-operation.
S:    September 18, 1926, Geneva.
R:    May 16, 1928, Belgrade.
D:    Three years.
      DURP, 1928, No. 61, p. 1352; Sluzbene Novine, 1928, No.
      129; NRGT, vol. 19, p. 15; LNTS, vol. 78, p. 414.
      Hereto:
Exchange of Notes Concerning an Extension for Another Three
Years:  December 3, 1930.
      NRGT, vol. 25, p. 326; LNTS, vol. 104, p. 514.

YUGOSLAVIA.
Settlement and Arbitration Agreement.
S:    September 18, 1926, Geneva.
R:    May 16, 1928, Belgrade.
D:    Five years.
      DURP, 1928, No. 61, p. 1356; NRGT, vol. 19, p. 16;
      LNTS, vol. 78, p. 420.

ITALY.
Payments Agreement.
S:    December 18, 1926, Warsaw.
R:    July 5, 1929, Warsaw.
      DURP, 1929, No. 58, pp. 454-455; LNTS, vol. 93, p. 313.
         Poland asked for credit to pay her debts to Italy.

NORWAY.
Trade and Navigation Agreement.
S:    December 22, 1926, Warsaw.
R:    August 30, 1927, Oslo.
D:    One year with automatic extension.
      DURP, 1927, No. 84, p. 1188; NRGT, vol. 28, p. 573.
      Hereto:
Supplement Protocol.
S:    April 26, 1928.
      DURP, 1929, No. 31.

GERMANY.
Agreement Concerning the Exchange of Official Documents
and Archives.
S:    December 22, 1926, Berlin.
R:    October 18, 1927, Warsaw.
        DURP, 1927, No. 96, p. 1332; LNTS, vol. 68, p. 263.


NORWAY.
Commerce and Navigation Treaty with the Final Protocol.
S:    December 22, 1926, Warsaw.
R:    August 30, 1927, Oslo.
        LNTS, vol. 66, p. 359.

-1927-

GERMANY.
Agreement Concerning the Administration of Warta River in
Areas where the River Corresponds with the Boundary.
S:    February 16, 1927, Poznan.
R:    February 13, 1928, Warsaw.
        DURP, 1928, No. 26, p. 450; LNTS, vol. 71, p. 369.


ESTONIA.
Trade and Navigation Agreement.
S:    February 19, 1927, Tallinn.
R:    March 25, 1931, Warsaw.
D:    One year with automatic extension.
        DURP, 1931, No. 38, p. 611; NRGT, vol. 28, p. 838;
        LNTS,    vol. 115, p. 177.
        Hereto:
Supplement Protocol.
S:    July 5, 1929, Tallinn.
R:    March 25, 1931, Warsaw.
        NRGT, vol. 28, p. 848; LNTS, vol. 115, p. 197.


YUGOSLAVIA.
Consular Convention.
S:    March 6, 1927, Belgrade.
R:    December 2, 1931, Warsaw.
        LNTS, vol. 126, p. 67.


PERSIA. (IRAN)
Treaty of Friendship.

S:     March 19, 1927, Teheran.
R:     October 7, 1930, Warsaw.
       DURP, 1930, No. 73, P. 923; NRGT, vol. 28, p. 665;
       LNTS, vol. 109, p. 87.

## PERSIA.
Trade Agreement.
S:     March 19, 1927, Teheran.
R:     October 7, 1930, Warsaw.
D:     Two years with the right for subsequent extension.
       DURP, 1930, No. 63, p. 928; DHA, 1931, p. 55; LNTS,
       vol. 109, p. 53.
       Hereto:
Supplement Agreement.
S:     November 4, 1930, Warsaw.
       DURP, 1931, No. 59, p. 995; DHA, 1931, p. 2485.

## CZECHOSLOVAKIA.
Convention Concerning Railway Traffic.
S:     May 30, 1927, Prague.
R:     November 23, 1929, Warsaw.
       LNTS, vol. 98, p. 233.

## AFGHANISTAN.
Treaty of Friendship.
S:     November 3, 1927, Ankara.
R:     April 30, 1928, Warsaw.
       DURP, 1928, No. 55, p. 1185; NRGT, vol. 20, p. 354;
       LNTS, vol. 74, p. 83.

       Came into force on May 15, 1928.

## GERMANY.
Agreement and Final Protocol. Regulation of Fishing in
Boundary Waters.
S:     December 10, 1927, Berlin.
R:     May 28, 1931, Warsaw.
       LNTS, vol. 120, p. 299.

## LATVIA.
Provisional Commercial Agreement.
S:     December 22, 1927, Riga.
R:     March 18, 1931, Riga.
       LNTS, vol. 115, p. 123.

Superseded by the Treaty of Commerce and Navigation
of February 12, 1929.

USSR.
Agreement Concerning Exchange of Political Prisoners.
S:    December 27, 1927, Warsaw.
    Shapiro, I, p. 357.
    Hereto:
Protocol Concerning the Transportation of Political Prisoners.
S:    August 3, 1932, Moscow.
    Shapiro, II, p. 56.

-1928-

BELGIUM.
Consular Convention.
S:    June 12, 1928, Brussels.
R:    August 6, 1931, Warsaw.
    LNTS, vol. 123, p. 25.

USA.
Conciliation and Arbitration Treaty.
S:    August 16, 1928, Washington.
R:    January 4, 1930, Warsaw.
    DURP, 1930, No. 4, p. 23; LNTS, vol. 99, pp. 403, 409.

(FIFTY-EIGHT STATES.)
Briand-Kellog Pact.
S:    August 27, 1928, Paris.
R:    By Poland, March 25, 1929.
    DURP, 1929, No. 29, p. 479; NRGT, vol. 21, p. 3.

LUXEMBURG.
Conciliation and Arbitration Treaty.
S:    October 29, 1928, Luxemburg.
R:    December 3, 1930, Luxemburg.
    LNTS, vol. III, p. 71.

LITHUANIA.
Provisional Agreement Concerning Traffic of Population in
Border Areas.
S:    November 7, 1928, Königsberg.
R:    April 19, 1929, Kaunas.
    DURP, 1929, No. 29, p. 486; LNTS, vol. 89, p. 171.

HUNGARY.
Conciliation and Arbitration Treaty.
S:    November 30, 1928, Warsaw.
R:    November 29, 1930, Budapest.
D:    Three years with the right for subsequent extension.
      NRGT, vol. 22, p. 327; LNTS, vol. 100, p. 67.

SPAIN.
Conciliation, Judicial Settlement, and Arbitration Treaty.
S:    December 3, 1928, Madrid.
R:    March 1, 1930, Warsaw.
D:    Three years with the right for subsequent extension.
      DURP, 1930, No. 20, p. 195; NRGT, vol. 22, p. 331;
      LNTS, vol. 101, p. 501.

-1929-

USSR, ESTONIA, LATVIA, RUMANIA.
Protocol Concerning the Enforcement of Briand-Kellog Pact
of August 27, 1928 ("Litvinov-Protocol"); Renunciation of War
as an Instrument of National Policy.
S:    February 9, 1929, Moscow.
R:    By Poland, March 30, 1929.
      DURP, 1929, No. 29, p. 479; NRGT, vol. 23, p. 327;
      LNTS, vol. 89, No. 2028, pp. 369-375; Documents, vol. 1,
      pp. 12-14.

LATVIA.
Treaty of Commerce and Navigation.
S:    February 12, 1929, Riga.
R:    March 18, 1931, Warsaw.
D:    One year with automatic extension.
      DHA, 1929, p. 24; LNTS, vol. 115, p. 135.
      Substitutes the Trade Agreement of December 22, 1927.

CHINA.
Treaty of Friendship; Trade and Navigation Agreement.
S:    September 18, 1929, Nanking.
R:    May 2, 1931, Warsaw.
      DURP, 1931, No. 62, p. 1040; LNTS, vol. 120, p. 331.
Additional Protocol of July 1, 1930.
      LNTS, vol. 120, p. 343.

CHILE.
Settlement Agreement.
S:   October 19, 1929, Santiago.
R:   December 18, 1930, Warsaw.
D:   Three years with the right for subsequent extension.
     DURP, No. 13, p. 126; NRGT, vol. 24, p. 394; LNTS,
     vol. 113, p. 79.

RUMANIA.
Settlement and Arbitration Agreement.
S:   October 24, 1929, Bucharest.
R:   February 25, 1930, Warsaw.
D:   Five years with the right for subsequent extension.
     DURP, 1930, No. 20, p. 188; NRGT, vol. 22, p. 354;
     LNTS, vol. 100, p. 299.

RUMANIA.
Agreement Concerning Railway Traffic.
S:   October 30, 1929, Bucharest.
R:   July 3, 1931, Warsaw.
     LNTS, vol. 121, p. 167.

NORWAY.
Conciliation, Arbitration, and Judicial Settlement Treaty.
S:   December 9, 1929, Oslo.
R:   April 26, 1930, Warsaw.
D:   Five years.
     DURP, 1931, No. 39, p. 639; NRGT, vol. 23, p. 69;
     LNTS, vol. 101, p. 325.

RUMANIA.
Consular Convention and Final Protocol.
S:   December 17, 1929, Bucharest.
R:   June 9, 1931, Warsaw.
     LNTS, vol. 119, p. 333.

GERMANY, DENMARK, FREE CITY OF DANZIG, SWEDEN.
Agreement Regarding the Regulation of Plaice and Flounder
Fishing in the Baltic Sea, with Final Protocol.
S:   December 17, 1929, Berlin.
Deposit of ratification at Berlin:  Poland and Free City of
Danzig, March 2, 1931.
     LNTS, vol. 115, p. 95.

RUMANIA.
Convention and Final Protocol.   Mutual Assistance and Legal
Protection in Civil Matters.
S:   December 19, 1929, Bucharest.
R:   May 9, 1932, Warsaw.
     LNTS, vol. 130, p. 205.

CZECHOSLOVAKIA.
Convention Concerning the Operation of the Municipal Services
of the Former Commune of Teschen, with Final Protocol.
S:   December 21, 1929, Olomouc.
R:   March 26, 1931, Warsaw.
     LNTS, vol. 115, p. 202.

PORTUGAL.
Trade and Navigation Agreement.
S:   December 28, 1929, Lisbon.
R:   March 7, 1931, Warsaw.
D:   One year with the right for subsequent extension.
     DURP, 1931, No. 31, p. 591; LNTS, vol. 117, p. 363.

BULGARIA.
Settlement and Arbitration Agreement.
S:   December 31, 1929, Warsaw.
R:   February 12, 1931, Sofia.
D:   Three years.
     NRGT, vol. 25, p. 20; LNTS, vol. 113, p. 89.

-1930-

FRANCE.
Agreement Concerning Polish Debt to France, Unpaid Balances
of Costs of Occupation of the Plebiscite Areas in Upper Silesia,
Marienwerder, and Allenstein.
S:   January 20, 1930, The Hague.
     LNTS, vol. 126, p. 117.

     Similar agreements were concluded with Italy and Great
Britain.

GREECE.
Trade and Navigation Agreement.
S:   April 10, 1930, Warsaw.
R:   June 18, 1931, Athens.

D:   One year with automatic extension.
     DURP, 1931, No. 63, p. 1060; NRGT, vol. 37, p. 298;
     LNTS, vol. 120, p. 369.
Superseded Trade Agreement of April 17, 1925.
     (DURP, 1925, No. 97.)
     Hereto:
Supplement Agreement.
S:   March 11, 1938, Athens.
     DURP, 1938, No. 29; LNTS, vol. 194, p. 13.

AUSTRIA.
Aerial Navigation Treaty.
S:   April 10, 1930, Vienna.
R:   August 21, 1930, Warsaw.
     LNTS, vol. 108, p. 289.

NETHERLANDS.
Judicial Settlement, Arbitration, and Conciliation Treaty.
S:   April 12, 1930, The Hague.
R:   January 27, 1931, Warsaw.
     LNTS, vol. 113, p. 65.

EGYPT.
Provisional Trade Agreement.
S:   April 22, 1930, Cairo.
R:   May 4, 1931, Cairo.
     DURP, 1931, No. 50, p. 793; LNTS, vol. 118, p. 413.

RUMANIA.
Trade and Navigation Agreement.
S:   June 23, 1930, Warsaw.
R:   August 23, 1932, Bucharest.
D:   Two years with automatic extension.
     DURP, 1932, No. 84, p. 1577; NRGT, vol. 33, p. 741.

ITALY.
Trade and Veterinary Agreement.
S:   July 22, 1930, Rome.
R:   July 19, 1931, Rome.
     DURP, 1931, No. 65, p. 1096.

FRANCE.
Convention and Protocol of Signature.  Commercial Airways.

S:    August 2, 1930, Warsaw.
R:    February 18, 1931, Paris.
      LNTS, vol. 114, p. 93.

BELGIUM.
Veterinary Convention
S:    December 18, 1930, Brussels.
R:    May 2, 1938, Warsaw.
      LNTS, vol. 197, p. 329.
      Hereto:
Protocol Amending Article 4 of above Convention.
S:    October 13, 1937, Brussels.
      LNTS, vol. 197, p. 329.

                    -1931-

RUMANIA.
Defense Treaty.
S:    January 15, 1931, Geneva.
R:    March 26, 1931, Bucharest.
D:    Five years.
      NRGT, vol. 30, p. 35; LNTS, vol. 115, p. 171.

        Superseded the Treaty of January 26, 1926.

        The authentic text of the existing Military Understand-
ing (clauses) between Poland and Rumania was not disclosed.

BULGARIA.
Convention.  Operation of Regular Air Lines.
S:    April 7, 1931, Sofia.
R:    January 25, 1932, Warsaw.
      LNTS, vol. 127, p. 45.

GREECE.
Convention.  Operation of Regular Air Lines.
S:    April 22, 1931, Athens.
R:    April 4, 1932, Warsaw.
      LNTS, vol. 129, p. 313.

GREAT BRITAIN, INDIA.
Trade Agreement.
S:    May 8, 1931, Warsaw.
R:    May 31, 1932, London.
      DURP, 1932, No. 55, p. 1069; NRGT, vol. 34, p. 522.

USA.
Treaty of Friendship and Trade. Consular Agreement.
S: June 15, 1931, Washington.
R: June 9, 1933, Warsaw.
D: One year with the right for subsequent extension.
   DURP, 1933, No. 49, p. 875; NRGT, vol. 34, p. 572.
Also Declaration Concerning the Access to the Free City of
Danzig.
S: March 9, 1934, Washington.
   NRGT, vol. 34, p. 590; American J. Suppl., vol. 28
   (1934) p. 124.


TURKEY.
Trade and Navigation Agreement.
S: August 29, 1931, Ankara.
R: August 30, 1934, Warsaw.
   DURP, 1934, No. 82, p. 1471.


-1932-


GREECE.
Treaty of Friendship; Settlement and Arbitration Agreement.
S: January 4, 1932, Warsaw.
R: July 2, 1932, Athens.
D: Five years.
   DURP, 1932, No. 66, p. 1285; NRGT, vol. 27, p. 671.


USSR.
Agreement Concerning Border Regime.
S: April 10, 1932, Moscow.
R: September 4, 1933, Warsaw.
D: Five years.
   DURP, 1933, No. 74, p. 1245; Sobranie, 1934, vol. 2,
   p. 246.


USSR.
Non-Aggression Treaty.
S: July 25, 1932, Moscow.
R: December 23, 1932, Warsaw.
D: Three years.
   DURP, No. 115, pp. 25-33; Sobranie, 1933, vol. 2, p. 98;
   NRGT, vol. 28, p. 329; LNTS, vol. 136, p. 38.

Art. 1: The two contracting Parties, recording the fact that they have renounced war as an instrument of national policy in their mutual relations, reciprocally undertake to refrain from taking any aggressive action against, or invading the territory of, the other Party, either alone or in conjunction with other Powers.

Any act of violence attacking the integrity and inviolability of the territory or the political independence of the other contracting Party shall be regarded as contrary to the undertakings contained in the present Article, even if such acts are committed without declaration of war and avoid all possible warlike manifestations.

In addition, Article 3 prohibited all understandings of an aggressive character with third countries directed against one of the signatories.

Hereto:

As an Essential Part of the Treaty: Arbitration Agreement.
S:    November 23, 1932, Moscow.
      DURP, 1932, No. 115, p. 2533; Sobranie, 1933, vol. 2,
      p. 99; LNTS, vol. 136, p. 136.
Protocol Prolonging Treaty until December 31, 1945.
S:    May 5, 1934, Moscow.
      DURP, 1934, No. 53; Sobranie, 1934, vol. 2, p. 142;
      LNTS, vol. 157, p. 431.

      (Treaty was revoked by the Soviet Government on September 17, 1939, after the collapse of the Polish resistance.)
PWB, p. 243.

-1933-

BRAZIL.
Settlement Agreement.
S:    January 27, 1933, Rio de Janeiro.
R:    September 13, 1933, Warsaw.
D:    Three years.
      DURP, 1933, No. 89, p. 1726; NRGT, vol. 28, p. 371.

GERMANY, FREE CITY OF DANZIG.
Agreement Concerning the Forwarding of Military Transports in Transit between East Prussia and the rest of Germany.
S:    February 13, 1933, Berlin.
R:    June 27, 1934, Warsaw.

DURP, 1934, No. 61, p. 1035; RGB1, 1934, No. 34; NRGT, vol. 35, p. 876.

Hereto:

Agreement Concerning Transport of Prisoners.

DURP, 1934, No. 67, p. 1199.


USSR.

Agreement Concerning the Settlement of Border Disputes.

S:   June 3, 1933, Moscow.

R:   September 20, 1933, Warsaw.

D:   Five years.

DURP, 1933, No. 90, p. 1734; Sobranie, 1933, vol. 2, p. 292; NRGT, vol. 29, p. 344; LNTS, vol. 142, p. 265.


USSR, ESTONIA, LATVIA, RUMANIA AND OTHERS.

Convention for the Disarmament - Draft.

S:   July 3 and 4, 1933, Soviet Embassy, London;
     Poland joined on October 16, 1933.
     DURP, 1933, No. 93, p. 1770; Sbornik 8 (1935), p. 27;
     NRGT, vol. 29, p. 33; LNTS, vol. 147, p. 67.

The meaning of the term "aggressor" was laid down in Article 2 of the Convention, which read: Accordingly, the aggressor in any international conflict shall, subject to the agreements in force between the parties to the dispute, be considered to be the State which is the first to commit any of the following actions:

(1)  Declaration of war upon another State

(2)  Invasion by its armed forces, with or without a declaration of war, of the territory of another State

(3)  Attack by its land, naval, or air forces, with or without a declaration of war, on the territory, vessels, or aircraft of another state

This Article was supplemented by Article 3, which stressed that there could be justification for such aggression: No political, military, economic, or other conditions may serve as an excuse or justification for the aggression referred to in Article 2.

However, the Convention never came into force due to lack of ratification by some of the contracting parties.


AUSTRIA.

Trade Agreement.

S:   October 11, 1933, Vienna.
R:   December 31, 1934, Warsaw.
     DURP, 1935, No. 2, p. 8; BGRO, 1933, No. 152, and
     1934, No. 10.

     Agreement was annulled by the German-Polish Econom-
ics Agreement of July 1, 1938.

-1934-

LUXEMBURG.
Agreement Concerning Extradition and the Assistance in Legal
Procedures.
S:   January 22, 1934, Luxemburg.
R:   February 3, 1936, Brussels.
     DURP, 1936, No. 16, p. 284.

GERMANY.
Non-Aggression Pact.
S:   January 26, 1934, Berlin.
R:   February 24, 1934, Warsaw.
D:   Ten years.
     DURP, 1934, No. 16, p. 276; RGB1, 1934, No. 15, p. 117;
     PWB, p. 25; AA, 1939, No. 2, p. 35; NRGT, vol. 28, p. 643.

CZECHOSLOVAKIA.
Trade and Navigation Agreement.
S:   February 10, 1934, Prague.
R:   February 18, 1937, Warsaw.
     DURP, 1937, No. 22, Appendix; LNTS, vol. 183, p. 213.
Superseded Preliminary Trade Agreement of October 6, 1933.
     DURP, 1934, No. 73, p. 1370; NRGT, vol. 38, p. 593.
Superseded by Agreement of July 4, 1947.
     UNTS, vol. 85, p. 212.

USSR.
Customs Agreement Concerning Delivery of Goods with Lists
of Goods.
S:   June 22, 1934, Warsaw.
     DURP, 1935, No. 53, p. 902.
     Hereto:
Annual Settlements through Exchange of Notes.
S:   December 1, 1934, for 1935.

DURP, 1935, No. 53
S:    March 3, 1936, for 1936.
DURP, 1936, No. 21.
S:    December 15, 1937, for the first quarter of 1938.
DURP, 1937, No. 90.

     Further, in connection with the Trade Agreement:
Agreement Concerning the Recognition of Ships' Tonnage (bulk);
Agreement Concerning Port-Deliveries (through Exchange of
Notes), of March 31 and December 4, 1936.
DURP, 1937, No. 3.


USSR.
Exchange of Notes between the Polish Government and the
Soviet Government in Connection with the Entry of the USSR
into the League of Nations.
S:    September 10, 1934, Moscow.
Official Documents, p. 180.

     Notes exchange the view that the relations between the
two countries will continue on the basis of all existing agreements between them, including the Pact of Non-Aggression
and the Convention for Definition of Aggression.


SPAIN.
Trade and Navigation Agreement.
S:    December 14, 1934, Madrid.
R:    April 8, 1936, Warsaw.
DURP, 1936, No. 35, p. 598.


-1935-


GREAT BRITAIN.
Trade Agreement.
S:    February 27, 1935, London.
R:    July 24, 1935, Warsaw.
D:    Until December 31, 1936, with the right for subsequent
      extension.


CANADA.
Trade Agreement.
S:    July 3, 1935, Ottawa.
R:    July 31, 1936, Warsaw.
D:    One year with automatic extension.

ITALY.
Consular Convention.
S:    July 10, 1935, Rome.
R:    May 7, 1936, Warsaw.
      DURP, 1935, No. 43, p. 720.


GERMANY.
Economic Treaty and Agreement Concerning Payments in Exchange of Goods.
S:    November 4, 1935, Warsaw.
R:    November 19, 1936, Berlin.
D:    One year with annual extension.
      DURP, 1935, No. 83, p. 1330; RGB1, 1935, No. 50, pp.
      767, 810.
Replaced Agreement Concerning the Reciprocal Exchange of Goods of October 11, 1934.
      RGB1, 1934, No. 50, DURP, 1935, No. 96.
      Hereto:
Supplement Agreements.
S:    July 18, 1936.
      DURP, 1936, No. 68.
S:    October 19, 1936.
      DURP, 1936, No. 83.
S:    December 21, 1936.
      DURP, 1936, No. 94.
Agreement Concerning the Extension of the Treaty. Payment's Agreement.
S:    February 20, 1937, Warsaw.
      DURP, 1937, No. 14; RGB1, 1937, No. 3.
Supplementary Agreement.
S:    November 29, 1937.
      DURP, 1937, No. 14.


-1936-


CANADA.
Trade Convention.
S:    February 20, 1936, Ottawa.
R:    July 31, 1936, Warsaw.
D:    One year with the right for subsequent extension.
      DURP, 1936, No. 61, p. 980.

ESTONIA.
Protocol Concerning Tariff between Two Countries.

S:    March 27, 1935, Warsaw.
R:    May 23, 1936, Tallinn.
      DURP, 1936, No. 53, p. 860.


USSR.
Harbor Payments Agreement.
S:    March 31, 1936, Moscow.
R:    December 4, 1936, Warsaw.
      DURP, 1937, No. 3, p. 33.


HUNGARY.
Convention Concerning Extradition.
S:    April 24, 1936, Budapest.
R:    June 14, 1937, Warsaw.
      DURP, 1937, No. 66, p. 1282.


USSR.
Agreement Concerning Legal Status of the Soviet's Trade
Delegation in Poland.
S:    June 14, 1936, Warsaw.
      DURP, 1939, No. 24, p. 438; VT, 1939, No. 5/6, p. 107;
      Shapiro II, p. 165.


FINLAND.
Protocol Concerning Tariff between two countries.
S:    July 16, 1936, Warsaw.
      DURP, 1936, No. 63, p. 1032.


FRANCE.
Provisional Trade Agreement.
S:    July 18, 1936, Paris.
D:    One year.
      DURP, 1936, No. 66, p. 1068.
      Hereto:
Protocol to the Provisional Trade Agreement.
S:    July 18, 1936, Paris.
      DURP, 1936, No. 90, p. 1460.


RUMANIA.
Convention Concerning Intellectual Co-operation.
S:    November 27, 1936, Warsaw.
R:    April 14, 1937, Bucharest.
      DURP, 1937, No. 36, p. 741.

-1937-

IRAQ.
Preliminary Trade Agreement.
S:　March 6, 1937, Baghdad.
　　DURP, 1937, No. 37, p. 751.

RUMANIA.
Convention Concerning the Payments in Tourist Traffic between
Two Countries.
S:　April 24, 1937, Bucharest.
R:　June 5, 1937, Warsaw.
D:　One year with 12 months' extension.
　　DURP, 1937, No. 43, p. 856.

FRANCE.
Trade and Navigation Agreement.
S:　May 22, 1937, Paris.
D:　One year with automatic extension
　　DURP, 1937, No. 54, p. 1006.
Superseded Provisional Trade Agreement of July 18, 1936.
　　DURP, 1936, No. 66.
　　Hereto:
Payment Agreement.
S:　December 29, 1937, Paris.
　　DURP, 1938, No. 14.

GERMANY.
Declaration on Minorities.
S:　November 5, 1937, Warsaw.
　　Heike, p. 275.

LATVIA.
Veterinary Convention, Annexes and Final Protocol.
S:　November 16, 1937, Riga.
R:　June 5, 1939, Warsaw.
　　LNTS, vol. 197, p. 43.

SWITZERLAND.
Treaty and Final Protocol, Extradition and Judicial Assistance
in Criminal Matters.
S:　November 19, 1937, Geneva.
　　LNTS, vol. 195, p. 297.

-1938-

FINLAND.
Protocol. Intellectual Co-operation.
S:    February 14, 1938, Warsaw.
      LNTS, vol. 194, p. 175.

      Came into force February 14, 1938.


GREAT BRITAIN.
Agreement Concerning the Limitation of Naval Armaments.
S:    April 27, 1938, London.
R:    November 22, 1938, London.
D:    Until December 31, 1942.
      DURP, 1938, No. 97, p. 1442; NRGT, vol. 36, p. 717.
      Hereto:
Amendment Agreement with Exchange of Notes.
S:    July 7, 1938, London.
R:    November 22, 1938.
      LNTS, vol. 195, p. 59.


LITHUANIA.
Agreement Concerning Postal and Telegraph Communications.
S:    May 2, 1938, Kaunas.
R:    June 27, 1938, Warsaw.
      DURP, 1938, No. 47, p. 817; LNTS, vol. 191, p. 359.
      Hereto:
Convention. Navigation and Timber-Floating.
S:    May 14, 1938, Kaunas.
      British S.P., vol. 143, p. 567.
Agreement Concerning Railway Traffic.
S:    May 25, 1938, Warsaw.
R:    June 28, 1938, Kaunas.
      DURP, 1938, No. 44; LNTS, vol. 191, p. 391.


LATVIA.
Convention. Operation of Regular Air Lines of Communication.
S:    June 16, 1938, Warsaw.
      LNTS, vol. 196, p. 105.


GERMANY.
Economic Treaty, with Agreement Concerning Payments in
Exchange of Goods.

S:    July 1, 1938, Berlin.
D:    Until February 28, 1941.
      DURP, 1938, No. 62, p. 1022; RGB1, 1938, No. 36, p. 752;
      NRGT, vol. 39, pp. 794, 806.
      Hereto:
Supplementary Agreement.
S:    March 2, 1939, Warsaw.
      RGB1, 1939, No. 16; NRGT, vol. 39, p. 810.


CZECHOSLOVAKIA.
Decree Regarding the Reunion of Teschen with Poland.
Issued on October 11, 1938.
      DURP, 1938, No. 78; British S.P., vol. 142, p. 765.

      ("Article 1.   The recovered territory of Teschen,
Silesia, is an indivisible part of the Polish Republic.")


USSR.
Joint Communique Concerning Polish-Soviet Relations.
S:    November 26, 1938, Moscow.
      Shapiro, II, p. 196.

      Relations are to be continued on the basis of all the
existing agreements.   Both Governments are favorable to the
extension of their commercial relations.


-1939-

USSR.
Commercial Agreement; Clearing Agreement; Trade Agreement.
S:    February 19, 1939, Moscow.
      PWB, p. 235 (Communique).


GREAT BRITAIN.
Treaty of Mutual Assistance with a Secret Protocol.
S:    August 25, 1939, London.
D:    Five years.
      British S.P., vol. 143, p. 301; NRGT, vol. 38, p. 5;
      LNTS, vol. 199, p. 57.

      Came into force upon signature.   ("Art. 1: Should one of
the contracting Parties become engaged in hostilities with a
European Power in consequence of aggression by the latter
against that contracting Party, the other contracting Party
will at once give the contracting Party engaged in hostilities
all the support and assistance in its power. Art. 1a of the Pro-

tocol:") The Expression, "a European Power," employed in
the treaty, refers to Germany.

FRANCE.
Treaty of Mutual Assistance.
S:    September 4, 1939, Paris.
       NRGT, vol. 38, p. 7; PV, vol. 2, p. 1100; Official Docu-
       ments, p. 137.

FRANCE, GREAT BRITAIN.
Agreement Concerning a Loan to Poland.
S:    September 7, 1939, London.
       NRGT, vol. 38, p. 10; LNTS, vol. 198, p. 357.

USSR.
Note of the Soviet Government about the Entering of the Soviet
Forces into Poland.
Delivered:   September 17, 1939, Moscow (to the Polish Ambas-
sador).

       The note, which was not accepted, states: "During the
course of ten days' hostilities, Poland has lost all her industrial areas and cultural centers. Warsaw no longer exists as
the capital of Poland. The Polish Government has disinte-
grated, and no longer shows any sign of life. This means
that the Polish State and its Government have, in fact, ceased
to exist. Therefore the Agreements concluded between the
USSR and Poland have ceased to exist. Left to her own devices
and bereft of leadership, Poland has become a suitable field
for all manner of hazards and surprises, which may constitute
a threat to the USSR.

       For these reasons the Soviet Government, which hither-
to has preserved neutrality, cannot any longer observe a neutral attitude toward these facts. ... In these circumstances,
the Soviet Government has directed the High Command of the
Red Army to order the troops to cross the frontier and to take
under their protection the life and property of the population
of Western Ukraine and Western Belorussia. ..."

       (Kusnierz, Bronislaw. Stalin and the Poles: An Indict-
ment of the Soviet Leaders, London, 1949, p. 32.)

# GOVERNMENT OF THE POLISH REPUBLIC IN EXILE, 1939-1944

The Government of the Polish Republic in exile was formed on the mandate of the State's President Wladyslaw Raczkiewicz by Wladyslaw Sikorski on September 30, 1939, in Paris after the Polish-French Exchange of Notes, concerning the status of the Government of September 19, 1939. On June 20, 1940, the Government moved to London.

The cessation of Polish military resistance against the German Army, and in the eastern provinces of Poland, the invasion by the Red Army forced the Polish Government, including the Polish President, Ignancy Mościcki, and the Commander-in-Chief, Marshal Edward Rydz-Śmigly, to cross over on September 17, 1939, into the neutral territory of Rumania.

On September 30, 1939, the Government declared its resignation; Mościcki resigned his office in favor of Wladyslaw Raczkiewicz, according to Articles 13-26 of the Constitution.

-1939-

GREAT BRITAIN.
Agreement Concerning the Use of Polish Merchant Vessels by Great Britain (through Exchange of Notes).
S:    October 12 - November 25, 1939, London.
      NRGT, vol. 39, p. 340; Ronnefarth, p. 373.
Supplemented by Agreement Concerning the Formation of Units of Polish Navy in Great Britain.
S:    November 18, 1939, London.
      Ronnefarth, p. 373; LNTS, vol. 199, p. 65.

FRANCE, GREAT BRITAIN.
Secret Protocol Concerning the Employment of Polish Air Force.
S:    October 25, 1939, Paris.
      DCW, p. 370.

-1940-

FRANCE.
Military Agreement.
S:     January 4, 1940, Paris.
        DCW, p. 360; British S.P., vol. 144, p. 407.
Also on the same day, Agreement Concerning the Polish Air
Force; Protocol Regarding the Carrying Out of the Military
Agreements.
        DCW, pp. 363, 365.

        This annuls the Agreement of September 9, 1939, Con-
cerning the Formation of a Polish Division in France, with
Protocols of September 21, 1939, Regarding the Realization
of the Agreement.

GREAT BRITAIN.
Agreement Concerning the Political and Military Co-operation.
S:     July 18, 1940, London.
        WPA, vol. 1, p. 447; Ronnefarth, p. 373.

        Related to the Treaty of Mutual Assistance of August
25, 1939.

GREAT BRITAIN.
Agreement Concerning the Employment of Polish Military
Forces in Great Britain.
S:     August 5, 1940, London
        WPA, vol. 1, p. 447; DCW, p. 377.
        Hereto:
Protocol Concerning the Legal Status of the Polish Military
Forces.
S:     November 22, 1940, London.
        DCW, p. 383;
Supplement Protocol.
S:     April 6, 1944, London.
        DCW, p. 383;
Agreement Concerning the Supplying of the Polish Military
Forces with Military Equipment within the Framework of the
Lend-Lease Program.
S:     June 29, 1944, London.
        WPA, vol. 2, p. 1033.

CZECHOSLOVAKIA (GOVERNMENT-IN-EXILE).
Joint Declaration Concerning Political and Economic Co-

operation <u>During</u> the <u>War</u> and <u>in</u> the <u>Post</u>-war <u>Period</u>. (<u>Declaration</u> of <u>Alliance</u>.)
S:    November 11, 1940, London.
       WPA, vol. 1, p. 452; JCEA 1 (1941-42), p. 97; British
       S. P., vol. 144, p. 381; Wandycz (II), p. 128.

       Both Governments express the hope that in this cooperation, based on respect for the freedom of nations, the principles of democracy, and the dignity of man, they will also be joined by other countries in this part of the European continent.

-1941-

CANADA.
<u>Agreement</u> <u>Concerning</u> <u>the</u> <u>Organization</u> <u>of</u> <u>Polish</u> <u>Military</u>
<u>Forces</u> <u>for</u> <u>Overseas</u> <u>Duty</u>.
S:    April 5, 1941, London.
       WPA, vol. 1, p. 447.

USSR.
<u>Agreement</u> <u>Concerning</u> <u>the</u> <u>Restoration</u> <u>of</u> <u>Diplomatic</u> <u>Relations</u>.
S:    July 30, 1941, London.
A:    By the USSR, April 26, 1943.
       VPSS (V) 1, p. 138; WPA, vol. 1, p. 354; AFR, vol. 4,
       p. 260; Documents, vol. 1, pp. 141-142; British S.P.,
       vol. 144, p. 869.

       (1)  The Soviet-German Treaties of 1939, regarding territorial division in Poland, are no longer valid; (2) Diplomatic relations are re-established with the Polish Government in London; and the formation of a Polish Army from former prisoners-of-war, political prisoners, and deportees in Russia is agreed upon; (3) An amnesty is to be declared for all Polish subjects confined on Soviet territory, including prisoners-of-war.

       On April 26, 1943, the Soviet Government broke off diplomatic relations with the Government of the Polish Republic in Exile (Compare the Note of the People's Commissar for Foreign Affairs, V. M. Molotov, of the same day).
       For Text see: AFR, vol. 5, p. 532.

USSR.
<u>Military</u> <u>Agreement</u>.
S:    August 14, 1941, London.

A:   By the USSR, April 26, 1943.
     VPSS (V) 1, p. 146; WPA, vol. 1, p. 447; British S.P.,
     vol. 144, p. 870; Documents, col. 1, pp. 147-148.
Also Agreement Concerning the Release of Interned Polish
Troops and the Restitution of Polish Property in the Polish
East Provinces Occupied by the USSR.
S:   September 29, 1941, Moscow.
     MoHeAPol 8 (1941), p. 883.
Protocol on an Amnesty for all Polish Citizens on the Territory
of the USSR.

USSR.
Joint Declaration of Friendship and Mutual Assistance.
S:   December 4, 1941, Moscow.
     VPSS (V) 1, p. 191; WPA, vol. 1, p. 361; AFR, vol. 4,
     p. 261; British S.P., vol. 144, p. 873.

     "The two Governments will lend one another complete
military aid as long as the war lasts, and the armed forces of
the Polish Republic on the territories of the Soviet Union will
fight against the German robbers side by side with the Soviet
armies."

USSR.
Agreement Concerning Soviet Loan for the Provision of Polish
Citizens Living in the USSR.
S:   December 31, 1941, Kuibyshev.
A:   By the USSR, April 26, 1943.
     VPSS (V) 1, p. 193; SFP, vol. 1, p. 113.

                    -1942-

TWENTY-FIVE STATES.
Declaration of the United Nations.
S:   January 1, 1942, Washington.
     LNTS, vol. 204, p. 381; WPA, vol. 1, p. 1; British S.P.,
     vol. 144, p. 1071.
     Reaffirms the Principles of the Atlantic Charter.

USSR.
Agreement on the Loan of 300 Million Rubles for the Formation
and Maintenance of the Polish Army in Soviet Territory.
S:   January 22, 1942, Kuibyshev.
A:   By the USSR, April 26, 1943.

VPSS (V), 1, p. 276; SFP, vol. 1, p. 126; Documents, vol. 1, pp. 556-557.

CZECHOSLOVAKIA (GOVERNMENT-IN-EXILE).
Treaty of Alliance with Joint Declaration Concerning Economic, Military, and Cultural Co-operation.
S:    January 23, 1942, London.
        WPA, vol. 1, pp. 435, 467; AFR, vol. 4, pp. 273, 275; Czechoslovak Sources, No. 2; Wandycz (II), p. 133.

USA.
Exchange of Notes Constituting an Agreement Relating to the Service of Nations of One Country in the Armed Forces of the Other Country.
S:    March 20, December 14, 1942, and January 26, February 25, 1943, Washington.
        UNTS, vol. 13, No. 86, p. 395.

        Came into force on January 27, 1943, the date of the receipt by the U. S. Government of the Note from the Polish Government of January 26, 1943.

USA.
Mutual Aid Agreement within the Framework of the Lend-Lease Program.
S:    July 1, 1942, Washington.
        D. S. Bull., vol. 7, p. 577; American J. Suppl., vol. 36 (1942), 222.


                                    -1943-

USA.
Agreement Concerning the Military Service of Polish Citizens in the U. S. Army (through Exchange of Notes).
S:    January 27, 1943, Washington.
        AFR, vol. 5, p. 92; UNTS, vol. 13, p. 395.

        On June 30, 1943, Extended to 16 States of the United Nations.


FORTY-FOUR STATES.
Agreement Establishing the United Nations Relief and Rehabilitation Administration (UNRRA).
S:    November 9, 1943, Washington.
        AFR, vol. 6, p. 251; British S. P., vol. 145, p. 159.

Government-in-Exile of the Polish Republic further participates in the following multilateral agreements within the framework of the United Nations and the Allied Powers respectively:

Inter-Allied Declaration Condemning Acts of Dispossession Committed in Territories Under Enemy Occupation (January 5, 1943, London);

Final Act of the United Nations Conference on Food and Agriculture (June 3, 1943, Hot Springs, Virginia);

Final Act of the Conference on Finance (July 22, 1944, Bretton Woods);

Agreement Concerning the Principles of Co-ordinated Control of Mercantile Navigation (August 5, 1944, London);

Inter-Allied Agreement Concerning the Air Service (December 7, 1944, Chicago);

International Conference Concerning Health (January 5, 1945, Washington.)

British S.P., vol. 145, pp. 805-979.

## POLISH COMMITTEE OF NATIONAL LIBERATION, 1944-1945

### (Polski Komitet Wyzwolenia Narodowego)

The Polish Committee of National Liberation was formed on July 21, 1944, in Chelm; from July 25, 1944 it resided in Lublin; on January 1, 1945, it was transformed into "Polish Provisional Government" (Polski Rząd Tymczasowy) and moved to Warsaw on January 18, 1945. This Government was installed by the Soviet Union in spite of the presence of the legal Exile Government in London.

July 25, 1944, the Soviet Government established diplomatic relations with the so-called "Lublin Committee."

-1944-

USSR.
Statement of the Soviet Government on the Soviet-Polish Relations.
January 10, 1944.
    (Izvestiia) January 11, 1944; Meissner, No. 18, p. 23.

USSR.
Statement of the Ministry of Foreign Affairs of the USSR Concerning Relations between the USSR and Poland.
July 25, 1944.
    DAFR, vol. 7, p. 854.

USSR.
Agreement of Friendship and Political and Military Co-operation.
S:    July 26, 1944, Moscow.
    WPA, vol. 2, p. 770; AFR, vol. 7, p. 854.
Agreement Concerning the Relations between the Soviet High Command and the Polish Administrative Authorities after the Entry of Soviet Army into Polish Territory.
S:    July 26, 1944, Moscow.
USSR: V.M. Molotov.

Poland:  E. Osóbka-Morawski.
       DAFR, vol. 7, p. 854.

-1945-

USSR.
Treaty of Friendship, Mutual Assistance, and Post-war Co-
operation.
S:     April 21, 1945, Moscow.
USSR:  J. Stalin.
Poland:  Edward Osóbka-Morawski.
R:     September 20, 1945, Warsaw.
D:     Twenty years.
       UNTS, 1948, vol. 12, No. 70, pp. 391, 403; British S.P.,
       vol. 145, p. 1166.

       Came into force on April 21, 1945, the date of signature,
in accordance with Article 8.

       The Treaty is directed against Germany and toward
maintaining and strengthening a firm and lasting friendship of
both Parties during and after the war.  Both Parties agree not
to enter into any alliance or take part in any coalition directed
against the other party.  Assurance of the continuance of the
co-operation for the strengthening of the economic and cultural
ties between the two countries.

POLISH PEOPLE'S REPUBLIC, 1945-1960

(Polska Republika Ludowa)

On June 25, the Provisional Government of the National
Unity was formed with the participation of the Polish Exile
Group, headed by S. Mikolajczyk; and, on February 6, 1947,
after the January election, it was replaced by the Government
of Cyrankiewicz (PPS) which then officially constituted the
Polish People's Republic.

-1945-

USSR.
Agreement Concerning the Right to Choose Nationality and Re-
settlement.
S:    July 6, 1945, Moscow.
      WPA, vol. 2, p. 1057; Meissner, p. 107; British S.P.,
      vol. 155, p. 840.

USSR.
Trade Agreement with Protocol Concerning the Legal Status of
the Soviet Trade Missions in Poland.
S:    July 7, 1945, Moscow.
R:    December 29, 1945, Warsaw.
D:    Unlimited.
      DURP, 1945, No. 195; Korolenko, p. 261; Dewar, p. 40.
      Hereto:
Annual Agreement Concerning the Exchange of Goods.
S:    April 12, 1946.
      (Keesing's CA, 1946, 717 C);

USSR.
Treaty Concerning the Polish-Soviet State Frontier.
S:    August 16, 1945, Moscow.
Poland: W. Osóbka-Morawski.
USSR: V. Molotov.
R:    February 5, 1946, Warsaw.

54

Izvestiia, August 17, 1945; UNTS, 1948, vol. 10, No. 61, p. 193 (maps included); DURP, 1947, No. 35, p. 557; British S.P., vol. 145, p. 1170.

Came into force on February 5, 1946.

In conformity with the decision made at the Crimean Conference, the new State border shall follow the "Curzon Line," with deviations of from 5 to 8 kilometers in favor of Poland in certain regions.

The following additional territory shall be ceded to Poland:
(1) The territory east of the "Curzon Line" as far as the Western Bug and the river Solokija and South of the town of Krylow, with a maximum deviation of 30 kilometers in favor of Poland;
(2) Part of the territory of the Forest of Bialowieże, in the district of Niemirow-Ialowka east of the "Curzon Line," including Niemirow, Hajnowka, Bialowieże, and Ialowka, with a maximum deviation of 17 kilometers in favor of Poland.
UNTS, 1947, vol. 10, No. 61, p. 193 (includes map with new border).

Treaty was signed by Edward Osóbka-Morawski for the President of the National Council of the Polish People's Republic and by V. Molotov for the Presidium of the Supreme Soviet of the USSR.

USSR.
Agreement Concerning the Reparations for Damages Caused by the German Occupation (Reparation Agreement).
S:    August 16, 1945, Moscow.
       ETA, p. 33; UNYB, 1946, p. 183.
       Hereto:
Agreement Concerning the Newly Established Polish Share of the German Reparation Benefits.
S:    April 30, 1946.
       British S.P., vol. 145, p. 1168.

SWEDEN.
Trade and Payment Agreement with Swedish Credit Grant.
S:    August 20, 1945.
       WPA, vol. 2, p. 1058; Keesing's CA, 1945, 385 C.

It was preceded by an <u>Agreement</u> <u>Concerning</u> <u>the</u> <u>Exchange</u> <u>of</u>
<u>Goods.</u>
S:    July 9, 1945.
      WPA, vol. 2, p. 1057.

HUNGARY.
<u>Trade</u> <u>Agreement.</u>
S:    October 4, 1945.
      WPA, vol. 2, p. 1058.
      Hereto:
<u>Trade</u> <u>Protocol.</u>
S:    June 28, 1946.
      (Ust. Gosp., No. 4 (1948), p. 65.)

FIFTY STATES.
<u>Charter</u> of the <u>United</u> <u>Nations.</u>
S:    June 26, 1945, San Francisco.
      D. S. Bull., vol. 12, p. 626; DURP, 1947, No. 23, p. 261.

USA.
<u>Exchange</u> <u>of</u> <u>Notes</u> <u>Constituting</u> an <u>Agreement</u> <u>Relating</u> <u>to</u> <u>the</u>
<u>Granting</u> <u>of</u> <u>Certain</u> <u>Reciprocal</u> <u>Customs</u> <u>Privileges</u> <u>for</u> <u>Foreign</u>
<u>Service</u> <u>Personnel.</u>
S:    October 5 and October 30, 1945, Warsaw.
      UNTS, 1948, vol. 15, No. 238, p. 225.

        Came into force on October 30, 1945, by the exchange
of said notes.

YUGOSLAVIA.
<u>Protocol</u> <u>Concerning</u> <u>Provisional</u> <u>Economic</u> <u>Relations.</u>
S:    November 23, 1945, Warsaw.
      UNTS, 1951, vol. 115, No. 1555, p. 3.

        Came into force on November 23, 1945.

        Prices to be charged for the goods shall be fixed ac-
cording to the latest quotations on the London Stock Exchange.

-1946-

YUGOSLAVIA.
<u>Protocol</u> (With Additional Protocol) <u>Concerning</u> <u>the</u> <u>Emigration</u>
<u>of</u> <u>Poles</u> <u>from</u> <u>Yugoslavia.</u>

S:    January 2, 1946, Belgrade.
      UNTS, 1951, vol. 115, No. 1566, p. 21.
           Came into force on January 2, 1946.    Emigration shall
be voluntary.


CZECHOSLOVAKIA.
Agreement Concerning Air Communication (With Annex).
S:    January 24, 1946, Prague.
R:    November 13, 1947, Warsaw.
      DURP, 1948, No. 4, p. 133; UNTS, 1949, vol. 25, No. 363,
      p. 181; British S.P., vol. 152, p. 49.


SOVIET MILITARY GOVERNMENT IN GERMANY.
Trade Agreement.
S:    February 2, 1946.
      Hereto:
Trade Agreement for 1947.
S:    March 29, 1947.
      Rzeczpospolita, March 29, 1947.
Trade Agreement for 1948.
S:    March 15, 1948.
      (Keesing's CA, 1948, 1421 H; NfA, March 17, 1948;)
With Supplementary Agreement of September 28, 1948.
      (Tägl. Rundschau, September 29, 1948.)
Trade Agreement for 1949.
S:    March 28, 1949.
      (Keesing's CA, 1949, 1871 G);
With Supplementary Agreement of December 29, 1949.
      (Keesing's CA, 1949, 2182 G).


CZECHOSLOVAKIA.
Agreement Concerning Mutual Return of Property Removed
after the Outbreak of War.
S:    February 12, 1946, Prague.
R:    November 13, 1947, Warsaw.
      UNTS, 1949, vol. 25, No. 364, p. 207; DURP, 1948, No. 4,
      p. 139.


GREAT BRITAIN (BRITISH ARMY OF THE RHINE).
Agreement between British and Soviet Representatives of the
Combined Repatriation Executive Concerning Completion of the
Evacuation of German Population from Poland.

S:    February 14, 1946.
      (Eur.Arch. 2 (1947), p. 824.)

YUGOSLAVIA.
Convention on Cultural Collaboration.
S:    March 16, 1946, Warsaw.
R:    June 7, 1946, Belgrade.
D:    Five years.
A:    By Poland, September 8, 1949.
      DURP, 1947, No. 26, p. 392; UNTS, 1947, vol. 10, No.
      139, p. 11.

      Establishment of scientific institutes which shall under-
take a comprehensive study of life and culture of the country
and a Yugoslav-Polish Joint Commission for implementation of
the aims of this Convention.

YUGOSLAVIA.
Treaty of Friendship and Mutual Assistance.
S:    March 18, 1946, Warsaw.
Poland:  Edward Osóbka-Morawski.
Yugoslavia:  Jozef Broz-Tito.
R:    April 15, 1946, Belgrade.
D:    Twenty years.
A:    By Poland, September 30, 1949.
      DURP, 1947, No. 26, p. 389; UNTS, 1946-47, vol. 1, No.
      13, p. 53.

USSR.
Postal Convention.
S:    March 20, 1946, Moscow.
      (PP, 1946, No. 5, p. 258.)

USA.
Exchange of Notes Constituting an Agreement to Economic and
Financial Co-operation.
S:    April 24, 1946, Washington.
      UNTS, 1947, vol. 4, No. 42, p. 155.

      Came into force on April 24, 1946, by signature.

      Opening of credits of $40,000,000 to the Government of
National Unity and the satisfactory conclusion of arrangements
for extending credits up to $50,000,000 for the purchase by
Poland of U.S. surplus property held abroad.

BULGARIA.
Trade Agreement.
S:    April 29, 1946.
      (Ust.Gosp., No. 4 (1948), p. 65.)
      Hereto:
Trade Convention for 1947-48.
S:    September 9, 1947.
      (NFA, September 6, 1947.)


USSR.
Agreement Concerning:  (1)  The Annulment of Polish Financial
Obligations Incurred During the War; (2)  The Long-term
Credits for the Arming of the Polish Army; (3)  Provision of a
Credit Based on Soviet Gold Reserves; (4)  Food Supplies to
Poland.
S:    May 27, 1946, Moscow.
      (Pravda, May 26, 1946 (Communique); Izvestiia, May 28,
      1946; Times, May 28, 1946.)

      Joint Communique mentions further negotiations con-
cerning trade, cultural exchanges, and repatriation of population.  (See Agreement of July 6, 1945.)

GREAT BRITAIN.
Agreement for the Settlement of Outstanding Financial Ques-
tions (With Exchange of Notes).
S:    June 24, 1946, London.
R:    May 9, 1947, London.
      DURP, 1947, No. 63, p. 1049; UNTS, 1947, vol. 11, No.
      149, p. 59; British S.P., vol. 156, p. 702.

      Great Britain discharges the claim for repayment of
the 73 million sterling in respect of amounts spent on war
material for the Polish Armed Forces in the West.


BELGIUM, CANADA, ... (11 states).
Agreement with Regard to Former German-owned Patents in
their Possession or Control.
S:    July 27, 1946, London.
R:    By Poland, December 3, 1947.
      DURP, 1948, No. 9, p. 221.


USA.
Exchange of Notes Constituting an Agreement Relating to Crim-

inal Offenses Committed by Members of the Armed Forces of
the Two Countries.
S:    August 5 and 29, 1946, Warsaw.
Exchange of Notes Constituting an Agreement Amending the
Above-Mentioned Agreement.
S:    February 6 and April 3 and 14, 1947, Warsaw.
      UNTS, 1953, vol. 160, No. 2097, p. 11.


FIFTY STATES.
Constitution of the United Nations Educational, Scientific, and
Cultural Organization (UNESCO).
S:    November 16, 1945, London.
Joined by Poland: November 6, 1946.
      UNTS, vol. 4, p. 275.

         On December 5, 1952, Poland stepped out.


NORWAY.
Payments Agreement.
S:    December 31, 1946, Warsaw.
R:    January 1, 1947, Oslo.
D:    One year.
      UNTS, 1948, vol. 15, Nos. 234, 235, p. 203.

         Payments by Norway to Poland and by Poland to Norway
shall be settled in Norwegian crowns.

         The Norges Bank and the Narodowy Bank Polski shall
make, by mutual agreement, the necessary arrangements to
insure application of the present agreement.
      Hereto:
Annual Settlement for 1948.
S:    February 4, 1948.
      (Eur.Arch. 3 (1948), p. 1187.)
Annual Settlement for 1949.
S:    January 8, 1949.
      (NFA, January 19, 1949.)
Annual Settlement for 1950.
S:    December 24, 1949.
      BCB, February 25, 1950.
Annual Settlement for 1951.
S:    January 16, 1951.
      VWD, January 19, 1951.

Annual Settlement for 1952-53.
S:    April 11, 1952.
      NU, May 15, 1952.
With Short-term Agreement Concerning Coal Deliveries of
June and September 1952.
      VWD, June 6, 1952, and September 21, 1959.
Annual Settlement for 1953-54.
S:    June 20, 1953.
      VWD, June 21, 1953.
Extended for 1954-55 in June 1954.
      VWD, July 1, 1954.


                            -1947-


BELGIUM, BRAZIL, ... (24 states).
Agreement Concerning Conservation or Restoration of the
Rights of Industrial Property which was Attained by the Second
World War.
S:    February 8, 1947, Neuchâtel.
R:    By Poland, December 3, 1947.
      DURP, 1948, No. 17, p. 327.


USA, GREAT BRITAIN, FRANCE, USSR, ITALY, AND OTHERS.
Peace Treaty with Italy.
S:    February 10, 1947, Paris.
R:    By Poland, February 4, 1948.
      UNTS, vol 49, p. 3; QuPV, vol. 1, p. 65; DURP, 1949,
      No. 50, Pos. 378 (Annex).


FRANCE.
Convention Concerning Payment of Death and Disability Pen-
sions to the Victims of the 1939-45 War (With Protocol).
S:    February 11, 1947, Paris.
      DURP, 1947, No. 73, p. 1219; UNTS, 1948, vol. 12, No.
      189, p. 287.


FRANCE.
Convention Concerning Cultural Co-operation.
S:    February 19, 1947, Paris.
R:    June 13, 1947, Warsaw.
      DURP, 1947, No. 62, p. 1044; UNTS, 1948, vol. 12, No.
      181, p. 96.

The purpose of this Convention is:

(1)  To establish chairs and lectureships in the French language and literature in Poland and the Polish language and literature in France, as well as institutes for promoting the study of relations between the two nations;

(2)  To encourage reciprocal visits to the universities and scientific institutions of the two countries by establishing grants for students and research workers;

(3)  To encourage the translations of both literatures and scientific masterpieces;

(4)  To facilitate relations and co-operation between representatives of science, literature, daily newspapers, and other publications.


SWEDEN.

Trade and Payment Agreement Concerning Credit Aid for the Reconstruction of Polish Economy.
S:    February 19, 1947.
D:    One year.
      (NfA, March 8, 1947.)
      Hereto:
Annual Settlement for 1948-49.
S:    April 22, 1948, Warsaw.
      DURP, 1949, No. 5, p. 27; UNTS, vol. 26, p. 400.
Protocol Concerning Prolongation.
S:    May 7, 1949.
      (NfA, May 14, 1949.)
Settlement for 1949-50.
S:    October 20, 1949.
      (NZZ, November 4, 1949.)
Settlement for 1950-51.
S:    November 1, 1950.
      (FDN, 1950, Nos. 21, 22.)
Supplement Agreement
S:    April 27, 1951.
      (VWD, May 4, 1951.)
Settlement for 1951-52.
S:    December 4, 1951.
      (FDN, 1951, No. 24.)
Short-term Agreement Concerning Coal Deliveries for
June 2, 1952.
      (Keesing's CA, 1952, 3500 H.)

Deliveries of October 1952.
    (VWD, October 12, 1952.)
Deliveries of March 2, 1953.
    (VWD, March 17, 1953.)
Settlement for 1953-54.
S:    March 23 and May 2, 1953.
    (BOT, June 6, 1953.)
Settlement for 1954-55.
S:    May 14, 1954.
    (FDN, 1954, No. 10; VWD, May 20, 1954.)

USSR.
Agreement Concerning Economic Aid and Technical Collaboration.
S:    March 6, 1947, Moscow.
    (Eur. Arch. 1 (1946-47) p. 546.)

CZECHOSLOVAKIA.
Treaty of Friendship and Mutual Aid (With Additional Protocol).
S:    March 10, 1947, Warsaw.
R:    July 4, 1947, Prague.
D:    Twenty years.
Poland:  J. Cyrankiewicz.
CSR:  C. Gottwald.
    Dokumenty, p. 245; UNTS, 1949, vol. 25, No. 365, p. 231;
    DURP, 1948, No. 7, p. 165; British S. P., vol. 149, p. 408.

    Came into force on signature.

SWEDEN.
Agreement Concerning the Regulation of Commercial Exchanges;
Agreement Respecting the Adjustment of Payments and Additional Agreement Concerning the Participation of Sweden in the
Reconstruction of Polish Economy, in Exchange for the Provision of Polish Coal, Coke, etc.
S:    March 18, 1947, Stockholm.
R:    June 4, 1947, Stockholm.
D:    One year.
    DURP, 1947, No. 73, p. 1205; UNTS, 1948, vol. 12, No.
    190, p. 295.

BELGIUM.
Technical Agreement on Co-operation between Social Insurance

Organizations.
S:    March 24, 1947, Brussels.
      DURP, 1948, No. 7, p. 169; UNTS, 1948, vol. 18, No.
      297, p. 279.
      Came into force on April 1, 1947.

In accordance with this Agreement, Belgium insurance organizations shall proceed to resume payment of annuities, pensions, and benefits due, under the law governing compensations for industrial accidents, old age, disability, and death insurance, to beneficiaries resident in the other country.

GREAT BRITAIN.
Provisional Trade and Payment Agreement.
S:    April 24, 1947, London.
D:    Three years.
      (BOT, March 6, 1948.)
      Hereto:
Supplement Agreement Fixing the Delivery Quotas for 1946.
S:    March 2, 1948.
      (Keesing's CA, 1948, 1404 A.)

YUGOSLAVIA.
Treaty on Economic Co-operation and Exchange of Goods (With Protocol and Annex).
S:    May 24, 1947, Warsaw.
      UNTS, 1951, vol. 115, No. 1557, p. 37.
Agreement on the Exchange of Goods Over a Period of Five Years.
S:    May 24, 1947, Warsaw.
A:    By Poland, July 6, 1949.
      UNTS, 1951, vol. 115, No. 1560, p. 89.
Agreement for the Provisional Settlement of Non-commercial Payments.
S:    May 24, 1947, Warsaw.
D:    One year.
      UNTS, 1951, vol. 115, No. 1558, p. 69.
      Came into force on signature
Protocol Regarding the Liquidation of Deliveries in Default under the Trade Agreement of January 18, 1946, and the Additional Protocols, Nos. 1 and 2, dated August 29, 1946.
S:    May 24, 1946, Warsaw.
      UNTS, 1951, vol. 115, No. 1559, p. 83.

Hereto:
Trade Agreement for 1948.
S:    April 14, 1948.
      (NfA, April 17, 1948.)
Trade Agreement for 1949.
S:    January 18, 1949.
      (NZZ, January 20, 1949.)

AUSTRIA.
Trade Agreement.
S:    May 28, 1947.
D:    One year.
      (Handelsblatt, June 19, 1947.)
      Hereto:
Annual Trade and Payment Agreement for 1948-49.
S:    July 7, 1948.
      (NfA, July 17, 1948.)
Agreement for 1949-50.
S:    July 1, 1949.
      (Keesing's CA, 1949, 2012 B.)
Agreement for 1950-51.
S:    August 1, 1950.
      (AO, August 24, 1950.)
Convention Concerning Coal Deliveries.
S:    March 9, 1951.
      (Keesing's CA, 1951, 2851 F.)
Agreement for 1951-52.
S:    August 1, 1951.
      (Keesing's CA, 1951, 3053 G.)
Agreement for 1953-54.
S:    April 23, 1953.
      (IW, 1953, No. 18.)
Supplement Protocol of October 5, 1953.
      (NZZ, October 14, 1953.)
Agreement for 1954-55.
S:    May 14, 1954.
      (VWD, May 17, 1954; IW, May 28, 1954.)

BULGARIA.
Agreement Concerning Cultural Co-operation.
S:    June 28, 1947, Warsaw.
R:    January 12, 1948, Sofia.

D:    Five years.
        DURP, 1948, No. 11, p. 256; UNTS, 1948, vol. 5, No.
        230, p. 123.

        Both parties agree to establish chairs and lectureships
in Bulgarian language and literature in Poland and in Polish
language and literature in Bulgaria, to afford scholars of both
countries freedom of scientific research in scientific research
institutes of the other country, to encourage exchange studies
in the universities and educational institutions of both countries,
to encourage translations into Polish and Bulgarian languages,
to facilitate mutually the activities of press agencies and correspondents.

        Setting up a Polish-Bulgarian Mixed Commission.

CZECHOSLOVAKIA.
Agreement Concerning Cultural Co-operation.
S:    July 4, 1947, Prague.
R:    July 2, 1948, Warsaw.
D:    Five years.
        DURP, 1948, No. 47, p. 951; UNTS, 1949, vol. 25, No.
        366, p. 249.

        Both parties agree to establish chairs and lectureships
in Czech and Slovak languages and literatures in Poland and in
Polish language and literature in Czechoslovakia to afford
scholars of both countries freedom of scientific research in
scientific research institutes of the other country, to encourage exchange studies in the universities and educational institutions of both countries, to encourage translations into Polish
and into Czech and Slovak languages, to facilitate mutually
the activities of press agencies and correspondents.

        Setting up a Polish-Czechoslovakian Mixed Commission.

CZECHOSLOVAKIA.
Convention Insuring Economic Co-operation (With Annexes).
S:    July 4, 1947, Prague.
R:    December 7, 1948, Warsaw.
D:    Five years.
        DURP, 1950, No. 8, p. 93; UNTS, 1951, vol. 88, No.
        1146, p. 62; British S.P., vol. 149, p. 441.

Annexes:
(1)    Treaty of Commerce,
(2)    Agreement on the Exchange of Goods,

(3) Protocol Concerning Guaranteed Supplies of Coal, Zinc, and Electric Power by Poland to Czechoslovakia for a Period of Five Years,
(4) Agreement Concerning Deliveries of Capital Goods from Czechoslovakia to Poland,
(5) Payments Agreement,
(6) Communications Agreement,
(7) Agreement Concerning Financial Co-operation,
(8) Agreement Concerning Industrial Co-operation,
(9) Agreement Concerning Co-operation in Agriculture, Forestry and Food Production,
(10) Agreement Concerning Scientific and Technical Co-operation,
(11) Protocol Concerning Direct Co-operation in the Construction and Expansion of Certain Economic Enterprises,
(12) Agreement Concerning Co-operation in Economic Planning and Statistics,
(13) Final Protocol to the Convention,
(14) Statutes of Polish-Czechoslovak Economic Co-operation Council,
(15) Protocol Concerning Mediation and Arbitration Procedure.
Hereto:
Agreement Concerning the Exchange of Goods for 1948-49.
S:    July 10, 1948.
      (Keesing's CA, 1948, 1566 B.)
With Supplementary Protocol Concerning Prolongation.
S:    June 20, 1949.
      (Keesing's CA, 1949, 1981 B.)
Agreement for 1950.
S:    November 26, 1949.
      (NZZ, November 29, 1949; Keesing's CA, 1949, 2146 B.)

CZECHOSLOVAKIA.
Agreement Concerning Minorities.
S:    July 8, 1947.
      (Meissner, p. 107; Keesing's CA, 1947, 1137 B.)

RUMANIA.
Agreement Concerning Air Communications (With Annex).
S:    August 9, 1947, Bucharest.
R:    October 25, 1947, Warsaw.
D:    Five years.
      DURP, 1947, No. 73, p. 1223; UNTS, 1948, vol. 12, No. 193, p. 363.

FRANCE.
Trade Agreement.
S:     August 21, 1947.
       (Keesing's CA, 1948, 1427 K; Times, March 20, 1948.)
Entered into force together with a Payment Agreement of November, 1947, by a Protocol of March 19, 1948.
       (Keesing's CA, 1948, 1427 K.)
Protocol Concerning Extension until August, 1948.
S:     February 28, 1948.
       (NfA, March 13, 1948.)
Trade Agreement for 1949.
S:     December 30, 1948.
       (Keesing's CA, 1948, 1756 D.)

       Because of the arrest of French Consular official in Poland, the French Government, in a note of January 7, 1950, refused to conclude a trade agreement for 1950.

YUGOSLAVIA.
Agreement Concerning Air Communication.
S:     August 22, 1947, Belgrade.
R:     February 12, 1948, Belgrade.
A:     By Poland, Autumn, 1949.
       DURP, 1948, No. 13, p. 293; ETA, pp. 5, 8.

UNITED NATIONS INTERNATIONAL CHILDREN'S EMERGENCY FUND.
Agreement Concerning the Activities in Poland.
S:     August 23, 1947, Paris.
       UNTS, 1950, vol. 65, No. 815, p. 4.

HUNGARY.
Agreement Concerning Air Communication (With Annex).
S:     August 28, 1947, Bucharest.
R:     December 13, 1947, Warsaw.
       DURP, 1948, No. 16, p. 315; UNTS, 1948, vol. 15, No. 231, p. 145.

RUMANIA.
Trade Agreement, with Payments Protocol.
S:     September 9, 1947, Bucharest.
D:     One year.
It was preceded by an Exchange of Goods Agreement.
S:     July 7, 1945.

(Ust. Gosp., No. 4 (1948), p. 65); Keesing's CA, 1945, 318A.

USSR.
Parcel Post Agreement.
S:    October 1, 1947, Moscow.
      SDD, vol. 13, pp. 448-459.
      Hereto:
Exchange of Notes Modifying the Parcel Post Agreement.
S:    August 26 and September 17, 1953.
      SDD, vol. 13, p. 454.
Changes in the Parcel Post Agreement of October 1, 1947.
S:    February 7, 1957, Moscow.

YUGOSLAVIA.
Special Agreement on Trade and Payments.
S:    November 7, 1947, Belgrade.
      UNTS, 1951, vol. 115, No. 1561, p. 137.

ITALY.
Trade Agreement.
S:    December 31, 1947, Warsaw.
D:    One year.
      Hereto:
Trade Agreement for 1948-49.
S:    June 16, 1948.
      (Keesing's CA, 1948, 1534 A.)
It was preceded by an Agreement Concerning Economic Re-
lations for 1946.
S:    December 29, 1945.
      (Keesing's CA, 1945, 591 F.)

                    -1948-

YUGOSLAVIA.
Agreement Concerning the Construction of a Powder Factory
in Yugoslavia.
S:    January 21, 1948, Warsaw.
      UNTS, 1951, vol. 115, No. 1562, p. 155.

GREAT BRITAIN.
Exchange of Notes (With Minutes and Annex) Constituting an
Agreement Concerning Compensation for British Interests

Affected by the Polish Nationalization Law of January 3, 1946.
S:    January 24, 1948, Warsaw.
      UNTS, 1951, vol. 87, No. 1163, p. 3; British S.P., vol.
      151, p. 67.

         Came into force on January 24, 1948, by the exchange
of notes.


USSR.
Agreement Concerning Mutual Exchange of Goods from 1948
until 1952 to the Total Value of $1,000 Million.
S:    January 26, 1948, Moscow.
D:    Five years.
      (Izvestiia, January 27, 1948); VPSS, 1948, vol. 1, p. 49
      (Communique).
      Hereto:
Protocol Establishing Quotas for the Exchange for 1948.
S:    May 13, 1948.
      (NfA, May 22, 1948.)
Protocol for 1949.
S:    January 15, 1949.
      VPSS, 1949, p. 39.
Protocol for 1950.
S:    January 25, 1950.
      VPSS, 1950, p. 41.


USSR.
Agreement Concerning Delivery of Industrial Equipment to
Poland on a Credit Basis.
S:    January 26, 1948, Moscow.
D:    Nine years.
      VPSS, 1948, vol. 1, p. 49.


HUNGARY.
Cultural Convention.
S:    January 31, 1948, Budapest.
R:    October 6, 1948, Warsaw.
D:    Five years.
      DURP, 1948, No. 51, p. 1039; UNTS, 1949, vo. 25, No.
      368, p. 283.

         To support the establishment of a chair of Hungarian
literature and language or history in one of the Polish universi-

ties and a chair of Polish literature and language or history in
one of the Hungarian universities; to encourage the exchange
of scholars and students.

FINLAND.
Trade Agreement.
S:   February 5, 1948.
D:   One year.
     (NfA, February 14, 1948.)
     Hereto:
Agreement for 1950.
S:   December 4, 1949.
     (Keesing's CA, 2156 B.)
Agreement for 1951.
S:   January 10, 1951.
     (NU, March 1, 1951.)
Agreement for 1952.
S:   December 17, 1951.
     (BOT, February 23, 1952.)
Agreement for 1953.
S:   December, 1952.
     (BOT, February 28, 1953.)
Agreement for 1954.
S:   December 8, 1953.
     (BOT, December 26, 1953.)
Agreement for 1955.
S:   December 1954.
     (IW, 1954, No. 52.)

CZECHOSLOVAKIA, YUGOSLAVIA.
Declaration Concerning Germany.
S:   February 18, 1948, Prague.
     Zbiór Dok., 1948, No. 3, p. 97.

        Protest Against the Creation of the Federal Republic
of Germany.

FRANCE
Agreement Concerning the Repatriation of Polish Citizens
from France.
S:   February 23, 1948, Paris.
     (Keesing's CA, 1948, 1399 B.)

RUMANIA.
Agreement Concerning Cultural Co-operation.
S:    February 27, 1948, Warsaw.
R:    November 11, 1948, Bucharest.
      DURP, 1949, No. 51, p. 225; UNTS, 1950, vol. 46, No. 707, p. 143.

      To promote the establishment of an Institute of Polish Culture in Rumania and an Institute of Rumanian Culture in Poland; furthermore, to promote the establishment of chairs and readerships in both languages and in both literatures.

GREAT BRITAIN.
Sterling Payments Agreement.
S:    March 2, 1948, London.
D:    Five years.
      UNTS, 1950, vol. 77, No. 99, p. 47; British S.P., vol. 154, p. 220.

      Came into force on March 10, 1948.

      All trade and financial payments shall be settled in Sterling;
Protocol Concerning Prolongation.
S:    April 7, 1953.
      (FS, April 15, 1953.)

FRANCE.
Agreement Concerning Compensation for Nationalized French Property; Agreement Concerning the Recognition of Polish Pre-war Debts.
S:    March 19, 1948.
      (Times, March 29, 1948); British S.P., vol. 152, p. 369.

NETHERLANDS.
Trade Agreement.
S:    April 1, 1948.
D:    One year.
      (NfA, April 3, 1948); (Keesing's CA, 1948, 1448 G.)
      Hereto:
Annual Settlement for 1949.
S:    February 15, 1949.
      (Handelsblatt, March 22, 1949.)

Settlement for 1950.
S:    March 23, 1950.
      (EV, April 6, 1950.)
Settlement for 1952.
S:    November 28, 1951.
      (BOT, February 2, 1952.)

CZECHOSLOVAKIA.
Agreement on Co-operation in the Field of Social Policy and
Administration (With Final Protocol).
S:    April 5, 1948, Warsaw.
R:    October 1, 1948, Prague.
      DURP, 1949, No. 6, p. 35; UNTS, 1949, vol. 31, No. 481,
      p. 325.
Agreement Regarding Social Insurance.
S:    April 5, 1948, Warsaw.
R:    October 1, 1948, Prague.
      DURP, 1949, No. 6, p. 41; UNTS, 1949, vol. 31, No.
      482, p. 355.

USSR.
Convention Concerning the Quarantine of Agricultural Plants
and Their Protection from Pests and Diseases.
S:    April 8, 1948, Warsaw.
R:    October 22, 1948, Moscow.
      DURP, 1949, No. 2, p. 3; UNTS, 1949, vol. 26, No. 288,
      p. 191.

YUGOSLAVIA.
Trade Agreement for the Period of June 1, 1948, to Decem-
ber 31, 1948 (With Agreement on the Settlement of Payments;
Additional Protocol on Prices and Exchange of Letters).
S:    April 12, 1948, Warsaw.
      UNTS, 1951, vol. 115, No. 1563, p. 167.

HUNGARY.
Convention Concerning Economic Co-operation and Arrange-
ment Relating to the Application of the Said Convention.
S:    May 13, 1948, Budapest.
R:    September 6, 1948, Warsaw.
D:    Five years.

DURP, 1948, No. 51, p. 1044; UNTS, 1949, vol. 25, No. 369, p. 301; MELP, pp. 87-89.
    Establishment of a Polish-Hungarian Permanent Commission for Economic Co-operation.
    Hereto:
Trade and Payment Agreement for 1950.
S:    November 12, 1949.
    (NfA, November 19, 1949; Keesing's CA, 1949, 2130.)
Agreement for 1951.
S:    September 20, 1950.
    (NZZ, September 21, 1950; Keesing's CA, 1950, 2591.)
Long-term Convention Concerning Exchange of Goods for 1951-54.
S:    November, 1950.
    (VWD, November 13, 1950.)
Agreement for 1952.
S:    January 21, 1952.
    (VWD, January 22, 1952); Keesing's CA, 1952, 3305.
Agreement for 1953.
S:    January 20, 1953.
    (Inf., January 23, 1953.)
Agreement for 1954.
S:    March 31, 1954.
    (DpA, May-June, 1954.)


CZECHOSLOVAKIA.
Agreement Concerning the Establishment of a Czechoslovak Free Zone in the Port of Szczecin.
S:    May 14, 1948.
    (Keesing's CA, 1948, 1444 E.)


FRANCE.
Investment Agreement.
S:    May 26, 1948.
D:    Five years.
    (NfA, June 5, 1948; Keesing's CA, 1948, 1510 A.)
Supplement Protocol.
S:    September 17, 1951.
    (MO, October 13, 1951.)


BULGARIA.
Treaty of Friendship, Co-operation, and Mutual Assistance.

S:   May 29, 1948, Warsaw.
Poland:  J. Cyrankiewicz, Z. Modzelewski.
Bulgaria:  G. Dimitrov, V. Kolarov.
R:   September 17, 1948, Sofia.
D:   Twenty years.
     DURP, 1949, No. 2, p. 8; UNTS, 1949, vol. 26, No. 389,
     p. 213; Zbiór Dok., 1948, No. 6, p. 299; British S.P.,
     vol. 152, p. 243.

     Parties agree to take all action to prevent further ag-
gression by Germany or any other State which might be associated with Germany.

BULGARIA.
Agreement Concerning Economic Co-operation and Exchange
of Goods.
S:   May 30, 1948, Warsaw.
R:   January 12, 1949, Sofia.
D:   Five years.
     DURP, 1948, No. 44, p. 945; UNTS, 1949, vol. 37, No.
     574, p. 3; MELP, pp. 90-95; British S.P., vol. 152,
     p. 246.

     Establishment of a Permanent Commission to implement
this Agreement.
     Hereto:
Supplement Protocol Concerning Exchange of Goods.
S:   March 27, 1949.
     (Handelsblatt, May 10, 1949.)
Trade and Payment Agreement for 1950.
S:   October 5, 1949.
     (Keesing's CA, 2090 E.)
Agreement for 1951.
S:   March 23, 1951.
     (BNS, Nos. 3, 4, 1951.)
Agreement for 1952.
S:   March 22, 1952.)
     (VWD, March 24, 1952.)
Agreement for 1953.
S:   March 17, 1953.
     (VWD, March 26, 1953.)
Agreement for 1954.
S:   May 14, 1954.
     (VWD, May 17, 1954.)

AUSTRALIA.
Exchange of Notes Constituting an Agreement Concerning a
Gift of Wool for Post-UNRA Relief.
S:    June 3, 1948, New York.
      UNTS, 1948, vol. 16, No. 258, p. 189.

     The government of Australia will supply without charge
to Poland Australian wool to the value of L. A. 250.000 and
will also pay in relation thereto the costs of procurements,
storage, transportation, and shipping to the port of entry into
Poland.

FRANCE.
General Convention on Social Security; Supplementary Agree-
ments on the System of Social Security, on Method of Transfer,
and General Protocol Relative to the a/m Convention.
S:    June 8, 1948, Paris.
R:    March 1, 1949, Warsaw.
      DURP, 1949, No. 24, p. 511; UNTS, 1949, vol. 32, No.
      503, p. 251.

HUNGARY.
Treaty of Friendship, Co-operation, and Mutual Aid.
S:    June 18, 1948, Warsaw.
Poland:  J. Cyrankiewicz.
Hungary:  L. Dinnyes, E. Molnar.
R:    September 6, 1948, Budapest.
D:    Twenty years.
      DURP, 1948, No. 51, p. 1048; UNTS, 1949, vol. 25, No.
      370, p. 319.

USSR, ALBANIA, BULGARIA, CZECHOSLOVAKIA, YUGOSLA-
VIA, RUMANIA.
Declaration of the Ministers of the Foreign Affairs Concern-
ing the Decision of the Conference of London on Germany.
S:    June 24, 1948, Warsaw.
      Zbiór Dok., 1948, No. 7, p. 445.

USSR.
Agreement Concerning the Regime on the Polish-Soviet
Frontier (With Final Protocol); Convention Concerning the
Procedure for the Settlement of Frontier Disputes and Inci-
dents.

S:    July 8, 1948, Moscow.
R:    February 15, 1949, Warsaw.
D:    Five years.
      DURP, 1949, No. 43, p. 897; No. 43, p. 914; UNTS, 1949,
      vol. 37, No. 575, p. 25; No. 576, p. 107; VPSS, 1948,
      vol. 11, p. 16, and 1949, p. 80 (Communique).
      Hereto:
Protocol Concerning Some Changes in Agreement, of July 8,
1948.
S:    December 8, 1951, Moscow.
R:    March 28, 1952, Moscow.
      DURP, 1952, No. 23, p. 237.


TURKEY.
Trade Agreement.
S:    July 18, 1948, Ankara.
      (BT, 1948, No. 67/68.)
      Hereto:
Protocol Concerning Exchange of Goods for 1960.
S:    March 14, 1960, Ankara.
      (Trybuna Ludu, 3. 15. 62)


RUMANIA.
Agreement Concerning Economic Co-operation.
S:    September 10, 1948.
D:    Five years.
      Hereto:
Agreement Concerning the Extension of the Exchange of Goods.
S:    April 7, 1949.
      (PDB, April 9, 1949; Keesing's CA, 1949, 1895 A.)
Trade Agreement for 1950.
S:    January 5, 1950, Bucharest.
      (Keesing's CA, 1950, 2206 A.)
Supplement Protocol.
S:    July 2, 1950.
      (Keesing's CA, 1950, 2466 A.)
Agreement for 1951.
S:    April 21, 1951.
      (PDB, April 25, 1951; Keesing's CA, 1951, 2922 F.)
Agreement for 1953.
S:    March 10, 1953.
      (PDB, March 21, 1953.)

CZECHOSLOVAKIA.
Convention on Privileged Rail Transit from Czechoslovakia to Czechoslovakia through Glucholazy, Polish Territory (With Protocol of Signature.).
S:   November 12, 1948, Warsaw.
R:   July 7, 1949, Prague.
D:   Indeterminate Period.
     DURP, 1950, No. 15, p. 179; UNTS, 1951, vol. 84, No. 1141, p. 347.


ARGENTINA.
Trade Agreement.
S:   December 8, 1948.
     (Handelsblatt, January 25, 1949.)


DENMARK.
Agreement Concerning the Settlement of Payments.
S:   December 14, 1948, Warsaw.
     UNTS, 1951, vol. 81, No. 1060, p. 33.
Additional Protocol to this Agreement.
S:   December 7, 1949, Copenhagen.
     UNTS, 1951, vol. 81, p. 41.
It was preceded by a Trade Convention for 1945-46.
S:   August 29, 1945, Warsaw.
     (Keesing's CA, 1945, 408 K.)
     Hereto:
Trade Agreement for 1950.
S:   December 7, 1949.
     (BCB, January 25, 1950.)
Protocol Concerning the Exchange of Goods and the Settlement of Payments for the Period of October 1, 1950, to September 30, 1951.
S:   November 30, 1950, Warsaw.
     UNTS, 1951, vol. 81, No. 1061, p. 43.
Trade and Payments Agreement for Two Years.
S:   June 9, 1952, Copenhagen.
     (LKD, 1952, C, pp. 601, 610.)
And Convention for 1953-54.
S:   June 19, 1953.
     (LKD, August 5, 1953.)
Agreement Concerning Danish Interests in Poland.
S:   March 16, 1954.
     (LKD, 1954, No. 1.)

NORWAY.
Agreement Concerning the Exchange of Commodities.
S:    December 31, 1948, Warsaw.
      UNTS, 1949, vol. 29, No. 430, p. 3.

        Came into force on January 1, 1949, and shall remain
valid until December 31, 1949.    Granting most favorable
treatment in the issue of import and export.

-1949-

GREAT BRITAIN.
Trade and Finance Agreement.
S:    January 14, 1949, Warsaw.
D:    Five years.
      UNTS, 1951, vol. 83, No. 1100, p. 3; BOT, January 22
      and 29, 1949; British S.P., vol. 154, p. 230.

        Came into force on January 14, as from the date of
signature.
Agreement Relating to Money and Property Subjected to Special
Measures since September 1, 1939 (With Annex.)
S:    January 14, 1949, Warsaw.
      UNTS, 1951, vol. 83, No. 1101, p. 51.
        Came into force on January 14, 1949.
      Hereto:
Supplement Agreement for 1950.
S:    March 17, 1950.
      (Keesing's CA, 1950, 2303 A; BOT, March 25, 1950.)
Agreement for 1952.
S:    July 1952.
      (BOT, July 5, 1952.)
Agreement for 1953.
S:    January 1953.
      (BOT, January 31, 1953.)

YUGOSLAVIA.
Trade Agreement for the Period of January 1, 1949, to Decem-
ber 31, 1949 (With Agreement on the Settlement of Payments;
Additional Protocol on Prices; Protocol and Exchange of Let-
ters).
S:    January 16, 1949, Belgrade.
      UNTS, 1951, vol. 115, No. 1564, p. 241.

CZECHOSLOVAKIA.
Agreement Concerning Mutual Legal Relations in Civil and
Criminal Cases (With Additional Protocol).
S:    January 21, 1949, Warsaw.
R:    April 10,  1949, Prague.
      DURP, 1949, No. 20, p. 315; UNTS, 1949, vol. 31, No.
      48, p. 205; British S. P. , vol. 155, p. 300.
Convention Concerning the Protection of Agricultural Plants
from Pests and Diseases.
S:    January 22, 1949, Prague.
R:    September 1, 1949, Warsaw.
      UNTS, 1951, vol. 85, No. 1142, p. 3.


USSR, BULGARIA, CZECHOSLOVAKIA, HUNGARY, RU-
MANIA.
Establishment of the Council of Economic Co-operation.
S:    January 25, 1949, Moscow.
      VPSS, 1949, p. 44 (Communique); Izvestiia, January 25,
      1949.

      Acceeded by the German Democratic Republic on Sep-
tember 30, 1950.


RUMANIA.
Treaty of Friendship, Co-operation, and Mutual Assistance.
S:    January 26, 1949, Bucharest.
Poland: J. Cyrankiewicz, Z. Modzelewski.
Rumania: Petru Groza, A. Pauker.
R:    November 29, 1949, Warsaw.
D:    Twenty years.
      DURP, 1950, No. 11, p. 139; UNTS, 1951, vol. 85, No.
      1143, p. 21; British S. P. , vol. 155, p. 838.


PAKISTAN.
Trade Agreement.
S:    April 5, 1959.
D:    One year.
      (Handelsblatt, May 10, 1949.)
      Hereto:
Trade Agreement for 1952-1953.
S:    June, 1952.
      (VWD, June 30, 1952.)


CZECHOSLOVAKIA.
Agreement Concerning the Right to Choose Nationality and

Resettlement.
S:   May 6, 1949.
     (Meissner, p. 107.)

DENMARK.
Protocol No. 1 on Danish Interests and Assets in Poland (With Exchange of Letters).
S:   May 12, 1949, Warsaw.
     UNTS, 1951, vol. 87, No. 1172, p. 179.
        Came into force on May 12, 1949, as from the date of signature.

BULGARIA.
Agreement Concerning Air Communications (With Annex and Additional Protocol).
S:   May 16, 1949, Warsaw.
R:   October 1, 1949, Sofia.
     DURP, 1950, No. 11,   p. 131; UNTS, 1951, vol. 84, No. 1140, p. 313.
        It annuls and replaces all previous Polish-Bulgarian agreements concerning air communications.

ISRAEL.
Trade Agreement.
S:   May 20, 1949.
     (NZZ, May 25, 1949.)
     Hereto:
Protocol Concerning Extension until the End of 1950.
S:   May 31, 1950.
     (VWD, June 4, 1950.)
New Settlement for 1951-52.
S:   April 2, 1951.
     (VWD, April 4, 1951.)
Settlement for 1954-55.
S:   April 16, 1954.
     (VWD, April 26, 1954; Israel Commerce, August 7, 1954.)

ITALY.
Trade Agreement.
S:   June 15, 1949.
D:   Three years.
     (Keesing's CA, 1949, 1970 B.)
     Hereto:

Protocol Concerning Extension.
S:    March 23, 1952; January, 1953; April 15, 1953; July 1,
      1953; June 23, 1954.
      (Inf. April 10, 1952; January 22 and April 23, 1953; July
      17, 1954.

SWITZERLAND.
Trade and Payments Agreement; Agreement Concerning the
Settlement of the Polish Pre-war Debts.
S:    June 25, 1949, Warsaw.
D:    Five years.
      (PDB, June 27, 1949; Keesing's CA, 1949, 1986 J.)
It was preceded by Short-term Agreements of March 4, 1946,
and June 10, 1947.
      (NfA, June 14, 1947; Keesing's CA, 1947, 1111 H.)
      Hereto:
Protocol on Exchange of Goods for 1950-51.
S:    July 6, 1950, Bern.
      (VWD, July 7, 1950; Keesing's CA, 1950, 2471.)
Protocol for 1951-52.
S:    September 15, 1951.
      (NZZ, September 18, 1951.)

EGYPT.
Trade Agreement.
S:    June 28, 1949.
D:    One year.
      (NfA, June 29, 1949.)
      Hereto:
Protocols Concerning Extension.
S:    November 19, 1950.
      (VWD, November 20, 1950.)
S:    January 20, 1951.
      VWD, January 25, 1951.
S:    January 2, 1952.
      (VWD, January 3, 1952.)
With the participation of the USSR and Bulgaria: Multilateral
Agreement on Exchange of Goods for 1953.
S:    March 10, 1953, Cairo.
      (VWD, March 11, 1953.)

GERMAN FEDERAL REPUBLIC.
Trade and Payment Agreement (Concluded by the American,
British, and French Military Governments).

S:   June 30, and July 15, 1949 (Trade Agreement).
     July 8, 1949 (Payment Agreement), Frankfurt/Main.
D:   One year.
     (AHE, Nos. 122-150, November 13, 1950.)

     Volume of trade for both sides to a value of approxi-
mately $34,405,000. Duration of credit from July 1, 1949,
until June 30, 1950: for Trade Agreement, from August 1, 1959,
until July 31, 1950.
     Hereto:
Protocol for the Trade Agreement for the Period from July 1,
1950, until June 20, 1951 (Volume of trade for both sides to
a value of approximately $32,630,000).
S:   October 9, 1950, Frankfurt (by German Delegation).
     (AHE, Nos. 122-150, November 13, 1950.)
Protocol Concerning the Trade Traffic of the Trade Agree-
ment for the period from January 1, 1952, until June 30, 1953
(Volume of trade to a value of $120 million).
S:   March 20, 1952, Bonn.
     (AHE, Nos. 22-52.)
With Extended List of Goods through Goods Protocol until Sep-
tember 30, 1953.
S:   July 9, 1953.
     (AHE, Nos. 41-54, August 9, 1954.)
Protocol Concerning the Negotiations of the Mixed German-
Polish Commission Regarding the Trade and Payment, with
Extension to the List of Goods from July 9, 1953, and Exten-
sion of the Notice Date in Payments Settlement.
S:   July 19, 1954, Bonn.
     (AHE, Nos. 41-54, August 9, 1954.)

     Goods Protocol of the Trade Agreement was paragraphed.
February 17, 1955, Warsaw.


CZECHOSLOVAKIA.
Agreement Concerning Privileged Rail Transit from Poland to
Poland through Czechoslovakia, through Broumov-Mezimesti.
S:   July 2, 1949, Prague.
R:   May 15, 1951, Warsaw
D:   Indeterminate period.
     DURP, 1951, No. 48, p. 411; UNTS, 1951, vol. 260, No.
     3709, p. 179.


BULGARIA.
Convention (With Final Protocol) Concerning Veterinary

Matters.
S:    September 26, 1949, Warsaw.
R:    October 29, 1952, Sofia.
D:    Five years.
      DURP, 1952, No. 50, p. 552; UNTS, 1957, vol. 260, No.
      3712, p. 249.

CHINESE PEOPLE'S REPUBLIC.
Exchange of Notes Concerning the Recognition of the Chinese
People's Republic.
S:    October 4, 1949, Warsaw.
      Zbiór Dok., 1950, No. 2, p. 102.

HUNGARY.
Convention Concerning the Protection of Agricultural Plants
from Pests and Diseases.
S:    October 29, 1949, Budapest.
R:    September 18, 1950, Warsaw.
      DURP, 1951, No. 11, p. 97; UNTS, 1951, vol. 260, No.
      3705, p. 91.

ICELAND.
Trade Agreement.
S:    November 18, 1949.
D:    One year.
      (BCB, January 25, 1950.)
      Hereto:
New Annual Settlements for 1953.
S:    February 23, 1953.
      (PDB, March 9, 1953.)
Settlement for 1954.
S:    February 2, 1954.
      (Trybuna Ludu, February 4, 1954.)
Protocol on Exchange of Goods for 1960-61 and Payments
Agreement.
S:    October 1, 1960, Warsaw.
      (Sprawy Międzynarodowe, 1960, No. 11, p. 137.)

DENMARK.
Agreement Concerning the Exchange of Commodities (With
Additional Protocol).
S:    December 7, 1949, Copenhagen.

D:   One year with the right to be extended for another year.
     UNTS, 1951, vol. 81. No. 1059, p. 21.

     Came into force upon signature.

## GENEVA CONVENTION.
Agreement Concerning the Protection of Civilian  Persons in
Time of War.
S:   August 12, 1949.
Acceded by Poland:  December 8, 1949.
     (Arch. VR 2 (1950), p. 446.)

## NORWAY.
Payments Agreement.
S:   December 21, 1949, Oslo.
     UNTS, 1950, vol. 48, No. 725, p. 107.

     Came into force on December 21, 1949, by signature.
Payments should be settled in Norwegian crowns.

-1950-

## INDONESIA.
Recognition of the United States of Indonesia.
S:   February 4, 1950, Warsaw.
     Zbiór Dok. , 1950, No. 4, p. 406.

## DEMOCRATIC REPUBLIC OF VIETNAM.
Recognition of the Democratic Republic of Vietnam.
S:   February 4, 1950, Warsaw.
     Zbiór Dok. , 1950, No. 4, p. 412.

## BELGIUM, LUXEMBOURG.
Trade and Payments Agreement.
S:   March 18, 1950.
D:   One year with the right for extension.
     (L'Echo, May 27, 1950.)
     Hereto:
Protocol for 1954.
S:   December 17, 1953.
     (IC, January 16, 1954.)
It was preceded by the Agreement for 1949.
S:   November 13, 1948.

(Keesing's CA, 1949, 1705 H.)

GERMAN DEMOCRATIC REPUBLIC.
Agreement Concerning Scientific and Technical Collaboration.
S:　June 6, 1950, Warsaw.
D:　Five years.
　Zbiór Dok., 1950, No. 7, p. 611; DDDR, p. 332.

GERMAN DEMOCRATIC REPUBLIC.
Protocol Concerning Cultural Collaboration.
S:　June 6, 1950, Warsaw.
D:　One year with automatic extension.
　(Eur. Arch. 5 (1950), p. 3329); DDDR, p. 334.

GERMAN DEMOCRATIC REPUBLIC.
Agreement Concerning the Exchange of Goods and Payments;
Payments Agreement.
S:　June 6, 1950, Warsaw.
　Meissner, p. 129 (Communique); DDDR, p. 129.
　Hereto:
Agreement Concerning Reciprocal Exchange of Goods for 1951.
S:　May 19, 1951, Berlin.
　(VWD, May 21, 1951); DDDR, p. 366.

USSR.
Agreement Concerning Delivery of Industrial Equipment to
Poland on Credit during the Period of 1951-1958; Agreement
Concerning Reciprocal Deliveries of Goods during the Period
1953-1958; Protocol Concerning the Exchange of Goods for
1951 and 1952 on the Basis of the Agreement of January 26, 1948.
S:　June 29, 1950, Moscow.
Further, Poland was a participant in the so-called "Three-
way Trade Agreement"--a Supplementary Protocol of the Soviet-
Finnish Trade Treaty of December 1, 1947; Agreement Con-
cerning the Exchange of Goods for 1949-1950.
S:　June 29, 1949.
　VPSS, 1949, p. 114.
　Hereto:
Agreement for 1951-52.
S:　April 14, 1951.
　(Keesing's CA, 1951, 2900 J.) (For Text of the Soviet-
　Finnish Treaty, see: Korolenko, p. 282.)
Protocol Concerning the Quotas of Goods for 1951.

S:    March 9, 1951.
VWD, March 13 and 27, 1951.
Supplementary Protocol for 1951-52.
S:    September 15, 1951.
(NZZ, September 18, 1951.)
Protocol Concerning the Exchange of Goods for 1953.
S:    April 22, 1954.
(Izvestiia, April 23, 1953.)
Protocol for 1954.
S:    February 11, 1954.
(Pravda, February 12, 1954; VT, 1954, No. 2, p. 39.)
Trade Protocol for 1955.
S:    February 25, 1955.
(VT, 1955, No. 3, p. 28; Izvestiia, February 26, 1955.)
Trade Protocol for 1956.
S:    February 8, 1956, Moscow.
(Izvestiia, February 9, 1956.)
Trade Protocol for 1957.
S:    April 9, 1957, Moscow.
(Izvestiia, April 10, 1957.)
Trade Protocol for 1958.
S:    February 5, 1958, Moscow.
(Izvestiia, February 6, 1958.)
Trade Protocol for 1959.
S:    November 21, 1958, Moscow.
(Izvestiia, November 22, 1958.)

GERMAN DEMOCRATIC REPUBLIC.
Agreement Concerning the Demarcation of the Established and Existing Polish-German Frontier.
S:    July 6, 1950, Zgorzelec (Görlitz).
Poland: J. Cyrankiewicz, Stefan Wierlowski.
German Democratic Republic: Otto Grotewohl, G. Dertinger.
R:    November 28, 1950, Berlin.
DURP, 1951, No. 14, p. 117; DDDR, p. 342; UNTS, 1959, vol. 319, No. 4631, p. 93; Zbiór Dok., 1950, No. 8, p. 703.
Hereto:
Instrument Confirming the Demarcation of the State Frontier between Poland and Germany (With Annexes).
S:    January 27, 1951, Frankfurt/Oder.
R:    October 22, 1952, Warsaw.
DURP, 1952, No. 53, p. 581; UNTS, 1959, vol. 319, No.

4631, p. 100

ALBANIA.
Agreement Concerning Cultural Co-operation.
S:    December 2, 1950, Tirana.
R:    April 18, 1951, Warsaw.
D:    Five years.
      DURP, 1952, No. 29, p. 261; UNTS, 1957, vol. 260, No.
      3707, p. 131.

      Teaching on university level of history, literature and
languages of each side, cultural exhibitions, exchange of cultural activities; creation of mixed Polish-Albanian Commission
for supervising and execution of this agreement.

-1951-

INDIA.
Trade Agreement
S:    January 5, 1951.
D:    One year.
      (Indian Trade Journal, February 1, 1951.)
Annually Extended:   For 1954-1956.
S:    March 3, 1954.
      (DpA, 1954, No. 6.)
It was preceded by a Trade Agreement of April 21, 1949.
      (Handelsblatt, June 8, 1949.)

ALBANIA.
Trade and Payments Agreement.
S:    January 24, 1951.
D:    Five years.
      (VWD, January 29, 1951.)
It was preceded by Trade Protocols:  For 1949 of January 22,
1949 and for 1950 of December 1949.
      (NfA, January 26, 1949; BCB, January 25, 1950.)
      Hereto:
New Settlement for 1953-1955.
S:    March 2, 1953.
      (PDB, March 21, 1953.)
Settlement for 1954.
S:    March 20, 1954.
      (DpA, 1954, Nos. 6, 7.)

ALBANIA.
Agreement Concerning Scientific and Technical Collaboration.
S:    January 25, 1951, Warsaw.
R:    December 27, 1951, Tirana.
D:    Five years.
      DURP, 1952, No. 7, p. 65; UNTS, 1951, vol. 260, No.
      3710, p. 217.


CHINESE PEOPLE'S REPUBLIC.
Trade Agreement for 1951; Navigation Agreement Establishing
a Polish-Chinese Navigational Company; Convention on Postal
and Telephone-Telegraph Communications.
S:    February 1, 1951, Peking.
      Hereto:
Trade Agreement for 1952.
S:    July 15, 1952.
      (Keesing's CA, 1952, 3563 C.)
Agreement for 1953, With Annexes on Payments.
S:    May 25, 1953.
      (Trybuna Ludu, May 27, 1953.)
Agreement for 1954.
S:    February 19, 1954.
      (Pravda, February 21, 1954.)


GERMAN DEMOCRATIC REPUBLIC.
Agreement Concerning Postal and Telephone-Telegraph Com-
munications.
S:    February 2, 1951, Warsaw.
      DDDR, p. 335.


USSR.
Agreement Concerning Exchange of Territories.
S:    February 15, 1951, Moscow.
R:    June 5, 1951.
      (Pravda, June 6, 1951); VVS, SSSR, July 14, 1951, No. 23;
      DURP, 1952, No. 11, p. 125; British S.P., vol. 158, p. 291.

        Description of the new border line appears in an article
by G. Rhode: "Polnisch-Sowjetischer Gebietaustausch, "
Zeitschrift für Geopolitik, January 22, 1951, pp. 443-444.
(480 qkm of the area of Drohobych-oblast (Ukr. SSR) is exchanged for the equal in size area of Lublin-Voivodship
(Poland).)

CHINESE PEOPLE'S REPUBLIC.
Agreement Concerning Cultural Collaboration.
S:    April 3, 1951, Warsaw.
R:    January 25, 1952, Peking.
D:    Five years.
      DURP, 1952, No. 14, p. 153.

CZECHOSLOVAKIA.
Trade and Payments Agreement.
S:    April 26, 1951.
D:    Five years.
      (NZZ, May 9, 1951; Keesing's CA, 1951, 2922 A.)
      Hereto:
Annual Settlements Concerning the Exchange of Goods for 1952.
S:    February 29, 1952.
      (MO, 1952, No. 1496.)
Settlement for 1953.
S:    March 17, 1953, Prague.
      (VWD, March 26, 1953.)

INDONESIA.
Trade and Payments Agreement.
S:    June 17, 1951.
      (PDB, June 23, 1951.)
      Hereto:
Trade Agreement for 1953-1954.
S:    May 1, 1953.
      (NU, 1953, No. 18.)
Agreement for 1954-1955.
S:    July, 1954.
      (VWD, July 5, 1954; NZZ, July 7, 1954.)

FRANCE.
Trade Agreement.
S:    September 17, 1951.
D:    One year.
      (Keesing's CA, 1951, 3117 F.)
      Hereto:
New Settlements for 1952-1953.
S:    October 13, 1952.
      (MO, October 23, 1952.)
Settlement for 1953-1954.
S:    October 31, 1953.
      (MO, 1953, No. 1581.)

Settlement for 1954-1955.
S:   November 25, 1954.
     (MO, February 2, 1954.)
Settlement for 1957 (Volume: $51 Million).
S:   December 3, 1956, Paris.
     (Press Release, December 15, 1956.)

GERMAN DEMOCRATIC REPUBLIC.
Agreement Concerning Exchange of Goods and Payments.
S:   November 10, 1951, Warsaw.
D:   Four years.
     DDDR, p. 367; (VWD, November 11, 1951.)
     Hereto:
Agreement Concerning Payments for 1952-1953.
S:   January 18, 1952, Warsaw.
     DDDR, p. 368.
Protocol Concerning the Conditions of Trade Deliveries for
1953.
S:   December 19, 1952, Warsaw.
     DDR, p. 370; (VWD, December 21, 1952.)
Protocol Concerning the Exchange of Goods and Payments for
1954.
S:   January 28, 1954.
     DDDR, p. 371.
And Supplementary Protocol.
S:   July 20, 1954.
     (VWD, July 22, 1954.)

                        -1952-

GERMAN DEMOCRATIC REPUBLIC.
Agreement Concerning Cultural Collaboration.
S:   January 8, 1952, Berlin.
R:   May 9, 1952, Warsaw.
D:   Five years.
     DURP, 1952, No. 27, p. 281; DDDR, p. 367.

GERMAN DEMOCRATIC REPUBLIC.
Navigation Agreement for the Regulation of Inland Water Navi-
gation and Maintenance of Border Waterways.
S:   February 6, 1952, Berlin.
R:   December 2, 1952, Berlin.
     DURP, 1952, No. 40, p. 477; DDDR, p. 368.

DENMARK.
Payments Agreement.
S:    June 9, 1952.
D:    Until March 31, 1954.
       UNTS, 1952, vol. 135, No. 1823, p. 221.

        Came into force on signature.  Payments to be made in Danish crowns.

DENMARK.
Agreement Concerning the Exchange of Goods.
S:    June 9, 1952, Warsaw.
D:    Until November 30, 1953.
       UNTS, 1952, vol. 135, No. 1822, p. 209.

        Came into force on June 9, 1952.

BRAZIL.
Trade Agreement.
S:    September 24, 1952.
       (MO, December 25, 1952.)
       Hereto:
Trade Agreement.
S:    November 23, 1954.
       (BCB, 1954, No. 12.)

IRAN.
Trade and Payments Agreement.
S:    October, 1952.
       (VWD, October 20, 1952.)
       Hereto:
New Settlement.
S:    June 1953.
       (VWD, 1953, p. 192.)
Trade Agreement for 1960.
S:    April 16, 1960, Teheran.
       (Sprawy Międzynarodowe, 1960, No. 5, p. 132.)

        Increase in trade transaction to 44 million Zloty.

GREECE.
Trade Agreement.
S:    October 22, 1952.
D:    One year.
       (NZZ, October 27, 1952.)
       Hereto:

Trade and Payments Agreement for 1954.
S:    January 11, 1954.
      (BOT, February 13, 1954.)

ARGENTINA.
Trade and Payments Agreement.
S:    October 30, 1952.
D:    Two years.
      (FS, December 15, 1952.)
      Hereto:
Agreements Concerning Exchange of Goods.
S:    January 11, 1954, and April, 1954.
      (VWD, January 12, 1954; April 27, 1954.)
Agreement Concerning Exchange of Goods in 1955.
S:    February 24, 1955.
      (Press Release, February 24, 1955, No. 18.)

-1953-

DENMARK.
Protocol No. 2 on Danish Interests and Assets in Poland.
S:    February 26, 1953, Warsaw.
      UNTS, 1954, vol. 186, No. 2496, p. 301.

      Came into force on August 6, 1953.

      The Polish Government shall pay to the Danish Government the amount of $3,430,000 as full and final compensation for Danish property nationalized by the Polish Government.

SPAIN.
Trade Agreement for 1953.
S:    April, 1953.
      Hereto:
Compensation Agreement.
S:    April 17, 1954.
      (Financial Times, May 8, 1954.)

USSR, ALBANIA, CZECHOSLOVAKIA, BULGARIA, GERMAN DEMOCRATIC REPUBLIC, HUNGARY, RUMANIA, CHINESE PEOPLE'S REPUBLIC.
Agreement Concerning International Freight Communication.
S:    July 31, 1953, Moscow.
D:    Indefinite.
      (VT, 1954, No. 2, pp. 32-33.)

Came into force on January 1, 1954.

USSR.
Protocol Concerning Preparation and Exchange of Radio Programs.
S:     September 5, 1953, Warsaw.
Sbornik, vol. 14, pp. 312-313, and vol. 15, p. 89.

Came into force on September 20, 1953.
Supplements the Agreement of October 22, 1949, Concerning Collaboration in the Field of Radio Broadcasting.

CZECHOSLOVAKIA.
Agreement Concerning Joint Building of the Oder-Danube Canal.
S:     September 8, 1953.
(Keesing's CA, 1953, 4154 F.)

USSR.
Communique About the Meeting of the Mixed Soviet-Polish Commission on Scientific and Technical Collaboration.
November 4, 1953, Warsaw.
     (Pravda, November 5, 1953; Izvestiia, November 5, 1953; VT, 1953, No. 11, p. 39.)

KOREAN PEOPLE'S REPUBLIC.
Agreement Concerning Economic Assistance to North Korea.
S:     November 13, 1953, Warsaw.
     (Zbiór Dok., 1953, No. 12, p. 2511.)

-1954-

CHINESE PEOPLE'S REPUBLIC.
Agreement Concerning Scientific and Technical Collaboration.
S:     July 20, 1954, Warsaw.
     (Trybuna Ludu, July 22, 1954.)
Note of the Polish Government With the Suggestion to France to Conclude a Treaty of Alliance and Mutual Assistance.
August 27, 1954.
     (Keesing's CA, 1952-54, p. 13770 A.)

GREAT BRITAIN.
Trade and Payments Agreement.

S:   November 11, 1954, Warsaw.
D:   Two years.
     (BOT, November 11, 1954; NZZ, November 14, 1954;
     Keesing's CA, 1952-54, p. 13930 B.)

     (1)  Poland undertook to pay Britain L 5,465,000, of
which L 2,665,000 was in settlement of claims for British
property rights and interests affected by Polish nationalization,
and the remaining L 2,800,000 covered pre-war debts guaranteed by the then Polish Government, as well as other pre-war
banking and commercial debts.

     (2)  Trade Agreement provided for the import of Polish
bacon and for annual negotiations for an exchange of other
goods.   The Anglo-Polish Trade and Financial Agreement of
1949 had expired at the end of 1953.
     Hereto:
Agreement Concerning Increasing Quotas for the Importation
of Certain Polish Goods.
S:   December 22, 1955, London.
Agreement on Details of Anglo-Polish Trade in 1956.
S:   February 6, 1956, London.
     (Keesing's CA, 1956, p. 14956.)

AUSTRIA.
The Austrian and Polish Governments Announced that They Had
Agreed to Raise Their Legations in Warsaw and Vienna to the
Status of Embassies.
S:   December 1, 1954.
     (Trybuna Ludu, December 1, 1954.)

USSR, CZECHOSLOVAKIA, GERMAN DEMOCRATIC RE-
PUBLIC, HUNGARY, RUMANIA, BULGARIA, ALBANIA.
Joint Declaration Concerning Policies of the Western Powers
in Regard to Germany.
S:   December 2, 1954, Moscow.
     Izvestiia, December 3, 1954; Sbornik, vol. 16, pp. 53-65;
     UNTS, vol. 226, pp. 153-186.

FINLAND.
The Finnish and Polish Government Agreed to Raise Their
Legations in Helsinki and Warsaw to the Status of Embassies.
S:   December 2, 1954, Warsaw.

-1955-

GERMAN FEDERAL REPUBLIC.
The Polish Council of State Unanimously Adopted a Resolution
Ending the State of War with Germany.  Statement by the Gov-
ernment was Issued on January 31, 1955.
    (Keesing's CA, 1955, p. 14091; Press Release, February
    2, 1955, No. 9.)


YUGOSLAVIA.
Trade and Payments Agreement for 1955.
S:    February 12, 1955, Belgrade.
    (Trybuna Ludu, February 13, 1955.)

          Exchange of goods amounts to $7-8 million for each
side.
    Hereto:
Protocol for 1956.
S:    November 14, 1955, Warsaw.
    (Trybuna Ludu, November 15, 1955.)
Agreement Concerning Poland's Supply of the Industrial and
Transportation Goods for Yugoslavia.
S:    February 3, 1956, Warsaw.
    (Trybuna Ludu, February 4, 1956; PDB, February 10,
    1956.)
Protocol Concerning Goods Exchange for 1957.
S:    November 27, 1956, Belgrade.
    (PDB, November 30, 1956.)
Protocol for 1957-58.
S:    June 5, 1957, Belgrade.
    (Trybuna Ludu, June 6, 1957.)


USSR.
Agreement Concerning Direct Moscow-Warsaw Air Service.
S:    February 19, 1955, Warsaw.
    (Trybuna Ludu, February 19, 1955; Izvestiia, February
    19, 1955.)


USSR, ALBANIA, BULGARIA, CZECHOSLOVAKIA, GERMAN
DEMOCRATIC REPUBLIC, HUNGARY, RUMANIA.  (The
Chinese People's Republic was associated by a statement but
not as a signatory.)
Treaty of Friendship, Co-operation, and Mutual Assistance
(Warsaw Pact).

S:  May 14, 1955, Warsaw.
D:  Twenty years with extension of ten years for those signa-
    tories which have not denounced it one year before expir-
    ation.   (On November 1, 1956, Hungary announced its
    withdrawal.  For Text see:  DIA, 1956, pp. 474-475).
    VVS, 1955, No. 9, Art. 225; DURP, 1955, No. 30, p.
    301; American J., Suppl., vol. 49 (1955) 194-99.

    Came into force on June 4, 1955.

    The Treaty provides for the establishment of:
(1)  a Unified Command of the Armed Forces of the Signatories,
(2)  a Political Consultative Committee of each Signatory.
     Hereto:
Communique Concerning the Establishment of a Joint Command
of the Armed Forces of the Signatories to the Treaty of Friendship, Co-operation, and Mutual Assistance of May 14, 1955.
Adopted:  May 14, 1955, in Warsaw.
     Izvestiia, May 15, 1955; NT, 1955, No. 21, Suppl. p. 68.

     Announces the selection of Soviet Marshal I. S. Konev
to head the Joint Command, headquarters of the Staff, which
is to be established in Moscow.
Final Communique of the Warsaw Conference of States of the
Soviet Bloc.
Issued May 17, 1955.
     Pravda, May 15, 1955; NT, 1955, No. 21, Suppl., pp.
     68-70.
Final Protocol of the Political Consultative Committee Estab-
lished by the Warsaw Treaty of May 14, 1955.
S:  January 28, 1956, Prague.
    Izvestiia, January 29, 1956.

     Two permanent organs under the Committee established
in Moscow.
(1)  A Permanent Commission to handle recommendations in
     the field of Foreign Policy,
(2)  A Unified Secretariat with Representatives of all Member
     States.
     Hereto:
Declaration Concerning International Security by the States
participating in the Warsaw Treaty of May 14, 1955, of Friendship, Co-operation, and Mutual Assistance.
S:  January 28, 1956, Prague.
    Izvestiia, January 29, 1956; NT, 1956, No. 6, pp. 33-36.

CANADA.
Trade Agreement.
S:    May 24, 1955.
      (PDB, June 3, 1955.)

USSR.
Agreement Concerning Aid by the USSR to Poland in Regard
to Development of Research Concerning Atomic Energy for the
Needs of the National Economy.
S:    April 23, 1955, Moscow.
      (Pravda, April 30, 1955.)

GERMAN DEMOCRATIC REPUBLIC.
Agreement Concerning the Establishment of Civil Aviation.
S:    June 20, 1955, Berlin.
      (Trybuna Ludu, June 22, 1955); DDDR, vol. 3, p. 458.
      Hereto:
Agreement Concerning Direct Warsaw-Berlin Air Service.
S:    January 12, 1956, Warsaw.
      (PDB, January 20, 1956); DDDR, vol. 3, p. 503.

INDIA.
Joint Statement Issued June 25, 1955, by Prime Minister Józef
Cyrankiewicz and Prime Minister Jawaharlal Nehru on the Oc-
casion of Nehru's Visit to Poland on June 23 to 26, 1955.
S:    June 25, 1955, Warsaw.
      Trybuna Ludu, June 26, 1955; Press Release, June 29,
      1955, No. 59 A.

      Adoption of five principles in the relations between
the two Countries:
(1)   Mutual respect for each other's territorial integrity and
      sovereignty,
(2)   Nonaggression,
(3)   Noninterference in each other's internal affairs for any
      reason whatever, whether of an economic, political, or
      ideological character,
(4)   Equality and mutual benefit,
(5)   Peaceful coexistence.

GERMAN DEMOCRATIC REPUBLIC.
Joint Statement by the Polish and East German Governments
Declaring that the Frontier between Poland and Germany had
been "definitely and irrevocably" fixed on the rivers Oder and
Neisse.

(Keesing's CA, 1955, p. 14816.)

The Declaration was issued on the fifth anniversary of the Agreement signed at Zgorzelec in 1950, in which the Polish and East German Governments had recognized the Oder-Neisse Line as the definite frontier between the two countries.

GERMAN DEMOCRATIC REPUBLIC.
Agreement Concerning the Collaboration in the Field of Veterinary Medicine.
S:   July 9, 1955, Berlin.
    (Trybuna Ludu, July 11, 1955); DDDR, vol. 3, p. 449.

NETHERLANDS.
Trade and Payments Agreement.
S:   August 4, 1955, Warsaw.
    (Trybuna Ludu, August 8, 1955; PDB, August 19, 1955.)
    Hereto:
Agreement Concerning Exchange of Goods for 1956-1957.
S:   July 24, 1956.
    (Życie Warszawy, July 25, 1956; EV, July 31, 1956.)

GERMAN DEMOCRATIC REPUBLIC.
Sanitation Agreement.
S:   October 7, 1955, Warsaw.
    DDDR, vol. 3, p. 498.

SYRIA.
Trade Agreement.
S:   October 10, 1955, Damascus.
    (Trybuna Ludu, October 16, 1955; VWD, October 13, 1955.)

BURMA.
Trade Agreement.
S:   October 31, 1955, Rangoon.
D:   Three years (1956-1958).
    (Trybuna Ludu, November 3, 1955.)

Burma is to deliver rice and other agricultural products in return for Polish supplies of consumer goods, machinery, and ships.

A separate one-year Protocol provided for Polish purchases from Burma, in 1956, of 50,000 to 60,000 long tons of rice.

A Polish Trade Mission is being established in Rangoon.
Hereto:
Protocol Concerning Shipment of Rice.
S:    November, 1955.
      (BOT, January 21, 1956.)

GERMAN DEMOCRATIC REPUBLIC.
Agreement on Zgorzelec (Görlitz) and Szczecin (Stettin); Establishment of Consulates.
S:    November 8, 1955.
      (Keesing's CA, 1955, p. 14562.)

      Under this Agreement Poland agreed to return to the German Democratic Republic part of the city of Zgorzelec, on the right (Polish) bank of the Neisse River. The Agreement also provided for a joint German-Polish Commission to work out a plan for the common administration of the port of Szczecin. It was also agreed that Poland would open consulates in Leipzig, Dresden, Görlitz, Erfurt, and Rostock, and that East Germany would establish Consulates at Wroclaw (Breslau) and Gdańsk.

YUGOSLAVIA.
Economic Agreements.
(1)   Trade Agreement for 1956,
(2)   Agreement on Scientific and Technical Co-operation,
(3)   Air Communication Agreement,
(4)   Settlement of Mutual Debtors' and Creditors' Claims Covering the Period of 1945 to 1955,
(5)   Agreement Concerning Tourist Traffic.
S:    November 14, 1955, Warsaw.
      (Keesing's CA, 1955, p. 14557; Trybuna Ludu, November 15, 1955.)

PARAGUAY.
Trade Agreement for 1956.
S:    November 23, 1955, Asuncion.
      (Trybuna Ludu, November 26, 1955; VWD, November 28, 1955.)

CEYLON.
Trade Agreement.
S:    December 2, 1955, Colombo.
      (Trybuna Ludu, December 4, 1955; WD, 1956, No. 1.)

Hereto:
Protocol on Goods Exchange for 1957-1958.
S:   July 29, 1957, London.
    (Trybuna Ludu, July 31, 1957.)

YUGOSLAVIA.
Civil Aviation Agreement for Belgrade-Warsaw Services.
S:   December 11, 1955, Belgrade.
    (Keesing's CA, 1955, p. 14628; Trybuna Ludu, December
    13, 1955.)

CHINESE PEOPLE'S REPUBLIC.
Trade and Payments Agreement for 1956.
S:   December 21, 1955, Warsaw.
    (Press Release, January 3, 1956.)

      Agreement calls for the shipment by Poland of complete
industrial plants, transport equipment, rolled goods, farm
and industrial machinery.  China will send iron ore, non-
ferrous metals and ores, raw materials for the foodstuffs and
textile industries as well as tea, rice, tobacco, and fruits.

DEMOCRATIC REPUBLIC OF VIETNAM.
Agreement on Tele-communication Service.
S:   December 24, 1955, Hanoi.
    (PDB, February 3, 1956.)

                      -1956-

LEBANESE REPUBLIC.
Trade and Payments Agreement.
S:   January 4, 1956, Beirut.
    (Trybuna Ludu, January 5 and 6, 1956.)
    Hereto:
Protocol to the Trade and Payments Agreement.
S:   April 7, 1960, Warsaw.
    (Trybuna Ludu, April 8, 1960.)

      Polish industrial products for Lebanese's food articles.

GERMAN DEMOCRATIC REPUBLIC.
Agreement Concerning Collaboration for Security of the Navigation and Fishing in the Baltic Sea Region.

S:    January 13, 1956, Warsaw.
      (Trybuna Ludu, January 14, 1956); DDDR, vol. 3, p. 503.

CZECHOSLOVAKIA.
Communications Agreement.
S:    January 13, 1956, Prague.
R:    September 14, 1956, Warsaw.
      DURP, 1957, No. 9, p. 77; UNTS, 1957, vol. 265, No.
      3811, p. 157; PDB, January 20, 1956.

      Poland shall provide in Polish seaports the facilities
necessary for Czechoslovakia to derive the greatest possible
benefit from those ports.  Merchant vessels flying the Czechoslovak flag shall be permitted to use Polish seaports as technical shipping bases.

USSR.
Protocol Concerning Expansion of Telegraph and Telephone
Service, Radio Broadcasting, and Television.
S:    February 7, 1956, Moscow.
      (Izvestiia, February 8, 1956.)

DEMOCRATIC REPUBLIC OF VIETNAM.
Trade and Payments Agreement for 1956; Agreement on Polish
Economic Assistance to Vietnam; Agreement Concerning
Scientific and Technical Collaboration; Protocol on Navigation.
S:    February 7, 1956, Hanoi.
      (PDB, February 24, 1956.)
      Hereto:
Protocol Concerning Goods Exchange for 1957.
S:    February 2, 1957, Hanoi.
      (Trybuna Ludu, February 8, 1957.)

AUSTRIA.
Air Transport Agreement (With Annexes).
S:    February 8, 1956, Vienna.
R:    April 1, 1956.
      UNTS, 1959, vol. 337, No. 4770, p. 221; (PDB, February
      17, 1956.)

PAKISTAN.
Trade Agreement for 1956.
S:    February 10, 1956, Karachi.
      (Press Release, February 15, 1956.)

Agreement contains an automatic renewal clause. Poland will send machinery and industrial installations. Pakistan will supply rice, cotton, wool, metal ores, and tea.

PORTUGAL.
Trade and Payments Agreement for 1956.
S:   February 12, 1956, Warsaw.
(Trybuna Ludu, February 13, 1956.)

EGYPT.
Agreement Concerning Direct Cairo-Warsaw Air Service.
S:   February 22, 1956, Cairo.
(PDB, February 24, 1956.)

YUGOSLAVIA.
Protocol Concerning Railroad Traffic.
S:   March 17, 1956, Belgrade.
(PDB, March 30, 1956.)

USSR, ALBANIA, BULGARIA, GERMAN DEMOCRATIC
REPUBLIC, PEOPLE'S REPUBLIC OF MONGOLIA, RUMANIA,
CZECHOSLOVAKIA, HUNGARY.
Agreement Concerning the Establishment of United Institute
for Atomic Research.
S:   March 26, 1956, Moscow.
Izvestiia, July 12, 1956.

KOREAN PEOPLE'S REPUBLIC.
Trade and Payments Agreement.
S:   March 28, 1956, Pyongyang.
(Trybuna Ludu, March 30, 1956; PDB, April 6, 1956.)
At the preceding Protocols, Agreement Concerning the Exchange of Goods was settled.
S:   June 2, 1952.
(Meissner, p. 197.)
Hereto:
Trade and Payments Agreement for 1957.
S:   April 26, 1957, Warsaw.
(Trybuna Ludu, April 27, 1957.)

INDIA.
Trade Treaty.
S:   April 3, 1956, New Delhi.

D:    Four years.
      (Trybuna Ludu, April 5, 1956; PDB, April 13, 1956.)
      Hereto:
Agreement Concerning the Realization of the Trade Treaty.
S:    April 11, 1956, New Delhi.
      (Trybuna Ludu, April 27, 1956.)
Agreement Concerning the Organization of the Indian-Polish
Navigation Service.
S:    May 16, 1956, New Delhi.
      (Trybuna Ludu, May 17, 1956; VWD, May 24, 1956.)
Agreement Concerning the Lists of Goods for 1957.
S:    March 1, 1957, New Delhi.
      (Trybuna Ludu, March 2, 1957; PDB, March   18, 1957.)

KOREAN PEOPLE'S REPUBLIC.
Agreement Concerning Cultural Co-operation.
S:    May 11, 1956, Pyongyang.
R:    By Poland, October 18, 1956.
D:    Five years.
      DURP, 1957, No. 19, p. 197.
      Hereto:
Agreement Concerning the Realization of the Cultural Co-
operation for the years 1960-1961.
S:    January 22, 1960, Pyongyang.
      (Trybuna Ludu, January 23, 1960.)

EGYPT.
Agreement Concerning the Establishment of Embassies in
Cairo and Warsaw.
S:    June, 1956.
      (Keesing's CA, 1956, p. 14908.)

SWEDEN.
Civic Air Transport Agreement (With Annexes and Exchange of
Notes).
S:    June 8, 1956, Warsaw.
      UNTS, 1959, vol. 334, No. 4771, p. 257; (Trybuna Ludu,
      June 14, 1956.)

USA.
Agreement on Settlement for Lend-Lease and Certain Claims.
S:    June 28, 1956, Washington.
      UNTS, 1957, vol. 273, No. 3944, p. 79.

Came into force on June 28, 1956, upon signature. Settlement of the "Lend-lease Article" Agreement being in operation under the Act of March 11, 1941.

USSR.
Agreement Concerning Cultural Co-operation.
S:   June 30, 1956, Warsaw.
R:   November 22, 1956, Moscow.
D:   Five years.
      DURP, 1957, No. 16, p. 153; UNTS, 1957, vol. 259, No. 3694, p. 311; VVS, 1956, No. 23, Art. 509.

The two Parties shall foster all forms of co-operation and mutual exchange in the spheres of science, higher and other education, literature, the graphic arts, music, the theater, the moving pictures, the press, radio, television, sports, and tourism, and shall encourage the exchange of experience relating to the propagation of culture.

YUGOSLAVIA.
Agreement Concerning Cultural Co-operation.
S:   July 6, 1956, Belgrade.
R:   February 19, 1957, Warsaw.
D:   Five years.
      DURP, 1957, No. 20, p. 205; UNTS, 1957, vol. 281, No. 4076, p. 143.

Co-operation and mutual exchange in the fields of science, higher and other education, literature, music, the theater, sports, and cultural activities.

CZECHOSLOVAKIA.
Protocol Concerning the Economic Co-operation in the System of the "Council for Common Economic Assistance."
S:   July 11, 1956, Warsaw.
      (Trybuna Ludu, July 12, 1956; PDB, July 20, 1956.)
      Hereto:
Protocol Concerning Economic Co-operation.
S:   March 29, 1957, Prague.
      (Trybuna Ludu, March 30, 1957.)
Agreement Concerning the Formation of the Committee for Economic Co-operation.
S:   May 7, 1957, Prague.
      (Trybuna Ludu, May 8, 1957.)

AFGHANISTAN.
Trade and Payments Agreement.
S:    August 2, 1956, Kabul.
D:    Three years.
      (Życie Warszawy, August 5 and 6, 1956; NU, 1956, No.
      22.)
      Hereto:
Protocol on the Exchange of Goods for 1957-1958.
S:    August 6, 1957, Warsaw.
      (Trybuna Ludu, August 7, 1957.)
Protocol on the Exchange of Goods for 1960.
S:    February 28, 1960, Warsaw.
      (Trybuna Ludu, February 29, 1960.)

INDIA.
Tele-communications Agreement.
S:    September 29, 1956, New Delhi.
R:    October 29, 1956, Warsaw.
      UNTS, 1957, vol. 276, No. 3993, p. 305.

BELGIUM.
Agreement Concerning Air Transport (With Annexes).
S:    October 17, 1956, Brussels.
R:    January 1, 1957, Warsaw.
      UNTS, 1960, vol. 355, No. 5100, p. 279.

GERMAN FEDERAL REPUBLIC.
Trade and Payments Agreement for 1957.
S:    November 16, 1956, Bonn.
      (BAZ, January 3, 1957; Trybuna Ludu, November 17,
      1956.)

      The volume of trade for both parties amounted to $70
million.
      Hereto:
Protocol Concerning the German-Polish Economic Agreement.
S:    December 3, 1957, Warsaw.
      (Trybuna Ludu, December 4, 1957.)

      Extending of the Protocols from November 16, 1956,
until March 31, 1958.
Protocol Concerning Increase of Trade Volume of More than
100 Million Zlotys.
S:    April 13, 1960, Warsaw.
      (Trybuna Ludu, April 14, 1960.)

USSR.
Communique Concerning Negotiations of the Representatives
of the CP USSR and the Soviet Government with the Polish
members of CC PZPR and the Polish Government.  Joint
statement Concerning Political, Economic and Military Relations.
S:    November 18, 1956, Moscow.
USSR:  N.S. Khrushchev, N.A. Bulganin.
Poland:  Wladyslaw Gomulka, Józef Cyrankiewicz.
     Trybuna Ludu, November 19, 1956; Pravda, November
     19, 1956; NT, 1956, No. 48, p. 37; Press Release, Novem-
     ber 20, 1956.

     The joint Declaration contained among others an Agree-
ment Concerning the Annulment of Polish Debts, a Soviet assurance Concerning the Delivery of 1.4 Million Tons of Grain
in 1957, as well as a Soviet promise of credit to the amount of
700 million rubles.
Covers:
(1)  International Relations, Particularly Egypt, the Chinese
     People's Republic, and Hungary;
(2)  Economic Relations;
(3)  Political Relations between USSR and Poland;
(4)  Military Relations, Including Statement Defining the Status
     of Soviet Army Stationed in Poland;
(5)  Agreement on Principles to Govern the Liberation and
     Repatriation of Poles in Places of Detention in the USSR.

     Soviet troops will remain in Poland for the time being.
They will not interfere in Poland's internal affairs and will
not be moved from their stations without the Polish Government's consent.  The joint statement issued by the Polish and
Soviet leaders expressed "confidence that the Hungarian working class and the whole Hungarian nation will discover in themselves sufficient strength to defend the gains of the people's
democratic system." Both countries will support the "Revolutionary Workers' and Peasants' Government" in Hungary (i. e.,
the Kadar Regime) and considered that "certain U.N. resolu-
tions on Hungary were designed to direct world opinion from
the aggression against Egypt."

     Furthermore, the statement says on the Polish-Soviet
Relations:  "...The Polish-Soviet alliance ... constitutes a
lasting guarantee of their security.  This alliance is the most
important factor in the strengthening of the independence of

the Polish People's Republic and the integrity of the Oder-Neisse frontier. ..."

CATHOLIC CHURCH OF POLAND.
Agreement on Relations between Church and State; Restoration of Religious Education.
S:    December 7, 1956, Warsaw.
      Keesing's CA, 1957, p. 15312.

        The Joint Commission reached agreement on six principles governing Church-State relations, as summarized below:
(1)   The Government will annul the Decree of February 9, 1953, dealing with appointments to ecclesiastical posts;
(2)   The following principles were agreed upon with regard to religious instruction in the schools:
      (a)  Religious instruction will be provided in all primary and secondary schools as an extra-curricular subject;
      (b)  Such instruction will be voluntary and will be provided for all children whose parents express a desire for it;
      (c)  Teachers of religion will be appointed by the education authorities in agreement with the Church and would be paid by the Ministry of Education;
      (d)  Inspection of religious instruction will be carried out by both Church and State authorities;
(3)   The Ministry of Health will issue directives for the religious care of the sick;
(4)   There will also be religious care for prisoners, including the appointment of prison chaplains;
(5)   Nuns removed in 1953 from the Opole, Wroclaw, and Katowice voevodships will be allowed to return there, while those who wish to leave Poland will be allowed to do so; parish priests who had been removed from their parishes in the Western voevodships will also be allowed to return;
(6)   The Episcopate and the Government had reached agreement on the appointment of five new Biships, nominated by the Holy See, to dioceses in Western Poland.

USSR.
Treaty Concerning the Legal Status of Soviet Troops Temporarily Stationed in Poland.
S:    December 17, 1956, Warsaw.
R:    By USSR, February 11, 1957, Moscow.
      By Poland, February 1, 1957.

(Pravda, December 18, 1956; Trybuna Ludu, December
18, 1956); VVS, 1957, No. 7, Art. 192; DURP, 1957, No.
29, p. 379; UNTS, vol. 266, p. 179; American J., vol. 52
(1958) 221-227.
Poland: M. Rapacki, Foreign Minister, and General M. Spychal-
ski, Defense Minister.
USSR: M. Shepilov, Foreign Minister, and Marshal Zhukov,
Defense Minister.

Came into force on February 27, 1957, and remained
in force as long as Soviet troops remain in Poland. Provides
that the number of Soviet troops in Poland and their location
shall be defined by special agreements. Movements of troops
and their training and maneuvers outside the base area to re-
quire Polish agreement. Agreements on special subjects have
to be signed (legal questions, transportations, custom regulations). A Mixed Soviet-Polish Commission to be established
with headquarters in Warsaw to settle disputes which arise
under the Treaty.

GREAT BRITAIN.
Trade Agreement for 1957-1959.
S:    December 31, 1956, Warsaw.
      (Keesing's CA, 1957, p. 15578; PDB, January 5, 1957.)

      It provided that:
(1)   Import quotas would be negotiated annually;
(2)   Poland would purchase L 15,750,000 worth of goods from
      Great Britain during 1957;
(3)   The British market would remain open without restriction
      to imports of a number of Polish products.

      Trading lists for 1957 envisaged an increase in Anglo-
Polish trade to an overall value of L 64,000,000, compared to
L 47,500,000 during 11 months of 1956 and L 43,200,000 in
1954.


-1957-


CHINESE PEOPLE'S REPUBLIC.
Joint Statement on Policy.
Issued January 12, 1957, in Warsaw on the occasion of the
visit of Chou En-lai to Poland and other countries.
      (Trybuna Ludu, January 17, 1957; PDB, January 19, 1957;
      Zbiór Dok., 1957, No. 1, p. 3; Keesing's CA, 1957, p.
      15463; Press Release, January 18, 1957.)

A Joint Statement emphasizing that relations between
Socialist countries should be based on the principle of equality
between them.

URUGUAY.
Payments Agreement for 1957.
S:    January 23, 1957, Montevideo.
      (Trybuna Ludu, January 25, 1957.)

GERMAN DEMOCRATIC REPUBLIC.
Agreement (With Final Protocol) Concerning Legal Relations
in Civil, Family, and Criminal Cases.
S:    February 1, 1957, Warsaw.
R:    October 11, 1957, Berlin.
      DURP, 1958, No. 27, p. 401; UNTS, 1959, vol. 319, No.
      4632, p. 115.

EGYPT.
Cultural Agreement.
S:    February 2, 1957, Cairo.
R:    April 29, 1958, Warsaw.
      DURP, 1958, No. 42, p. 593; UNTS, 1959, vol. 319, No.
      4633, p. 221.

      The two Parties will accord mutual assistance in all
that may encourage scientific and artistic co-operation between
them. Exchange of university professors and scientists engaged in scientific research and between institutes and universities of both countries is provided.

USSR.
Protocol Concerning Cultural Collaboration in 1957.
S:    February 6, 1957, Moscow.
      (Izvestiia, February 7, 1957.)

JAPAN.
Agreement Concerning the Re-establishment of Normal Rela-
tions.
S:    February 8, 1957, New York.
R:    May 18, 1957, Warsaw.
      DURP, 1957, No. 49, p. 545; UNTS, 1958, vol. 318, No.
      4620, p. 251.

      Re-establishment of diplomatic relations and exchange
of diplomatic representatives with the rank of ambassador.

Japan and Poland undertake not to intervene, whether directly
or indirectly, in each other's internal affairs, regardless of
economic, political or ideological reasons.

MONGOLIAN PEOPLE'S REPUBLIC.
Agreement on Cultural Co-operation.
S:   February 15, 1957, Warsaw.
     (Trybuna Ludu, February 16, 1957.)

USSR.
Protocol of the Eleventh Meeting of the Soviet-Polish Commis-
sion for Scientific and Technical Collaboration.
S:   March 3, 1957, Moscow.
     (Izvestiia, March 7, 1957; BSE, 1958, p. 35.)

USSR.
Treaty Concerning Demarcation of the Existing Soviet-Polish
State Frontier in the Sector Adjoining the Baltic Sea (With
two maps).
S:   March 5, 1957, Moscow.
R:   May 4, 1957, Warsaw.
     DURP, 1958, No. 37, p. 532; UNTS, 1957, vol. 274, No.
     3963, p. 133.

     Treaty provides for the establishment of a Mixed Soviet-
Polish Frontier Demarcation Commission to complete work
within six months from date the treaty becomes effective.

BURMA.
Joint Declaration on the Occasion of the Visit of the Polish
Government Delegation to Burma.
S:   March 21, 1957, Rangoon.
     (Zbiór Dok., 1957, No. 3, p. 302.)

CAMBODIA.
Joint Communique of the Delegation of the Polish Government
and the Government of Cambodia.
S:   March 24, 1957, Phnom Penh.
     (Zbiór Dok., 1957, No. 3, p. 307.)

USSR.
Agreement on the Time Limits and Procedure of Further
Repatriation of Persons of Polish Nationality from the USSR.
S:   March 25, 1957, Moscow.

R:     July 10, 1957, Warsaw.
       DURP, 1957, No. 47, p. 529; UNTS, 1957, vol. 281, No.
       4075, p. 121.

(1)    The right of repatriation is extended to:
       (a)  All persons who were Polish nationals on September
            17, 1939,
       (b)  The wives, children, and parents living with such
            repatriots in one household, even if they had not been
            Polish nationals on September 17, 1939,
       (c)  Children of such persons born after September 17,
            1939, who had no close relatives in the USSR and
            whose relatives were or would be residing in Poland,
            or repatriation had been applied for by the Polish
            authorities,
       (d)  Persons of Jewish nationality who possessed Polish
            citizenship on September 17, 1939;
(2)    Persons entitled to repatriation who are at present in
       Soviet prison or labor camps will be released or trans-
       ferred to the Polish authorities, regardless of their terms
       of detention;
(3)    Repatriation will remain voluntary and applications will be
       accepted until October 1, 1958, The repatriation scheme
       will be completed by December 1, 1958.

       The number of persons affected by the Agreement was
not officially stated, but British, U.S., and French press reports from Warsaw determined the figure to be between 120,000
and 500,000.

USSR.
Agreement Concerning Scientific Collaboration in 1957 between
the Academies of Sciences of the USSR and Poland.
S:     March 27, 1957, Warsaw.
       (Pravda, March 29, 1957; Izvestiia, March 29, 1957.)

       Includes the fields of physics, chemistry, technology,
geology, and history.

INDIA.
Agreement Concerning Cultural Co-operation.
S:     March 27, 1957, New Delhi.
R:     August 12, 1958, Warsaw.
D:     Five years.
       DURP, 1958, No. 57, p. 753; Zbiór Dok., 1957, No. 4, p.
       468.

Also Joint Communique of the Prime Ministers of Both Governments.
　　　Zbiór Dok., 1957, No. 4, p. 462; UNTS, 1959, vol. 319,
　　　No. 4635, p. 263.

　　　Setting up the Commission with two sub-Commissions:
One with residence in Warsaw,
One with residence in New Delhi.

MONGOLIAN PEOPLE'S REPUBLIC.
Trade and Payments Agreement.
S:　March 30, 1957, Ulan Bator.
　　(Trybuna Ludu, March 31, 1957.)


YUGOSLAVIA.
Agreement Concerning Collaboration for the Peaceful Use of
Atomic Energy.
S:　April 4, 1957, Warsaw.
　　(Trybuna Ludu, April 5, 1957.)

DEMOCRATIC REPUBLIC OF VIETNAM.
Agreement Concerning Cultural Co-operation.
S:　April 6, 1957, Hanoi.
R:　June 2, 1958, Warsaw.
D:　Five years.
　　DURP, 1958, No. 53, p. 722.

DEMOCRATIC REPUBLIC OF VIETNAM.
Joint Declaration of the Prime Ministers on the Occasion of
the Visit of the Polish Government Delegation.
S:　April 6, 1957, Hanoi.
　　(Zbiór Dok., 1957, No. 4, p. 473; Trybuna Ludu, April
　　7, 1957.)


CZECHOSLOVAKIA.
Agreement for the Establishment of an Economic Co-operation
Committee.
S:　April 7, 1957, Prague.
　　(Keesing's CA, 1958, p. 16290); Dokumenty, p. 259.
　　Hereto:
Protocol Concerning Czechoslovak-Polish Economical Co-
operation.
S:　April 17, 1958, Prague.
　　Dokumenty, p. 261.

Agreement Concerning Economic and Technical Co-operation
for 1960-61.
S:      April 21, 1960, Ostrawica.
        (Sprawy Międzynarodowe, 1960, No. 5, p. 132.)

CHINESE PEOPLE'S REPUBLIC.
Joint Statement Signed by Premier Józef Cyrankiewicz and
Premier Chou En-lai in Peking on April 11, 1957.
S:      April 11, 1957, Peking.
        (Trybuna Ludu, April 12, 1957; Zbiór Dok., 1957, No. 4,
        p. 483; Press Release, April 13, 1957.)

        The two Parties fully support the reasonable aspiration
of the German people for the unification of Germany and support the efforts made by the German Democratic Republic in
this direction.  The Government of the People's Republic of
China reaffirms that the existing Western border of Poland on
the Oder and Neisse is a border of peace between Poland and
Germany which is in the interest of European security and
which must not be altered.

KOREAN PEOPLE'S REPUBLIC.
Joint Declaration of the Prime Ministers on the Occasion of
the Visit of the Polish Government Delegation.
S:      April 17, 1957, Pyongyang.
        (Trybuna Ludu, April 18, 1957; Zbiór Dok., 1957, No. 4,
        p. 494.)

GERMAN DEMOCRATIC REPUBLIC.
Agreement Concerning Co-operation in the Construction of
Brown Coal Open-cast Mines.
S:      April 17, 1957, Berlin.
        (PDB, April 27, 1957.)

MONGOLIAN PEOPLE'S REPUBLIC.
Joint Declaration of the Prime Ministers on the Occasion of the
Visit of Polish Government Delegation.
S:      April 18, 1957, Ulan Bator.
        (Zbiór Dok., 1957, No. 4, p. 503.)

USA.
Ford Foundation Grant to Poland for Cultural Exchanges with
the West.
S:      April, 1957.
        (Keesing's CA, 1957, p. 15638.)

A grant of $500,000 to finance an exchange of scholars, writers, and other academic workers between Poland, the USA, and Western Europe.

AFGHANISTAN.
Joint Statement on the Occasion of the Visit of the Prime Minister of Afghanistan, H.R.H. Sardar Mohammed Daud, to Poland.
S:    April 30, 1957, Warsaw.
(Trybuna Ludu, May 1, 1957; Zbiór Dok., 1957, No. 4, p. 533; Press Release, May 2, 1957.)

Both sides express the conviction that the visit of the Prime Minister of Afghanistan will contribute towards further strengthening of relations between the two countries and will serve the cause of peaceful international co-operation.

CZECHOSLOVAKIA.
Joint Polish-Czechoslovak Declaration.
S:    May 7, 1957, Prague.
(Trybuna Ludu, May 8, 1957; Press Release, May 9, 1957.)

In the fall of systematic revisionist attacks against the peace frontier on the Oder and Neisse, conducted from West Germany and supported by various official circles, both sides consider it essential to state that this question is settled once and for all. The government of Czechoslovakia fully shares the attitude taken by the Polish Government with regard to the inviolability of the Oder and Neisse frontier and gives Poland its unlimited support. Both Governments are of the opinion that the unification of Germany is a question to be settled by the Germans themselves.

USSR, GERMAN DEMOCRATIC REPUBLIC.
Protocol Concerning an Increase of the Relative Role of Maritime Transport in Foreign Trade and Concerning Organization of Freight Transportation on the Internal Waterways of the USSR, Poland, and the German Democratic Republic.
S:    May 22, 1957, Moscow.
(VT, 1957, No. 7, p. 36; Trybuna Ludu, May 23, 1957.)

USA.
Surplus Agricultural Commodities Agreement.
S:    June 7, 1957, Washington.
UNTS, 1958, vol. 291, No. 4243, p. 41; Trybuna Ludu, June 8, 1957; New York Times, May 8, 1957.

Came into force on June 7, 1957, upon signature.

(1) The USA will extend to Poland a "line of credit" of $30,000,000 to be administered by the U.S. Export-Import Bank for the purchase of agricultural products and mining equipment and the payment of transportation costs;

(2) The U.S. Government will also sell wheat, cotton, fats, and oils to Poland for about $18,900,000. Payments will be made in Polish currency (at the rate of 24 zlotys to the dollar), and the zloty balances could be used for a variety of purposes in Poland, including the payment of the expenses of the U.S. Embassy in Warsaw.

Finally, both Governments agreed:

(1) To start negotiations early in 1958 for a lump-sum settlement of American property claims resulting from nationalization measures and other property requisitionings by Poland;

(2) To begin discussion at an early date on the release of pre-war Polish assets in the USA which had been blocked under U.S. regulations and whose value was estimated at less than $2,000,000.

GERMAN DEMOCRATIC REPUBLIC.
Joint Declaration of the Prime Ministers on the Occasion of the Visit of the Polish Party and Governmental Delegation.
S:     June 22, 1957, Moscow.
(Trybuna Ludu, June 21, 1957; ND, June 21, 1957.)

USSR.
Agreement Concerning Co-operation in the Field of Radio and Television Services.
S:     June 22, 1957, Moscow.
(Trybuna Ludu, June 21, 1957; Izvestiia, June 23, 1957.)

SPAIN.
Payments Agreement.
S:     July 5, 1957, Paris.
(Trybuna Ludu, July 6, 1957.)

FRANCE.
Cultural Agreement.
S:     July 9, 1957, Paris.
(Trybuna Ludu, July 10, 1957; PDB, July 18, 1957;

Keesing's CA, 1957, p. 15668; Press Release, July 10, 1957.)

Agreement provides for the free movement of nationals of either country within the other, the mutual importation of books, newspapers, and periodicals, the promotion of the teaching of the French and Polish languages, broadcast and television exchanges, and an increase in the number of scholarships and scientific fellowships.

GERMAN DEMOCRATIC REPUBLIC.
Agreement Concerning Collaboration in the Question of Social Security and Social Welfare; Treaty on Co-operation in Social Policy.
S:    July 13, 1957, Warsaw.
R:    February 28, 1958, Berlin.
D:    Three years.
      DURP, 1958, No. 51, p. 689; UNTS, 1959, vol. 319, No. 4634, p. 229; ND, July 14, 1957.

USSR.
Agreement Concerning Exchange of Students and Research Workers.
S:    August 23, 1957, Warsaw.
      (BSE, 1958, p. 37.)

YUGOSLAVIA.
Joint Declaration Signed by President J. Broz-Tito and Wladyslaw Gomulka.
S:    September 16, 1957, Belgrade.
      (Trybuna Ludu, September 17, 1957; Press Release, September 17, 1957; Keesing's CA, 1957, p. 15807.)

The Statement announces, inter alia:
(1)   Increased co-operation between the two parties,
(2)   Closer governmental consultation,
(3)   The formation of a Joint Commission for Economic Co-operation,
(4)   Yugoslav recognition of the Oder-Neisse Line as the Western frontier of Poland,
(5)   The joint support of both countries for the Soviet thesis that there were two German States and that German reunification could only come about through direct talks between the German Federal Republic with the German Democratic Republic.

GERMAN DEMOCRATIC REPUBLIC.
Agreement Concerning Collaboration by the Use of Atomic
Energy for Peaceful Purposes.
S:    September 17, 1957, Berlin.
      (Trybuna Ludu, September 18, 1957; ND, September 18,
      1957.)

MONGOLIAN PEOPLE'S REPUBLIC.
Joint Polish-Mongolian Declaration.
S:    September 19, 1957, Warsaw, on the occasion of the visit
      of the Mongolian Delegation led by Prime Minister Tsedenbal
      Yumzhagin.
      (Press Release, September 20, 1957.)

      Both sides pledge their support for the struggle of the
peoples of the Near and Middle East for their national independence, and declare themselves against colonialism endeavoring
to interfere in the internal affairs of these countries, as is the
case with regard to Syria.

FRANCE.
Agreement on Exchange of Scientists.
S:    October 24, 1957, Warsaw.
D:    1957-1958.
      (Keesing's CA, 1957, p. 15826.)

USSR.
Agreement Concerning Legal Assistance in Cases Arising out
of the Temporary Stationing of Soviet Troops in Poland.
S:    October 26, 1957, Warsaw.
      DURP, 1958, No. 37, p. 535; VVS, 1958, No. 6, Art. 126;
      Izvestiia, October 27, 1957.

CZECHOSLOVAKIA.
Agreement Concerning the Problems of Water Transport and
Mutual Assistance in Transit Traffic.
S:    November 12, 1957, Warsaw.
      (Trybuna Ludu, November 13, 1957.)

GERMAN DEMOCRATIC REPUBLIC.
Consular Convention.
S:    November 25, 1957, Warsaw.
R:    October 31, 1958, Berlin.
      DURP, 1959, No. 7, p. 49; UNTS, 1959, vol. 340, No.
      4862, p. 99; ND, November 26, 1957.

GREAT BRITAIN.
Agreement on Direct London-Warsaw Air Service.
S:   November 27, 1957.
     (Keesing's CA, 1957, p. 15906.)
     Effective not later than April 1, 1958.

CZECHOSLOVAKIA.
Agreement Concerning the Co-operation in the area of Industrial Machinery.
S:   December 11, 1957, Prague.
     (Trybuna Ludu, December 12, 1957.)

USSR.
Treaty Concerning Legal Assistance and Relations in Civil, Family, and Criminal Cases.
S:   December 28, 1957, Warsaw.
R:   June 8, 1958, Moscow.
D:   Five years.
     DURP, 1958, No. 32, p. 468; UNTS, 1959, vol. 320, No. 4638, p. 3; Izvestiia, December 29, 1957; Trybuna Ludu, December 12, 1957.

-1958-

YUGOSLAVIA.
Agreement Concerning Social Insurance, with Additional Protocol and Agreement Concerning Co-operation in the Field of Social Policy.
S:   January 16, 1958, Warsaw.
R:   December 9, 1958, Belgrade.
     DURP, 1959, No. 19, pp. 301, 309; UNTS, 1959, vol. 340, Nos. 4863, 4864, pp. 137, 181.

     The contracting Parties shall co-operate in all problems and in all sectors of social policy in order to intensify social progress in their own States and at the international level.

USSR.
Consular Convention.
S:   January 21, 1958, Warsaw.
R:   June 8, 1958, Moscow.
D:   Unlimited period.
     DURP, 1958, No. 32, p. 457; UNTS, 1959, vol. 319, No. 4637, p. 291.

This Convention renounces the Consular Convention concluded on July 18, 1924.

USSR.
Convention Regulating the Citizenship of Persons Having Dual Citizenship.
S:    January 21, 1958, Warsaw.
R:    May 8, 1958, Moscow.
      DURP, 1958, No. 32, p. 451; UNTS, 1959, vol. 319, No. 4636, p. 277.

Persons resident in the territory of one contracting Party whom both contracting Parties, under their legislation, regard as their citizens, may, in accordance with this convention, opt for the citizenship of either Party.

USSR.
Agreement on Soviet Technical Aid for Polish Atomic Energy Development.
S:    January 22, 1958, Moscow.
      (Keesing's CA, 1958, p. 16106.)

Under its terms, the Soviet Union will assist Poland in designing and building her second experimental reactor and her first atomic power station.

CZECHOSLOVAKIA.
Agreement Concerning Railroad Communication System.
S:    January 31, 1958, Prague.
R:    May 31, 1958, Warsaw.
D:    Five years.
      DURP, 1958, No. 53, p. 709.

USA.
Agreement Concerning Increased U.S. Economic Aid, Sale of U.S. Surplus Farm Products, Large U.S. Credit.
S:    February 15, 1958, Washington.
      UNTS, 1958, vol. 307, No. 4452, p. 217; (Keesing's CA, 1958, p. 16039.)

Came into force on February 15, 1958, upon signature.
Agreement provides for:
(1)   The sale to Poland of U.S. surplus farm products worth $73,000,000 at world market prices, against payment in zlotys;

(2)  The extension to Poland of a $25,000,000 credit for the purchase of additional agricultural products, raw materials, machinery, and medical equipment.

YUGOSLAVIA.
Agreement on Creation of Committee for Economic Co-operation.
S:  February 20, 1958, Warsaw.
    (Keesing's CA, 1958, p. 16074.)

    The Agreement implemented a decision made by President Tito and W. Gomulka during the latter's visit to Belgrade in September, 1957.

USSR.
Agreement on Mutual Commodity Supplies for 1958-1960.
S:  February, 1958, Moscow.
    (Keesing's CA, 1959, p. 16572.)

    Under this Agreement, the Polish-Soviet trade is expected to increase by 1960 to about 30,000,000,000 rubles (approximately $750,000,000) and the Soviet share in Poland's total foreign trade during the three year period to 28 per cent. The USSR will supply Poland chiefly with raw materials. Polish exports to the USSR will mostly consist of machinery and equipment.

USSR.
Protocol Concerning the Delimination of Polish and Soviet Territorial Waters in the Gulf of Gdańsk of the Baltic Sea.
S:  March 18, 1958, Warsaw.
R:  July 29, 1958, Moscow.
    DURP, 1958, No. 76, p. 947.

CZECHOSLOVAKIA.
Agreement Concerning the Settlement of Outstanding Property Matters.
S:  March 29, 1958, Prague.
R:  January 9, 1959, Warsaw.
    DURP, 1959, No. 19, p. 312; UNTS, 1959, vol. 340, No. 4865, p. 199.

    Settlement of the outstanding property matters relating to the period before May 9, 1945.

INDIA.
Protocol Concerning Indian-Polish Trade Agreement; List of

Goods for 1958.
S:    March 31, 1958, New Delhi.
      (Trybuna Ludu, April 2, 1958.)

      Poland will export machines, chemical products, and
others. India will supply iron, tea, and leather.
      Hereto:
Protocol on Exchange of Goods for 1962-65.
S:    May 7, 1960, New Delhi.
      (Trybuna Ludu, May 8, 1960.)

RUMANIA.
Trade and Payments Agreement for 1958.
S:    April 1, 1958, Bucharest.
      (Trybuna Ludu, April 3, 1958.)

      Volume of trade exchange for 1958 should be increased
by 15 per cent compared with 1957. Poland will export coke,
machinery, and motors. Rumania will supply oil, gas, cement,
and wine.
      Hereto:
Trade and Payments Agreement for 1961-65.
S:    May 28, 1960, Bucharest.
      (Sprawy Międzynarodowe, 1960, No. 7-8, p. 189.)

      Increase of trade up to 65 per cent.

BULGARIA.
Payments Agreement for 1958-1960 and Trade Agreement for
1958.
S:    April 2, 1958, Sofia.
      (Trybuna Ludu, April 3, 1958.)

      Increase in trade for 1958 by 50 per cent compared with
1957.
      Hereto:
Trade Agreement for 1961-65.
S:    March 27, 1960, Warsaw.
      (Trybuna Ludu, March 28, 1960.)

      Poland will deliver several industrial types of equipment.
Trade will double.

RUMANIA.
Protocol Concerning Polish Aid in Building a Factory for Cel-
lulose in Braila, Rumania.

S:    April 3, 1958, Bucharest.
      (Trybuna Ludu, April 4, 1958.)

      Annual production is expected to be 200,000 tons.

CHINESE PEOPLE'S REPUBLIC.
Agreement Concerning Trade Exchange for 1959-1962.
S:    April 7, 1958, Peking.
      (Trybuna Ludu, April 8 and 9, 1958.)

      Poland will supply transport vehicles, agricultural
machinery, and 17 industrial factories.  China will export iron
ore, wolfram, tea, dry fruits, rice, and silk.
      Hereto:
Protocol on the Exchange of Goods for 1960-61.
S:    February 11, 1960.
      (Trybuna Ludu, February 12, 1960.)

USSR.
General Understanding on Trade Exchanges for 1961-1965.
S:    April 9, 1958, Moscow.
      (Keesing's CA, 1959, p. 16572; Trybuna Ludu, April 11,
      1958.)

      USSR will export iron ore, manganese and chrome ores,
tins, concentrates, grain, cotton, flax, and others to Poland.
Polish supplies to the USSR will include coal, coke, steel
pipes, zinc, sea-going ships, building material, machinery,
sugar refining plant, and others.

JAPAN.
Treaty on Commerce.
S:    April 26, 1958, Tokyo.
R:    January 16, 1959, Warsaw.
D:    Five years.
      DURP, 1959, No. 19, p. 316; UNTS, 1959, vol. 340, No.
      4866, p. 221.

      Parties have resolved to conclude this Treaty, envisaged
in Article 5 of the Agreement signed on February 8, 1957.
Most favored-nation treatment in all matters with respect to
customs duties and charges of all kinds.

BULGARIA.
Joint Declaration Signed in Sofia by the Delegation of the Central Committee of the Polish United Workers' Party, the Polish

Government, the Delegation of the Central Committee of the
Communist Party of Bulgaria, and the Bulgarian Government
on the World Policy and Trade Agreement.
S:    May 8, 1958, Sofia.
      (Press Release, May 10, 1958; Trybuna Ludu, May 9,
      1958.)

        The two delegations stated that the idea of peaceful co-
existence and of the settlement of controversial questions
through negotiations are mobilizing the evermore powerful
social forces of all nations towards the struggle against the
danger of destructive nuclear war for disarmament and peace.

        Increase in trade of 50 per cent compared to 1957.

HUNGARY.

Joint Declaration of the Delegation of the Polish United Worker's
Party and the CC of the Hungarian Socialist Worker's Party and
both Governments.
S:    May 12, 1958, Budapest.
      (Press Release, May 13, 1958; Trybuna Ludu, May 14,
      1958.)

        The declaration stated that the arming of the German
Federal Republic with atomic and rocket weapons is particularly dangerous in Europe.  The Hungarian Government fully
supports the proposal of the Polish People's Republic for the
creation of an atom-free zone in Middle Europe.  The co-
existence policy is basic for both countries.  The platforms of
both Communist countries are identical.  Close economical
co-operation will be continued.

RUMANIA.

Joint Declaration of the Delegation of the Polish United Workers'
Party and the Polish Government and the Delegations of Ru-
manian Workers' Party and Government.
S:    May 14, 1958, Bucharest.
      (Press Release, May 19, 1958; Trybuna Ludu, May 15,
      1958.)

        The Declaration states that the Governments of Poland
and Rumania, serving the vital interests of their nations, are
conducting, together with the Soviet Union, the Chinese People's
Republic, and the other Socialist countries, a consistent foreign policy in defense of peace and peaceful co-existence with
all countries, regardless of their social systems.  Both coun-

tries protest against the equipment of the West German Army
with nuclear weapons.

USSR, ALBANIA, BULGARIA, CZECHOSLOVAKIA, GERMAN
DEMOCRATIC REPUBLIC, HUNGARY, RUMANIA.
Joint Declaration of the Meeting of the Warsaw Pact States.
S:   May 24, 1958, Moscow.
     Pravda, May 25, 1958; Trybuna Ludu, May 25, 1958.

     The reduction of armed forces by 490,000 men; evacu-
ation of Soviet troops from Rumania; withdrawal of one Soviet
division from Hungary; proposal of signing a nonaggression
pact with members of the North Atlantic Treaty Organization.

USA.
Exchange of Notes (With Memorandum) Constituting an Agree-
ment Relating to the Distribution of Publications.
S:   May 30, 1958, Warsaw.
     UNTS, 1958, vol. 315, No. 4572, p. 231.

     Came into force on May 30, 1958, with the exchange of
said notes.

CZECHOSLOVAKIA.
Agreement Concerning the Final Demarcation of the State
Frontier.
S:   June 13, 1958, Warsaw.
R:   February 14, 1959, Prague.
     DURP, 1959, No. 25, p. 369; UNTS, 1960, vol. 354, No.
     5064, p. 221.

     Acceptance of the frontier line between Czechoslovakia
and Poland which was worked out by a special Czechoslovak-
Polish Mixed Commission.

USSR.
Agreement for Soviet Technical Assistance to Poland in Con-
structing an Oil Refinery.
S:   August 23, 1958, Moscow.
     (Keesing's CA, 1959, p. 16573.)

     Under this Agreement, the Soviet Union will give techni-
cal and designing assistance in building an oil refinery in Poland, which is planned to achieve an output of 2,000,000 tons
of crude oil in the first stage (1963-1964), of 4,000,000 tons

in the second stage (1966-1967), and of about 8, 000, 000 tons
annually in the final stage (1975).    Construction will start in
1960.

USA.
Agreement on the Reopening of Consulates in Chicago and
Poznan.
S:    October 18, 1958, Washington.
      (Keesing's CA, 1958, p. 16480.)

        Formerly Poland had consulates in Chicago, New York,
Detroit, Pittsburgh, and San Francisco, while the USA had
consular offices in  Poznan, Cracow, and Gdynia.    All these
were closed down in 1954, although the U. S. and Polish Governments continued to maintain embassies in each other's capitals.

USSR.
Joint Declaration on the Occasion of the Visit of a Delegation
of the Polish People's Republic to the Soviet Union from October 24 to November 12, 1958.
S:    November 12, 1958, Moscow.
      Izvestiia, November 13, 1958; Trybuna Ludu, November
      13,  1958; Press Release, November 14, 1958.

        In the opinion of the two delegations a most dangerous
symptom of the present world situation is the policy of the
ruling circles of the Atlantic Pact and its dominating force,
the United States of America, aimed at converting Western
Europe into an arsenal of atomic weapons.    Both delegations
fully support the fair and sovereign right of the Chinese people
to liberate and unite all their lands including Taiwan and the
offshore islands.

YUGOSLAVIA.
Consular Convention.
S:    November 17, 1958, Belgrade.
R:    June 12, 1959, Warsaw.
      DURP, 1959, No. 51, p. 591.

NORWAY.
Agreement Concerning Cultural Co-operation.
S:    December 17, 1958, Warsaw.
R:    May 5, 1959, Oslo.
      DURP, 1959, No. 38, p. 475.

MONGOLIAN PEOPLE'S REPUBLIC.
Agreement Concerning Cultural Co-operation.
S:    December 23, 1958, Warsaw.
R:    October 20, 1960, Ulan Bator.
D:    Five years.
      DURP, 1960, No. 19, p. 181.

      Agreement provides for the exchange of professors,
students, and the co-operation of cultural institutions of both
Parties.
      Hereto:
Agreement Concerning the Realization of the Cultural Co-
operation.
S:    January 30, 1960, Ulan Bator.
      (Trybuna Ludu, February 1, 1960.)

-1959-

IRAQ.
Agreement on Economic, Scientific, and Technical Co-operation.
S:    January 1, 1959, Baghdad.
      (Keesing's CA, 1959, p. 16742); Zbiór Umów, pp. 9-11.

      Under the Trade Agreement, Poland will export to Iraq
complete industrial schemes and installations; such as, sugar
plants, cold stores, and ice factories.   Iraq's supplies to Poland will include grain, hides, dried fruit, and other commodities.

      The Economic and Technical Co-operation Agreement
provided that Poland would send scientific, technical, and other
specialists as consultants to Iraq.    Polish specialists will also
be employed in State institutions, colleges, offices, and factories.

CANADA.
Agreement on Partial Release of Polish Art Treasures Depos-
ited in Canada.
S:    January 8, 1959, Ottawa.
      (Keesing's CA, 1959, p. 16635.)

      Art treasures had been secretly removed from Poland
at the time of the German invasion and brought to Canada for
safekeeping.

USSR.
Preliminary Protocol Concerning Cultural Co-operation.
S:    January 10, 1959, Moscow.
      (Pravda, January 11, 1959.)

        Envisages collaboration in 1959 between the Ministries
of Culture of the USSR and Poland in the fields of theater, music, circus, cinema, visual art, and publishing.

USSR.
Protocol Concerning the Establishment of Permanent Collabor-
ation between the Capitals of the Two States.
S:    January 25 (?), 1959, Warsaw.
      (Pravda, January 26, 1959.)

HUNGARY.
Agreement Concerning Co-operation in the Question of Social
Policy.
S:    February 14, 1959, Warsaw.
R:    October 23, 1959, Budapest.
      DURP, 1959, No. 67, p. 711; Zbiór Umów, pp. 12-23.
      Also:
Agreement Concerning Legal Procedure in the Questions of
Civil and Criminal Affairs.
S:    March 6, 1959, Budapest.
R:    January 27, 1960, Warsaw.
      Zbiór Umów, pp. 24-56.

        This agreement substitutes the agreement of April 24,
1936.

USSR.
Agreement Concerning Trade Expansion.
S:    February 19, 1959, Moscow.
      (Pravda, February 20, 1959.)

        Soviet watches, bicycles, technological equipment,
matches, herring, canned fish, in exchange for Polish knit
goods, footwear, furniture, pianos, crystal, woolens, paints,
etc.

USSR.
Agreement Concerning Soviet Technical Aid.
S:    March 3, 1959, Moscow.
      (Izvestiia, March 5, 1959.)

Provides for Soviet aid in the development of Poland's oil, gas, and copper ore industries; necessary equipment to be delivered 1959-1964.

HUNGARY.
Agreement Concerning Legal Relations in Civil, Family Affairs and Criminal Cases.
S:   March 6, 1959, Budapest.
R:   January 27, 1960, Warsaw.
D:   Five years.
     DURP, 1960, No. 8, p. 73.

IRAQ.
Agreement on Cultural and Scientific Co-operation.
S:   April 2, 1959, Warsaw.
R:   December 9, 1959, Baghdad.
     DURP, 1960, No. 13, p. 133; Zbiór Umów, pp. 57-59.

Agreement provides for co-operation between scientific, cultural, and educational institutions; exchanges of scientists and representatives of educational and cultural organizations.

GREAT BRITAIN.
Exchange of Notes Constituting an Agreement Concerning the Introduction of Air Services.
S:   April 3, 1959, Warsaw.
     UNTS, 1960, vol. 351, p. 295.

Came into force on April 3, 1959, with the exchange of said notes.

USSR.
Agreement Concerning Soviet Technical Aid in Construction of a Communications Line and Production of Communications Equipment.
S:   April 3, 1959, Moscow.
     (VT, 1960, No. 2, p. 56.)

BELORUSSIAN SSR.
Agreement Concerning Reciprocal Exchange of Delegations between the Grodno and Brest Regions of the BSSR and the Bialystok and Lublin Provinces of Poland.
S:   April 3, 1959, Warsaw.
     (Izvestiia, April 5, 1959.)

GERMAN DEMOCRATIC REPUBLIC.
Protocol Concerning the Establishment of the Cultural and Informational Centers in Warsaw and Berlin.
S:    May 6, 1959, Warsaw.
D:    One year with the right for extension.
(Zbiór Umów, pp. 64-68.)

HUNGARY.
Consular Convention.
S:    May 20, 1959, Warsaw.
R:    November 6, 1959, Budapest.
D:    Five years, with the right for extension.
      DURP, 1959, No. 68, p. 719; Zbiór Umów, pp. 69-76.

      This convention substitutes the Convention of April 24, 1936.

U.S.A.
Agreement on U.S. Economic Aid; Surplus Agricultural Commodities Agreement (With Exchange of Notes).
S:    June 10, 1959, Washington.
      UNTS, 1959, vol. 347, No. 4989, p. 41; Keesing's CA, 1959, p. 16887.

      Agreement provides:
(1)  The sale to Poland of U.S. surplus farm products to a total value of $44,000,000, payment to be made in zlotys;
(2)  The extension to Poland of a "line of credit" of $6,000,000, of which $2,000,000 will be used for Polish purchases of antipoliomyelitis vaccine and $4,000,000 to pay the balance of the freight charges on the agricultural products. The loan will carry interest at 4 1/2 per cent per annum and will be payable in dollars.

BULGARIA.
Agreement Concerning Collaboration in the Questions of Custom.
S:    June 20, 1959, Sofia.
R:    October 1, 1959, Warsaw.
D:    Three years with the right for extension for another three years.
      Zbiór Umów, pp. 77-89.

CZECHOSLOVAKIA.
Convention Concerning Minor Frontier Traffic.

S:    July 4, 1959, Prague.
R:    March 12, 1960, Warsaw.
      DURP, 1960, No. 27, p. 261; UNTS, 1960, vol. 363, No.
      5210, p. 333; Zbiór Umów, pp. 81-89.

USSR.
Joint Statement on German Question and Berlin.
S:    July 22, 1959, Warsaw.
      Trybuna Ludu, July 23, 1959; Press Release, July 23,
      1959; (Keesing's CA, 1959, p. 16919.)

      A joint statement, signed by N. Khruschchev, W.
Gomulka, and J. Cyrankiewicz, deals largely with the German
Question.  The statement also reaffirmed Soviet and Polish
support for nonaggression pacts between Eastern and Western
Germany and between the NATO and Warsaw Pact countries,
reduction of the armed forces of both blocs, and the establish-
ment of nuclear-free zones in Central Europe, the Baltic and
Scandinavian area, and the Balkans.

      Addressing a meeting at Szczecin on July 17, N. Khrush-
chev reaffirmed the Soviet guarantee of the Oder-Neisse frontier.

GERMAN DEMOCRATIC REPUBLIC.
Agreement Concerning Railway Traffic on the line Hagenwerder--
Krzewina Zgorzelecka--Hirschfelde--Zittau--Porajów.
S:    September 23, 1959, Berlin.
R:    December 31, 1959, Warsaw.
D:    Unlimited.
      Zbiór Umów, pp. 90-99.

UNITED NATIONS SPECIAL FUND.
Agreement Concerning Assistance from the Special Fund.
S:    October 15, 1959, New York.
      UNTS, 1959, vol. 344, No. 4951.

      Came into force on October 15, 1959.

      This Agreement embodies the conditions under which the
special fund shall provide the Government of Poland with assistance and also lays down basic conditions under which pro-
jects will be executed.

USSR.
Trade Protocol for 1960.

S:    November 6, 1959, Moscow.
      (VT, 1960, No. 2, p. 57; Pravda, November 7, 1959.)
      Volume of planned exchange to exceed three billion
rubles.

GERMAN DEMOCRATIC REPUBLIC.
Agreement Concerning Regulation and Preservation of the Neisse
River.
S:    November 10, 1959, Berlin.
R:    January 27, 1960, Warsaw.
D:    Forty years.
      Zbiór Umów, pp. 100-105.


FRANCE.
Note Exchange Concerning Some Exemptions from Taxes
S:    November 12, 1959, Warsaw.
      Zbiór Umów, pp. 106-109.


USSR, ALBANIA, BULGARIA, HUNGARY, GERMAN DEMO-
CRATIC REPUBLIC, RUMANIA, CZECHOSLOVAKIA.
Charter of the Council for Mutual Economic Assistance.
S:    December 14, 1959, Sofia.
      UNTS, 1960, vol. 368, No. 5245, p. 253.

      Came into force on April 13, 1960.


CZECHOSLOVAKIA.
Agreement Concerning Mutual Collaboration in the Mining Res-
cues.
S:    December 16, 1959, Katowice.
R:    May 17, 1960, Prague.
D:    Five years.
      Zbiór Umów, pp. 110-114.


CZECHOSLOVAKIA.
Agreement Concerning Cultural Co-operation between the Po-
lish Academy of Science and the Slovakian Academy of Science.
S:    December 16, 1959, Warsaw.
      (Trybuna Ludu, December 16, 1962.); UNTS, 1960, vol.
      372, No. 5300, p. 223.


USSR, GERMAN DEMOCRATIC REPUBLIC.
Agreement Concerning the Construction of Oil Pipe from the

USSR to East Germany.
S:    December 18, 1959, Moscow.
      (Trybuna Ludu, December 19, 1959.)

GHANA.
Establishment of Diplomatic Relations and Consular Agreement.
S:    December 31, 1959.
      (Trybuna Ludu, January 1, 1960.)

-1960-

DEMOCRATIC REPUBLIC OF VIETNAM.
Trade and Payments Agreement for 1960.
S:    January 13, 1960, Warsaw.
      (Trybuna Ludu, January 14, 1960.)

HUNGARY.
Agreement Concerning the Use of the Atomic Energy for Peaceful Purposes.
S:    January 15, 1960, Budapest.
      (Trybuna Ludu, January 16, 1960.)

HUNGARY.
Protocol Concerning the Exchange of Goods for 1960.
S:    January 18, 1960, Warsaw.
      (Trybuna Ludu, January 19, 1960.)
      Hereto:
Trade Agreement for 1965-1970.
S:    July 6, 1960, Warsaw.
      (Sprawy Międzynarodowe,1960, No. 9, p. 146.)

RUMANIA.
Agreement Concerning the Realization of Cultural Co-operation
for the years 1960-1961.
S:    January 26, 1960, Bucharest.
      (Trybuna Ludu, January 27, 1960.)

GERMAN DEMOCRATIC REPUBLIC.
Agreement Concerning Co-operation in the Field of Atomic
Energy.
S:    February 4, 1960, Berlin.
      (Trybuna Ludu, February 5, 1960.)

UKRAINIAN SSR.
Protocol Concerning the Traffic and Exchange of Experts of
Agriculture and of Other Areas.
S:    February 6, 1960, Lublin.
(Sprawy Międzynarodowe, 1960, No. 2, p. 138.)

USA.
Agreement on the Sale of U.S. Surplus Wheat.
S:    February 10, 1960, Washington.
(Keesing's CA, 1960, p. 17277.)

      USA will sell to Poland a further 22,000,000 bushels of
wheat under the U.S. Farm Surplus Disposal Program, at a
total cost of about $41,500,000. Payment will be made in Po-
lish zlotys, which the USA will use for defraying its embassy
and other expenses in Poland. The Agreement brought the
amount of U.S. farm surplus products purchased by Poland
since 1957 to $235,600,000.

CZECHOSLOVAKIA.
Agreement Concerning the Exchange of Goods for 1960-61;
Payments Agreement.
S:    February 11, 1960, Prague.
(Trybuna Ludu, February 12, 1960.)

CZECHOSLOVAKIA, HUNGARY, GERMAN DEMOCRATIC
REPUBLIC.
Agreement on the Creation of a Television Network--Intervision.
S:    February 12, 1960, Warsaw.
(Keesing's CA, 1960, p. 17264.)

YUGOSLAVIA.
Agreement Concerning the Realization of the Cultural Co-
operation for the years 1960-1961.
S:    February 15, 1960, Warsaw.
(Trybuna Ludu, February 15, 1960.)

FRANCE.
Trade Agreement for 1960.
S:    February 17, 1960, Paris.
(Trybuna Ludu, February 18, 1960.)

      Value of trade in 1960 will reach $13 million on each
side.

USSR.
Agreement Concerning Collaboration in the Question of Custom.
S:    February 19, 1960, Warsaw.
Zbiór Umów, 1960, p. 11.

DENMARK.
Protocol Concerning the Exchange of Goods for 1960.
S:    February 20, 1960, Copenhagen.
(Trybuna Ludu, February 21, 1960.)

Poland's export to Denmark will increase to $14, 330.

USSR.
Protocol Concerning the Exchange of Goods for 1961-1965.
S:    March 10, 1960, Warsaw.
(Trybuna Ludu, March 11, 1960.)

BRAZIL.
Trade Agreement
S:    March 21, 1960, Rio de Janeiro.
D:    Five years.
(Trybuna Ludu, March 22, 1960.)

Granting of credits up to four million dollars for each
side.

CUBA.
Trade and Payments Agreement.
S·    March 21, 1960, Havanna.
(Trybuna Ludu, April 1, 1960.)

Poland will deliver industrial equipment, agricultural
machinery for Cuba's sugar and tobacco.

GERMAN DEMOCRATIC REPUBLIC.
Agreement Concerning Economic and Technical Co-operation.
S:    April 22, 1960, Warsaw.
Zbiór Umów, 1960, p. 20.

Establishment of a permanent Commission for Economic
and Technical Co-operation.
Hereto:
Protocol on Exchange of Goods for 1960.
(Sprawy Międzynarodowe, 1960, No. 5, p. 133.)

Increase of trade up to six per cent.

GREECE.
Agreement on Resumption of Full Diplomatic Relations; Economic Agreement.
S:    May 2, 1960, Athens.
(Keesing's CA, 1960, p. 17419.)

     Economic Agreement provided for the construction by a Polish concern of a sugar beet factory in the Serrai area with a capacity of up to 2,000 tons daily, at a total cost of 90,000,000 drachmas ($4,200,000); 90 per cent of the expenditure will be paid in the form of Greek products to be exported to Poland, notably tobacco, while the remaining ten per cent will be paid in foreign currency.

YUGOSLAVIA.
Agreement Concerning Co-operation in the Field of Veterinary Medicine.
S:    May 5, 1960, Warsaw.
R:    October 24, 1960, Budapest.
     DURP, 1960, No. 50, p. 473; Zbiór Umów, 1960, p. 26.

SWEDEN.
Protocol on Exchange of Goods and Payments Agreement for 1960-61.
S:    May 6, 1960, Stockholm.
(Sprawy, Międzynardowe, 1960, No. 5, p. 133.)

CZECHOSLOVAKIA.
Consular Convention.
S:    May 17, 1960, Prague.
     Zbiór Umów, 1960, p. 39.

DENMARK.
Consular Convention.
S:    June 8, 1960, Copenhagen.
     Zbiór Umów, 1960, p. 49.

INDIA.
Shipping Agreement.
S:    June 27, 1960, New Delhi.

     It provides for the operation of a regular service between the two countries with 12 sailings each way annually by the Western Shipping Corporation of India and by Polish Ocean

Lines. A joint committee will be set up to review the working
of the Agreement.

## CUBA.
### Economic and Technical Agreements.
S:    July 1, 1960, Havana.
      Zbiór Umów, 1960, p. 71.

    It was also agreed to resume diplomatic relations be-
tween Cuba and Poland, suspended since the war. The Economic Agreement provided mainly for the delivery of Polish machinery and installations to Cuba.

## USA.
### Agreement, with Annex, regarding Claims of Nationals of the U.S.
S:    July 16, 1960, Washington.
      American J., vol. 55 (1961) 540-544; Zbiór Umów, 1960,
      p. 84.

    Poland undertook to pay the U.S. Government $40,000,000
(in annual installments of $2,000,000 over 20 years) as a lump-
sum settlement of the claims of American citizens whose property had been seized in Poland. The USA agreed, in return,
to release Polish assets worth about $1,000,000, which had
been frozen since World War II.

## USA.
### Agreement of Sale of U.S. Surplus Farm Products.
S:    July 21, 1960, Washington.
      UNTS, 1960, vol. 380, No. 5456, p. 157.

    The Agreement covers the sale of $61,500 worth of
wheat, $28,000,000 worth of cotton, $12,000,000 worth of
barley, and supplies of grain and sorghum, soya beans, tobacco, and dried milk. With $10,500,000 provided for ocean
freight charges, the total amount involved was $130,000,000,
bringing to $365,300,000 the value of U.S. Agricultural surplus
products sold by the USA to Poland since 1957.

## CZECHOSLOVAKIA.
### Agreement Concerning Economic and Technical Co-operation.
S:    September 10, 1960, Warsaw.
      Zbiór Umów, 1960, p. 110.

AFGHANISTAN.
Joint Declaration Concerning Polish-Afghanistan Relations Based on the Principle of Coexistence. Diplomatic Representation will be based on the level of Embassies. Trade Agreement for 1961-63; Agreement on Economic and Technical Cooperation.
S:    September 19, 1960, Kabul.
      Zbiór Umów, 1960, p. 116.

EGYPT.
Trade and Payments Agreement.
S:   November 4, 1960, Cairo.
D:   Three years.
     (Trybuna Ludu, November 5, 1960.)

GREECE.
Trade and Payments Agreement; Protocol on Exchange of Goods, for 1960-61.
S:   November 11, 1960, Athens.
D:   Three years.
     (Trybuna Ludu, November 12, 1960.)

     Value of goods exchanged in 1961 will amount to 56 million Zloty.

ITALY.
Trade Agreement; Agreement Concerning Technical Co-operation.
S:   November 27, 1960, Warsaw.
D:   Four years.

     Trade value for 1961 will be increased to $40 million. Annual increase for the next years up to 10 per cent.

GERMAN DEMOCRATIC REPUBLIC, USSR.
Agreement on Inland Shipping.
S:   November 28, 1960, Warsaw.
     (Keesing's CA, 1960, p. 17838.)

     The Agreement:
(1)  Provides for the opening of a permanent shipping line from Kaliningrad to the river ports in the Berlin area via Vistula, the Bydgoszcz Canal, the Notec River, and the Oder;
(2)  Sets out the conditions for transit shipments between Poland

and the Soviet Union;

(3)  Guarantees equal profits from shipments for the three
     countries.

# Part II

# SELECTED TEXTS OF TREATIES

TREATIES OF THE POLISH REPUBLIC,
1919-1939

1. Versailles Peace Treaty of June 28, 1919

(Excerpts)

(Article 27, point 7 was concerned with the determination
of boundaries between Germany and Poland.)

Article 87

Germany, in conformity with the action already taken
by the Allied and Associated Powers, recognizes the complete
independence of Poland, and renounces in her favour all rights
and title over the territory bounded by the Baltic Sea, the eastern frontier of Germany as laid down in Article 27 of Part II
(Boundaries of Germany) of the present Treaty up to a point
situated about 2 kilometres to the east of Larzendorf, then a
line to the acute angle which the northern boundary of Upper
Silesia makes about 3 kilometres northwest of Simmenau, then
the boundary of Upper Silesia to its meeting point with the old
frontier between Germany and Russia, then this frontier to the
point where it crosses the course of the Niemen, and the northern
frontier of East Prussia as laid down in Article 28 of Part II
aforesaid. The provisions of this Article do not, however,
apply to the territories of East Prussia and the Free City of
Danzig, as defined in Article 28 of Part II (Boundaries of Germany) and in Article 100 of Section XI (Danzig) of this Part.

The boundaries of Poland not laid down in the present
Treaty will be subsequently determined by the Principal Allied
and Associated Powers.

A Commission consisting of seven members, five of
whom shall be nominated by the Principal Allied and Associated
Powers, one by Germany, and one by Poland, shall be constituted fifteen days after the coming into force of the present
Treaty to delimit on the spot the frontier line between Poland
and Germany. The decisions of the Commission will be taken

143

by a majority of votes and shall be binding upon the parties
concerned.

. . .                    Article 93

        Poland accepts and agrees to embody in a Treaty with
the Principal Allied and Associated Powers such provisions as
may be deemed necessary by the said Powers to protect the
interest of inhabitants of Poland who differ from the majority
of the population in race, language, or religion.   Poland further accepts and agrees to embody in a Treaty with the said
Powers  such provisions as they may deem necessary to protect
freedom of transit and equitable treatment of the commerce of
other nations.

Article 94

        In the area between the southern frontier of East Prussia
as described in Article 28 of Part II of the present Treaty,  and
the line described below,  the inhabitants will be called upon to
indicate by a vote the state to which they wish to belong.   The
western and northern boundary of Region Allenstein to its junction with the boundary between the Kreise of Oletsko and Angen-
burg; thence junction with the old frontier of East Prussia.

        (Article 95 described the procedure of the plebiscite in
the area defined above.)

Article 96

        In the area comprising the Kreise of Stuhm and Rosen-
burg and the portion of the Kreise of Marienburg which is situated east of the Nogot and that of Marienwerder east of Vistula,
the inhabitants will be called upon to indicate by a vote,  to be
taken in each commune (Gemeinde),  whether they desire the
various communes situated in this territory to belong to Poland
or to East Prussia.

        (Article 97 described the procedure of the plebiscite in
the area defined above.)

Article 98

Germany and Poland undertake,  within one year of the

coming into force of this Treaty, to enter into conventions of which the terms, in case of difference, shall be settled by the Council of the League of Nations, with the object of securing, on the one hand to Germany full and adequate railroad, telegraphic, and telephonic facilities for communication between Poland and the Free City of Danzig over any German territory that may, on the right bank of the Vistula, intervene between Poland and the Free City of Danzig.

...                    Article 102

The Principal Allied and Associated Powers undertake to establish the town of Danzig, together with the rest of the territory described in Article 100, as a free city. It will be placed under the protection of the League of Nations.

...                    Article 104

The Principal Allied and Associated Powers undertake to negotiate a Treaty between the Polish Government and the Free City of Danzig, which shall come into force at the same time as the establishment of the said Free City, with the following objects:

(1) To effect the inclusion of the Free City of Danzig within the Polish Customs frontiers, and to establish a free area in the port;

(2) To ensure to Poland without any restriction the free use and service of all waterways, docks, basins, wharves, and other works within the territory of the Free City necessary for Polish imports and exports;

(3) To ensure to Poland the control and administration of the Vistula and of the whole railway system within the Free City, except such street and other railways as serve primarily the needs of the Free City, and of postal, telegraphic, and telephonic communication between Poland and the port of Danzig;

(4) To ensure to Poland the right to develop and improve the waterways, docks, basins, wharves, railways, and other works and means of communication mentioned in this Article, as well as to lease or purchase through appropriate processes such land and other property as may be necessary for these purposes;

(5) To provide against any discrimination within the Free City of Danzig to the detriment of citizens of Poland and other per-

sons of Polish origin or speech;
(6)  To provide that Polish Government shall undertake the conduct of the foreign relations of the Free City of Danzig as well
as the diplomatic protection of citizens of that city when abroad.

2.  Convention with the Free City of Danzig (Gdańsk) of November 9, 1920

(Excerpts)

Article 1

The diplomatic representative of the Polish government,
residing in Danzig, will be the mediator between the Polish
government and the government of the Free City.

Article 2

Poland will take upon herself all affairs of the Free City
pertaining to foreign affairs, as well as protection over the citizens of the Free City living abroad.   This protection will be
to the same extent as for all citizens of Poland.

The passports issued to the citizens of Danzig will assure Polish protection abroad only in cases where they have
visas from the representative of the Polish government in Danzig.

. . .                       Article 6

The Polish government will not approve any treaty or
agreement of international significance concerning the Free
City of Danzig without first asking the Free City for its opinion.
Absence of this consultation will be made known to the High
Commissar of the League of Nations.   In all cases the High
Commissar will have the power of veto over all treaties and/or
agreements of international significance which pertain to the
Free City of Danzig, if the Assembly of the League of Nations
will consider them as being opposed to this Treaty or to the
Status of the Free City.

. . .                       Article 8

The right to display a flag of the Free City will serve

only the establishments which are owned exclusively by citizens
of the Free City, including brotherhoods and organizations
which are registered in the Free City where the interest of citizens of the Free City predominates.

## Article 9

The Free City of Danzig and Poland will be under obligation, circumstances and their respective interests permitting,
to enact laws concerning the rights to banners.

## Article 10

The Free City is under obligation to treat the ships
under Polish flag in the Danzig port in the same manner as the
ships under a Free City banner.

... ## Article 13

The Free City of Danzig is surrounded by the Polish
boundary; Poland and the Free City represent a single area
under Polish laws and tariffs.

... ## Article 19

Under the name of "Authority of Port and Waterways of
Danzig" will be established an assembly consisting of an equal
number of Polish and Danzig commissars, whose number should
be no more than five from each side, and who will be elected
respectively through the Polish government and the government
of the Free City from among representatives of interests in
the two sides.

## Article 20

This Authority will function within the limits of the
Free City, controlling, governing, and regulating the port,
waterways, and those railroads which predominantly serve the
port, and that wealth and those establishments which serve
their purposes, excluding the wealth and establishments which
belong to the railroads.

## Article 21

The railways which are not mentioned in Article 20 will serve, together with the other railways, the needs of the Free City and will be controlled and regulated by Poland, which in turn will benefit and/or cover the costs.

...

## Article 26

The Authority will be under obligation to ensure for Poland free use of the port and communication centers, which were mentioned in Article 20, without any restrictions on means which are necessary to ensure transportation into Poland and from Poland; the Authority will be under obligation to use all centers necessary to ensure development and improvement of the port and of the means of communication.

...

## Article 29

Poland shall have the benefit of establishing postal, telegraph and telephone systems in Danzig and directly connected with Poland. This also includes communicational connections through Danzig port between Poland and countries abroad, as well as communication between Poland and Danzig.

...

## Article 33

The Free City of Danzig is under obligation to the racial, religious, and linquistic minorities on the same grounds as were established through Poland on her territory in accordance with the First Treaty ratified in Versailles on June 28, 1919, between Poland and the Allied and Associated Powers, especially to see to it that in legislative and administrative procedures neither side exhibits ill-will toward citizens of Poland and other individuals of Polish descent or language, as specified by Article 104, section 5 of the Versailles Treaty of peace with Germany.

Articles 14 to 19 of the Treaty ratified in Versailles between the Allied and Associated Powers and Poland on June 28, 1919, as well as Article 89 of the Treaty of Versailles with Germany, pertain to the Free City of Danzig with equal status.

...                       Article 39

Every dispute which may arise between Poland and the Free City in regard to this Treaty or all future agreements, obligations, or understandings, and all matters pertaining to the relationship between Poland and the Free City, will be referred to the Highest Commissar who, if such actions appear to be necessary, will refer them to the Assembly of the League of Nations.

November 9, 1920

(Dziennik Ustaw Rzecz, Polskiej, 1922, No. 13, Pos. 117.)

3. Political Agreement between France and Poland of February 19, 1921

The Polish Government and the French Government, both desirous of safeguarding, by the maintenance of the Treaties which both have signed or which may in the future be recognized by both parties, the peace of Europe, the security of their territories and their common political and economic interests, have agreed as follows:

(1) In order to co-ordinate their endeavours towards peace, the two Governments undertake to consult each other on all questions of foreign policy which concern both States, so far as those questions affect the settlement of international relations in the Spirit of the Treaties and in accordance with the Covenant of the League of Nations.

(2) In view of the fact that economic restoration is the essential preliminary condition of the re-establishment of international order and peace in Europe, the two Governments shall come to an understanding in this regard, with a view to concerted action and mutual support.

They will endeavour to develop their economic relations, and for this purpose will conclude special agreements and a Commercial Treaty.

(3) If, notwithstanding the sincerely peaceful views and intentions of the two Contracting States, either or both of them should be attacked without giving provocation, the two Governments shall take concerted measures for the defense of their territory and the protection of their legitimate interests, within the limits specified in the preamble.

(4)   The two Governments undertake to consult each other before concluding new agreements which will affect their policy in Central and Eastern Europe.

(5)   The present Agreement shall not come into force until the commercial agreements now in course of negotiation have been signed.

Paris, February 19, 1921

(Signed)   A. Briand
(Signed)   E. Sapieha

(LNTS, vol. 18, p. 13.)

4.   Convention between the Polish Republic and the Kingdom of Rumania of March 3, 1921

Being firmly resolved to safeguard a peace which was gained at the price of so many sacrifices, the Chief of the State of the Polish Republic and His Majesty the King of Rumania have agreed to conclude a Convention for a defensive alliance.

For this purpose they have named as their plenipotentiaries:

For the Chief of the State of the Polish Republic:

Prince Eustache Sapieha, His Minister for Foreign Affairs; and

For His Majesty the King of Rumania:

M. Take Jonesco, His Minister for Foreign Affairs,

Who, after exchanging their full powers, found in good and due form, agreed to the following articles:

Article 1

Poland and Rumania undertake to assist each other in the event of their being the object of an unprovoked attack on their present eastern frontiers.

Accordingly, if either State is the object of an unprovoked attack, the other shall consider itself in a state of war and shall render armed assistance.

Article 2

In order to co-ordinate their efforts to maintain peace,

both Governments undertake to consult together on such questions of foreign policy as concern their relations with their eastern neighbours.

### Article 3

A military Convention shall determine the manner in
which either country shall render assistance to the other should
the occasion arise.

This Convention shall be subject to the same conditions
as the present Convention as regards duration and denunciation.

### Article 4

If in spite of their efforts to maintain peace, the two
States are compelled to enter on a defensive war under the
terms of Article 1, each undertakes not to negotiate nor to conclude an armistice or a peace without the participation of the
other State.

### Article 5

The duration of the present Convention shall be five
years from the date of its signature, but either Government
shall be at liberty to denounce it after two years on giving the
other State six months' notice.

### Article 6

Neither of the High Contracting Parties shall be at
liberty to conclude an alliance with a third Power without having previously obtained the assent of the other Party.

Alliances with a view to the maintenance of treaties
already signed jointly by both Poland and Rumania are excepted
from this provision.

Such alliances must, however, be notified.

The Polish Government hereby declares that it is ac-
quainted with the agreements entered into by Rumania with the
other States with a view to upholding the Treaties of Trianon
and Neuilly, which agreements may be transformed into treaties of alliance.

The Rumanian Government hereby declares that it is ac-
quainted with the agreements entered into by Poland with the
French Republic.

## Article 7

The present Convention shall be communicated to the
League of Nations in accordance with the Treaty of Versailles.

## Article 8

The present Convention shall be ratified and the ratifications exchanged at Bucharest as soon as possible.

In witness whereof the Plenipotentiaries have signed the
present Convention and have thereto set their seal.

Done at Bucharest in Duplicate this third day of March,
1921.

(L. S.) Take Jonesco
(L. S.) E. Sapieha

(LNTS, vol. 7, p. 79)

## 5. Peace Treaty between Poland, RSFSR, and Ukrainian SSR of March 18, 1921

(Excerpts)

...                        Article 1

The two Contracting Parties declare that a state of war
has ceased to exist between them.

## Article 2

The two Contracting Parties, in accordance with the
principle of national self-determination, recognize the independence of the Ukraine and of White Ruthenia and agree and decide that the eastern frontier of Poland, that is to say, the
frontier between Poland on the one hand, and Russia, White
Ruthenia and the Ukraine on the other, shall be as follows:
(Description of the frontiers)...

...                         Article 3

     Russia and the Ukraine abandon all rights and claims to
the territories situated to the west of the frontier laid down by
Article 2 of the present Treaty. Poland, on the other hand,
abandons in favour of the Ukraine and of White Ruthenia all
rights and claims to the territory situated to the east of this
frontier. The two Contracting Parties agree that, in so far as
the territory situated to the west of the frontier fixed in Article
2 of the present Treaty includes districts which form the subject of a dispute between Poland and Lithuania, the question of
the attribution of these districts to one of those two States is a
matter which exclusively concerns Poland and Lithuania.

...                         Article 5

     Each of the Contracting Parties mutually undertakes to
respect in every way the political sovereignty of the other Party,
to abstain from interference in its internal affairs, and particularly to refrain from all agitation, propaganda or interference
of any kind, and not to encourage any such movement.

     Each of the Contracting Parties undertakes not to create
or protect organizations which are formed with the object of en-
couraging armed conflict against the other Contracting Party or
of undermining its territorial integrity, or of subverting by
force its political or social institutions, nor yet such organizations as claim to be the Government of the other Party or of
a part of the territories of the other Party. The Contracting
Parties, therefore, undertake to prevent such organizations,
their official representatives and other persons connected
therewith, from establishing themselves on their territory,
and to prohibit military recruiting and the entry into their territory, and transport across it, of armed forces, arms, muni-
tions and war material of any kind destined for such organizations.

...                         Article 10

     1. Each of the Contracting Parties guarantees to the
subjects of the other Party a full amnesty for political crimes
and offences. Attacks directed against the system of govern-

ment and the security of the State, as well as all acts committed in the interest of the other Party, shall be regarded as political crimes and offences within the meaning of this article.

2. The amnesty shall also apply to acts which have been made the subject of administrative proceedings or proceedings other than before a court of law and to contraventions of provisions in force as regards prisoners of war and interned civilians and, generally, as regards subjects of the other Party.

3. The putting into effect of the amnesty under points 1 and 2 of this Article, entails the obligation to institute no new judicial investigations, to discontinue proceedings which have already been instituted and to suspend execution of sentences which have already been passed.

4. The suspension of the execution of a sentence does not necessarily imply that the prisoner shall be set at liberty, but in such an event he must be immediately handed over, with all papers referring to his case, to the authorities of the State of which he is a national.

Nevertheless, if such person states that he desires not to be repatriated, or if the authorities of the country of which he is a national refuse to admit him, such person may be again placed in custody.

5. Persons against whom legal proceedings have been taken, or a preliminary judicial investigation had been instituted, or who have been summoned to appear before a court of justice for any breach of the law, or who have been sentenced for such an offence, shall forthwith be handed over, on application being made by the State of which they are nationals, together with all the papers relating to their case.

6. The amnesty referred to in this Article shall also apply to all the above-mentioned offences that have been committed up to the time when this Treaty is ratified.

Sentence of death passed upon persons found guilty of one of the offences referred to above shall be suspended as from the date of the signature of this Treaty. ...

(Dziennik Ustaw Rzecz. Polskiej, 1921, No. 49, Pos. 300.)

6. Treaty of Mutual Guarantee between France and Poland of

October <u>16</u>, <u>1925</u>

The President of the French Republic and the President
of the Polish Republic;

Equally desirous to see Europe spared from war by a
sincere observance of the undertakings arrived at this day with
a view to the maintenance of general peace;

Have resolved to guarantee their benefits to each other
reciprocally by a treaty concluded within the framework of the
Covenant of the League of Nations and of the treaties existing
between them;

And have to this effect nominated for their plenipotentiaries: ...

Who, after having exchanged their full powers, found in
good and due form, have agreed on the following provisions:

Article 1

In the event of Poland or France suffering from a failure
to observe the undertakings arrived at this day between them
and Germany with a view to the maintenance of general peace,
France, and reciprocally Poland, acting in application of Article 16 of the Covenant of the League of Nations, undertake to
lend each other immediately aid and assistance, if such a failure
is accompanied by an unprovoked recourse to arms.

In the event of the Council of the League of Nations, when
dealing with a question brought before it in accordance with the
said undertakings, being unable to succeed in making its report accepted by all its members other than the representatives
of the parties to the dispute, and in the event of Poland or France
being attacked without provocation, France, or reciprocally Poland, acting in application of Article 15, paragraph 7, of the
Covenant of the League of Nations, will immediately lend aid
and assistance.

Article 2

Nothing in the present treaty shall affect the rights and
obligations of the High Contracting Parties as members of the
League of Nations, or shall be interpreted as restricting the

duty of the League to take whatever action may be deemed wise and effectual to safeguard the peace of the world.

## Article 3

The present treaty shall be registered with the League of Nations, in accordance with the Covenant.

## Article 4

The present treaty shall be ratified. The ratifications will be deposited at Geneva with the League of Nations at the same time as the ratification of the treaty concluded this day between Germany, Belgium, France, Great Britain and Italy, and the ratification of the treaty concluded at the same time between Germany, and Poland.

It will enter into force and remain in force under the same conditions as the said treaties.

The present treaty done in a single copy will be deposited in the archives of the League of Nations, and the Secretary-General of the League will be requested to transmit certified copies to each of the high contracting parties.

Done at Locarno the 16th of October, 1925.

(American J., Suppl. vol. 20 (1926) 32-33.)

7. Pact of Friendship and Co-operation between Poland and Yugoslavia of September 18, 1926

THE PRESIDENT OF THE POLISH REPUBLIC and HIS MAJESTY THE KING OF THE SERBS, CROATS AND SLOVENES, being firmly resolved to safeguard peace, the maintenance of which is essential for political stability and the economic recovery of Europe, have agreed to conclude a Treaty of Friendship, which is a natural consequence of the friendly relations existing between the two countries. For this purpose they have appointed as their Plenipotentiaries:

THE PRESIDENT OF THE POLISH REPUBLIC:

M. August ZALESKI, Minister for Foreign Affairs;

HIS MAJESTY THE KING OF THE SERBS, CROATS AND SLOVENES:

M. Momtchilo NINTCHITCH, Doctor of Laws, Minister

for Foreign Affairs,

Who, having communicated their full powers, found in good and due form, have agreed upon the following provisions:

## Article 1

The continuance of the sincere friendship and permanent good understanding which happily already exists between the Polish Republic and the Kingdom of the Serbs, Croats and Slovenes is solemnly confirmed.

## Article 2

In order to co-ordinate their efforts for peace, the two Governments undertake to consult together regarding questions of foreign policy which, in their opinion, affect both Contracting Parties.

## Article 3

As regards other questions of foreign policy, the two Contracting Parties undertake, in the case of international difficulties, to proceed to an immediate exchange of views in the most friendly spirit.

## Article 4

The High Contracting Parties undertake to conclude as soon as possible an Arbitration Convention applicable to any disputes which may in the future arise between them and which it may not be possible to settle by friendly agreement through the diplomatic channel.

## Article 5

The present Pact shall remain in force for a period of three years as from the date of signature, but either of the Contracting Parties shall be free to denounce it after two years, by giving the other Party six months' notice.

## Article 6

The present Pact shall be communicated to the League

of Nations in conformity with Article 18 of the Covenant.

Article 7

The present Pact shall be ratified and the instruments of ratification exchanged at Belgrade as soon as possible.

In faith whereof the Plenipotentiaries have signed the present Treaty and have thereto affixed their seals.

Done at Geneva, in duplicate, on September 18, 1926.

(L. S.)  August ZALESKI
(L. S.)  M. NINTCHITCH

(LNTS, vol. 78, p. 415-17.)

8.  Protocol between Estonia, Latvia, Poland, Rumania, and the USSR of February 9, 1929

The Government of the Estonian Republic, the President of the Latvian Republic, the President of the Polish Republic, His Majesty the King of Rumania, and the Central Executive Committee of the Union of Soviet Socialist Republics, being desirous of promoting the maintenance of peace between their respective countries, and for this purpose of putting into force without delay, between the peoples of those countries, the Treaty for the renunciation of war as an instrument of national policy, signed at Paris on August 27, 1928, have decided to achieve this purpose by means of the present Protocol and have appointed as their Plenipotentiaries...

Who, having communicated their full powers, found in good and due form, have agreed as follows:

Article 1

The Treaty for the renunciation of war as an instrument of national policy, signed at Paris on August 27, 1928, a copy of which is attached to the present Protocol as an integral part of that instrument, shall come into force between the Contracting Parties after the ratification of the said Treaty of Paris of 1928 by the competent legislative bodies of the respective Contracting Parties.

Article 2

The entry into force in virtue of the present Protocol,

of the Treaty of Paris of 1928 in reciprocal relations between
the Parties to the present Protocol shall be valid independently
of the entry into force of the Treaty of Paris of 1928 as provided in Article 3 of the last-named Treaty.

## Article 3

1. The present Protocol shall be ratified by the competent legislative bodies of the Contracting Parties, in conformity
with the requirements of their respective constitutions.

2. The instruments of ratification shall be deposited
by each of the Contracting Parties with the Government of the
Union of Soviet Socialist Republics within one week of the ratification of the present Protocol by the respective Parties.

3. As from the date of the deposit of the instruments of
ratification by two of the Contracting Parties, the present Protocol shall come into force between those two Parties. In reciprocal relations between the other Contracting Parties and the
States for which it has already come into force, the Protocol
shall come into force as and when their instruments of ratification are deposited.

4. The Government of the Union of Soviet Socialist
Republics shall immediately notify the deposit of the several
ratifications to all the signatories to the present Protocol.

## Article 4

In order to give effect to Article 1 of the present Protocol, each of the High Contracting Parties, after ratification by
its legislative bodies of the Treaty of Paris of 1928, shall immediately notify the Government of the Union of Soviet Socialist
Republics and all other Parties to the present Protocol, through
the diplomatic channel.

## Article 5

The present Protocol shall be open for the accession of
the Governments of all countries. Notification of final accession shall be made to the address of the Government of the
Union of Soviet Socialist Republics, which shall duly notify all
the other Parties of the present Protocol. Immediately on re-
ceipt of such notification of accession, the present protocol
shall be put into force in reciprocal relations between the ac-

ceding State and all the other Parties to the present Protocol.

## Article 6

The entry into force, in virtue of the present Protocol, of the Treaty of Paris of 1928, in reciprocal relations between the acceding State and all other Parties to the said Protocol, shall be effected in the way laid down in Article 4 of the Protocol.

## Article 7

The present Protocol has been drawn up in a single copy, an authentic copy of which shall be communicated by the Government of the Union of Soviet Socialist Republics to each of the signatory or acceding States.

In faith whereof the above-mentioned Plenipotentiaries have signed the present Protocol and have affixed their seals thereto.

(Official Documents Concerning Polish-German and Polish-Soviet Relations, 1933-1939. Polish White Book. London, n. d., No. 150.)

9. Treaty of Guarantee between Poland and Rumania of January 15, 1931

THE PRESIDENT OF THE REPUBLIC OF POLAND AND HIS MAJESTY THE KING OF RUMANIA, noting the happy consolidation of the guarantees of general peace in Europe; being anxious to satisfy the desire of the nations for security; desirous of seeing their countries spared from war; and moreover sincerely desirous of giving to their peoples additional guarantees within the framework of the Covenant of the League of Nations and of the treaties of which they are signatories; have resolved to conclude a Treaty with this object and have appointed as their plenipotentiaries:

THE PRESIDENT OF THE REPUBLIC OF POLAND:

M. August ZALESKI, Minister for Foreign Affairs;

HIS MAJESTY THE KING OF RUMANIA:

M. G. G. MIRONESCO, His Prime Minister and Minister for Foreign Affairs;

Who having exchanged their full powers, found in good
and due form, have agreed on the following provisions:

## Article 1

Poland and Rumania undertake reciprocally to respect
and maintain their present territorial integrity and political independence against all external aggression.

## Article 2

In the event of Poland or Rumania being attacked without provocation, in violation of the obligations imposed by Articles 12, 13 and 15 of the Covenant of the League of Nations,
Rumania and, reciprocally, Poland, acting in application of
Article 16 of the Covenant of the League of Nations, will immediately lend aid and assistance.

In the event of the Council of the League of Nations, when
dealing with a question brought before it in accordance with the
said undertakings, being unable to succeed in securing accep-
tance of its report by all its members other than the representatives of the Parties to the dispute, and in the event of Poland or
Rumania being attacked without provocation, Rumania and, reciprocally, Poland, acting in application of Article 15, paragraph 7, of the Covenant of the League of Nations, will immediately lend aid and assistance.

In the event of a dispute under Article 17 of the Covenant
of the League of Nations arising, and of Poland or Rumania
being attacked without provocation, Rumania, and reciprocally,
Poland, will immediately lend aid and assistance.

The conditions of execution of the above-mentioned
stipulations shall be made the subject of technical arrangements.

## Article 3

If, in spite of their efforts to maintain peace, the two
States are compelled to enter on a defensive war under the
terms of Articles 1 and 2, each undertakes not to negotiate nor
to conclude an armistice or a peace without the participation
of the other State.

Article 4

In order to co-ordinate their efforts to maintain peace, both Governments undertake to consult together on such questions of foreign policy as concern the two Contracting Parties.

Article 5

Neither of the High Contracting Parties shall be at liberty to conclude an alliance with a third Power without having previously obtained the assent of the other Party.

Alliances with a view to the maintenance of Treaties already signed jointly by both Poland and Rumania are excepted from this provision.

Such alliances must, however, be notified.

Article 6

The present Treaty shall be valid for five years as from March 26, 1931. If it is not denounced by one of the High Contracting Parties at least one year before the expiration of this period, it shall be deemed to have been renewed by tacit agreement for a further period of five years and similarly thereafter.

Article 7

The present Treaty shall be ratified and the ratifications exchanged at Bucharest as soon as possible.

In faith whereof, the Plenipotentiaries have signed the present Treaty and thereto affixed their seals.

Done in duplicate, at Geneva, January 15, 1931.

(L. S.) August ZALESKI
(L. S.) G. G. MIRONESCO

(LNTS, vol. 115, pp. 173-175.)

10. Non-Aggression Pact between Poland and the USSR of July 25, 1932

The President of the Polish Republic, of the one part, and the Central Executive Committee of the Union of Soviet Socialist Republics, of the other part,

Desirous of maintaining the present state of peace between their countries, and convinced that the maintenance of
peace between them constitutes an important factor in the work
of preserving universal peace;

Considering that the Treaty of Peace of March 18, 1921,
constitutes, now as in the past, the basis of their reciprocal
relations and undertakings;

Convinced that the peaceful settlement of international
disputes and the exclusion of all that might be contrary to the
normal condition of relations between the States are the surest
means of arriving at the goal desired;

Declaring that none of the obligations hitherto assumed
by either of the Parties stands in the way of the peaceful development of their mutual relations or is incompatible with the present Pact;

Have decided to conclude the present Pact with the object of amplifying and completing the pact for the renunciation
of war signed at Paris on August 27, 1928, and put into force by
the Protocol signed at Moscow on February 9, 1929, and for
that purpose have designated as their Plenipotentiaries...

Who, after exchanging their full powers, found in good
and due form, have agreed on the following provisions:

Article 1

The two Contracting Parties, recording the fact that
they have renounced war as an instrument of national policy in
their mutual relations, reciprocally undertake to refrain from
taking any aggressive action against or invading the territory
of the other Party, either alone or in conjunction with other
Powers.

Any act of violence attacking the integrity and inviolability of the territory or the political independence of the other
Contracting Party shall be regarded as contrary to the undertakings contained in the present Article, even if such acts are
committed without declaration of war and avoid all possible
warlike manifestations.

Article 2

Should one of the Contracting Parties be attacked by a

Third State or by a group of other States, the other Contracting Party undertakes not to give aid or assistance, either directly or indirectly, to the aggressor State during the whole period of the conflict.

If one of the Contracting Parties commits an act of aggression against a third State, the other Contracting Party shall have the right to be released from the present Treaty without previous denunciation.

## Article 3

Each of the Contracting Parties undertakes not to be a party to any agreement openly hostile to the other Party from the point of view of aggression.

## Article 4

The undertakings provided for in Articles 1 and 2 of the present Pact shall in no case limit or modify the international rights and obligations of each Contracting Party under agreements concluded by it before the coming into force of the present Pact, so far as the said agreements contain no aggressive elements.

## Article 5

The two Contracting Parties, desirous of settling and solving, exclusively by peaceful means, any disputes and differences, of whatever nature or origin, which may arise between them, undertake to submit questions at issue, which it has not been possible to settle within a reasonable period by diplomatic channels, to a procedure of conciliation, in accordance with the provisions of the Convention for the application of the procedure of conciliation, which constitutes an integral part of the present Pact and shall be signed separately and ratified as soon as possible simultaneously with the Pact of Non-Aggression.

## Article 6

The present Pact shall be ratified as soon as possible, and the instruments of ratification shall be exchanged at Warsaw within thirty days following the ratification by Poland and the Union of Soviet Socialist Republics, after which the Pact shall come into force immediately.

### Article 7

The Pact is concluded for three years. If it is not denounced by one of the Contracting Parties, after previous notice of not less than six months before the expiration of that period, it shall be automatically renewed for a further period of two years.

### Article 8

The present Pact is drawn up in Polish and Russian, both texts being authentic.

In faith, whereof the above-named Plenipotentiaries have signed the present Pact and have thereto affixed their seals.

Done at Moscow, in two copies, July 25, 1932.

### Protocol of Signature No. 1

The Contracting Parties declare that Article 7 of the Pact of July 25, 1932, cannot be interpreted as meaning that the expiration of the time limit or denunciation before the expiration of the time period under Article 7 could have as a result of the limitation or cancellation of the obligations arising out of the Pact of Paris of 1928.

Done at Moscow, in two copies, July 25, 1932.

### Protocol of Signature No. 2

On signing the Pact of Non-Aggression this day, the two Parties having exchanged their views on the draft Conciliation Convention submitted by the Soviet Party, declare that they are convinced that there is no essential difference of opinion between them.

Done at Moscow, in two copies, July 25, 1932.

(Dz. U.R.P., 1932, No. 115/951/953. Transl. from Polish: Pol. Sov. R., No. 7.)

## 11. Polish-German Declaration of January 26, 1934

The Polish Government and the German Government consider that the time has come to introduce a new phase in the political relations between Germany and Poland by a direct understanding between State and State. They have, therefore, decided in the present Declaration to lay down the principles for the future development of these relations.

The two Governments base their action on the fact that the maintenance and guarantee of a lasting peace between their countries is an essential prerequisite for the general peace in Europe.

They have therefore decided to base their mutual relations on the principles laid down in the Pact of Paris of August 27, 1928, and propose to define more exactly the application of these principles in so far as the relations between Germany and Poland are concerned.

Each of the two Governments, therefore, lays it down that the international obligations undertaken by it towards a third party do not hinder the peaceful development of their mutual relations, do not conflict with the present Declaration, and are not affected by this Declaration. They establish, moreover, that this Declaration does not extend to those questions which under international law are to be regarded exclusively as the internal concern of either of the two States.

Both Governments announce their intention to settle directly all questions of whatever nature which concern their mutual relations.

Should any disputes arise between them and agreement thereon not be reached by direct negotiation, they will, in each particular case, on the basis of mutual agreement, seek a solution by other peaceful means, without prejudice to the possibility of applying, if necessary, those methods of procedure in which provision is made for such cases in other agreements in force between them. In no circumstances, however, will they proceed to the application of force for the purpose of reaching a decision in such disputes.

The guarantee of peace created by these principles will facilitate the great task of both Governments of finding a solution for problems of political, economic and social kinds,

based on a just and fair adjustment of the interests of both
parties.

Both Governments are convinced that the relations between their countries will in this manner develop fruitfully, and
will lead to the establishment of a neighbourly relationship
which will contribute to the well-being not only of both their
countries, but of the other peoples of Europe as well.

The present declaration shall be ratified, and the instruments of ratification shall be exchanged in Warsaw as soon as
possible.

The declaration is valid for a period of ten years,
reckoned from the day of the exchange of its instruments of
ratification.

If the declaration is not denounced by one of the two
Governments six months before the expiration of this period,
it will continue in force; but can then be denounced by either
Government at any time on notice of six months being given.
Made in duplicate in the German and Polish languages.

Berlin, January 26, 1934.

For the German Government:
FREIHERR VON NEURATH

For the Polish Government:
JÓZEF LIPSKI

(Official Documents Concerning Polish-German and Polish-
Soviet Relations, 1933-1939.  Polish White Book.  London n. d.,
No. 10.)

12.  Protocol Renewing the Pact of Non-Aggression of July 25,
1932, of May 5, 1934 with the USSR

The President of the Republic of Poland, and the Central
Executive Committee of the Union of Soviet Socialist Republics,

Being desirous of providing as firm a basis as possible
for the development of relations between their countries;

Being desirous of giving each other fresh proof of the
unchangeable character  and solidity of the pacific and friendly
relations happily established between them;

Moved by the desire to collaborate in the consolidation
of world peace and also for the stability and peaceful development of international relations in Eastern Europe;

Noting that the conclusion on July 25, 1932, at Moscow, of the Treaty between the Republic of Poland and the Union of Soviet Socialist Republics has had a beneficial influence on the development of their relations and on the solution of the above-mentioned problems;

Have decided to sign the present Protocol, and have for this purpose appointed as their Plenipotentiaries . . . .

Who, having communicated their full powers, found in good and true form, have agreed on the following provisions:

Article 1

In modification of the provisions of Article 7 of the Treaty of Non-Aggression concluded at Moscow on July 25, 1932, between the Republic of Poland and the Union of Soviet Socialist Republics concerning the date and manner in which that Treaty shall cease to have effect, the two Contracting Parties decide that it shall remain in force until December 31, 1945.

Each of the High Contracting Parties shall be entitled to denounce the Treaty by giving notice to that effect six months before the expiration of the above-mentioned period. If the Treaty is not denounced by either of the Contracting Parties, its period of validity shall be automatically prolonged for two years; similarly, the Treaty shall be regarded as prolonged on each occasion for a further period of two years, if it is not denounced by either of the Contracting Parties in the manner provided for in the present Article.

Article 2

The present Protocol is drawn up in duplicate, each copy being in the Polish and Russian languages and both texts being equally authentic.

The present Protocol shall be ratified as soon as possible, and the instruments of ratification shall be exchanged between the Contracting Parties at Warsaw.

The present Protocol shall come into force on the date of the exchange of the instruments of ratification.

In faith whereof the above-mentioned Plenipotentiaries have signed the present Protocol and have thereto affixed their seals.

Done at Moscow, in duplicate, in the Polish and Russian languages, the 5th day of May, 1934.

### Final Protocol

In connection with the signature on this date of the Protocol prolonging the Treaty of Non-Aggression between the Republic of Poland and the Union of Soviet Socialist Republics of July 25, 1932, each of the High Contracting Parties, having again examined all the provisions of the Peace Treaty concluded at Riga on March 18, 1921, which constitutes the basis of their mutual relations, declares that it has no obligations and is not bound by any declarations inconsistent with the provisions of the said Peace Treaty and in particular of Article 3 thereof.

Consequently, the Government of the Union of Soviet Socialist Republics confirms that the note from the People's Commissar, G. V. Chicherin, of September 28, 1926, to the Lithuanian Government cannot be interpreted to mean that the note implied any intention on the part of the Soviet Government to interfere in the settlement of the territorial questions mentioned therein.

Done at Moscow, in duplicate, in the Polish and Russian languages, the 5th day of May, 1934.

(Dz. U. R. P., 1934, No. 53/487/488.  Transl. from Polish: Official Documents..., No. 157.)

### 13.  Anglo-Polish Agreement of Mutual Assistance of August 25, 1939

The Government of the United Kingdom of Great Britain and Northern Ireland and the Polish Government,

Desiring to place on a permanent basis the collaboration between their respective countries resulting from the assurances of mutual assistance of a defensive character which they have already exchanged;

Have resolved to conclude an Agreement for that purpose and have appointed as their Plenipotentiaries:

The Government of the United Kingdom and Northern Ireland:

The Rt. Hon. Viscount Halifax, K. G. , G. C. S. I. , G. C. I. E. , Principal Secretary of State for Foreign Affairs;

The Polish Government:

His Excellency Count Edward Raczyński, Ambassador Extraordinary and Plenipotentiary of the Polish Republic in London;

Who, having exchanged their Full Powers, found in good and due form, have agreed on the following provisions:

## Article 1

Should one of the Contracting Parties become engaged in hostilities with a European Power in consequence of aggression by the latter against that Contracting Party, the other Contracting Party will at once give the Contracting Party engaged in hostilities all the support and assistance in its power.

## Article 2

(1) The provisions of Article 1 will also apply in the event of any action by a European power which clearly threatened, directly or indirectly, the independence of one of the Contracting Parties, and was of such a nature that the Party in question considered it vital to resist it with its armed forces.

(2) Should one of the Contracting Parties become engaged in hostilities with a European Power in consequence of action by the Power which threatened the independence or neutrality of another European State in such a way as to constitute a clear menace to the security of that Contracting Party, the provisions of Article 1 will apply, without prejudice, however, to the rights of the other European State concerned.

## Article 3

Should a European Power attempt to undermine the independence of one of the Contracting Parties by processes of economic penetration or in any other way, the Contracting Parties will support each other in resistance to such attempts. Should the European Power concerned thereupon embark on hostilities against one of the Contracting Parties, the provisions of Article 1 will apply.

## Article 4

The methods of applying the undertakings of mutual as-

sistance provided for by the present Agreement are established
between the competent naval, military and air authorities of
the Contracting Parties.

## Article 5

Without prejudice to the foregoing undertakings of the
Contracting Parties to give each other mutual support and assistance immediately on the outbreak of hostilities, they will
exchange complete and speedy information concerning any development which might threaten their independence and, in
particular, concerning any development which threatened to
call the said undertakings into operation.

## Article 6

(1)  The Contracting Parties will communicate to each
other the terms of any undertakings of assistance against aggression which they have already given or may in the future
give to other States.

(2)  Should either of the Contracting Parties intend to
give such an undertaking after the coming into force of the  present Agreement, the other Contracting Party shall, in order
to ensure the proper functioning of the agreement, be informed
thereof.

(3)  Any new undertaking which the Contracting Parties
may enter into in future shall neither limit their obligations
under the present Agreement nor indirectly create new obligations between the Contracting Party not participating in these
undertakings and the third State concerned.

## Article 7

Should the Contracting Parties be engaged in hostilities
in consequence of the application of the present Agreement,
they will not conclude an armistice or treaty of peace except by
mutual agreement.

## Article 8

(1)  The present Agreement shall remain in force for a
period of five years.

(2)  Unless denounced six months before the expiration

of this period it shall continue in force, each Contracting Party having thereafter the right to denounce it at any time by giving six months' notice to that effect.

(3)  The present Agreement shall come into force on signature.

In faith whereof the above-named Plenipotentiaries have signed the present Agreement and have affixed thereto their seals.

Done in English in duplicate, at London, the 25th of August, 1939.  A Polish text shall subsequently be agreed upon between the Contracting Parties and both texts will then be authentic.

(L. S. )  HALIFAX

(L. S. )  EDWARD RACZYŃSKI

(Official Documents . . . , No. 91. )


14.  Protocol of Mutual Assistance between Poland and France of September 4, 1939


## Article 1

The Polish Government and the French Government, desiring to assure the full efficacy of the Polish-French Alliance, and having especially in view the present situation of the League of Nations, agree to confirm that their mutual obligations of assistance in the event of aggression by a third Power continue to be founded on the agreements of Alliance in force.

At the same time they declare that henceforth they interpret the said Agreements as embodying the following obligations:  The undertaking of the two Contracting Parties mutually to render all aid and assistance in their power at once and from the outbreak of hostilities between one of the Contracting Parties and a European Power in consequence of that Power's aggression against the said Contracting Party, equally applies to the case of any action by a European Power which manifestly directly or indirectly threatens the independence of one of the Contracting Parties, and is of such a nature that the Party in question considers it vital to resist that aggression with its armed forces.

Should one of the Contracting Parties become engaged in hostilities with a European Power in consequence of action by that Power which threatened the independence or neutrality of another European State in such a way as to constitute a clear menace to the security of that Contracting Party, the Provisions of Article 1 will apply, without prejudice, however, to the rights of the other European State Concerned.

### Article 2

The methods of applying the undertakings of mutual assistance provided for by the present Agreement are established between the competent military, naval, and air authorities of the Contracting Parties.

### Article 3

(1) The Contracting Parties will communicate to each other the terms of any undertakings of assistance against aggression which they have already given or may in the future give to other States.

(2) Should either of the Contracting Parties intend to give such an undertaking after the coming into force of the present Agreement, the other Contracting Party shall, in order to ensure proper functioning of the Agreement, be informed thereof.

(3) Any new undertaking which the Contracting Parties may enter into in the future shall neither limit their obligations under the present Agreement nor indirectly create new obligations between the Contracting Party not participating in those undertakings and the third State concerned.

### Article 4

Should the Contracting Parties be engaged in hostilities in consequence of the application of the present Agreement, they will not conclude an armistice or treaty of peace except by mutual agreement.

The present Protocol, constituting an integral part of

the Polish-French Agreements of 1921 and 1925, shall remain in force as long as the said Agreements.

                              Juljusz Lukasiewicz
                              Georges Bonnet

(Official Documents..., No. 139.)

# TREATIES OF THE POLISH GOVERNMENT
# IN EXILE, 1939-1944

## 15. Polish-Soviet Agreement of July 30, 1941

The Government of the Republic of Poland and the Government of the Union of Soviet Socialist Republics have concluded the present Agreement and decided as follows:

1. The Government of the Union of Soviet Socialist Republics recognizes that the Soviet-German treaties of 1939 relative to territorial changes in Poland have lost their validity. The Government of the Republic of Poland declares that Poland is not bound by any Agreement with any third State directed against the USSR.

2. Diplomatic relations will be restored between the two Governments upon the signature of this Agreement and an exchange of ambassadors will follow immediately.

3. The two Governments mutually undertake to render one another aid and support of all kinds in the present war against Hitlerite Germany.

4. The Government of the Union of Soviet Socialist Republics expresses its consent to the formation on the territory of the Union of Soviet Socialist Republics of a Polish Army under a commander appointed by the Government of the Republic of Poland, in agreement with the Government of the Union of Soviet Socialist Republics. The Polish Army on the territory of the Union of Soviet Socialist Republics will be subordinated in operational matters to the Supreme Command of the USSR on which there will be a representative of the Polish Army. All details as to command, organization and employment of this force will be settled in a subsequent Agreement.

5. This Agreement will come into force immediately upon its signature and without ratification. The present Agreement is drawn up in two copies, each of them in the Russian and Polish languages. Both texts have equal force.

SECRET PROTOCOL

1.   Various claims both of public and private nature will
be dealt with in the course of further negotiations between the
two governments.

2.   This protocol enters into force simultaneously with
the Agreement of the 30th of July, 1941.

PROTOCOL

1.   As soon as diplomatic relations are re-established
the Government of the Union of Soviet Socialist Republics will
grant amnesty to all Polish Citizens who are at present deprived
of their freedom on the territory of the USSR either as prisoners
of war or on other adequate grounds.

2.   The present Protocol comes into force simultaneously
with the Agreement of July 30, 1941.

> I. Maisky
> Wladyslaw Sikorski

(Documents on Polish-Soviet Relations, 1939-1945, vol. I, p.
141-42.)

16.   Agreement between Poland and Czechoslovakia of January
23, 1942

In execution of the declaration of the Governments of
Poland and Czechoslovakia of November 11, 1940, whereby
both Governments decided that after the war Poland and Czechoslovakia shall form a Confederation of States in that area of
Europe with which the vital interests of the two countries are
bound, the Governments of Poland and Czechoslovakia conducted
uninterrupted negotiations on the subject of the method of bringing the above declaration to fruition.   At the same time both
Governments adopted a resolution expressing their satisfaction
with the conclusion of the Greek-Yugoslav agreement of January 15, 1942, and their conviction that the security and prosperity of the area of Europe situated between the Baltic and
Aegean Seas depend primarily on the collaboration of two con-
federations, the foundation of one of which has been laid by the
Polish-Czechoslovak agreement and of the other by the Greek-
Yugoslav agreement.   Both Governments reached agreement

with regard to a number of principles of the projected Confederation which were defined in the following declaration, London,
January 23, 1942:

The Governments of Poland and Czechoslovakia have
agreed on the following points with regard to the future Confederation of Poland Czechoslovakia.

1.  The two Governments desire that the Polish-
Czechoslovak Confederation should embrace other states of the
European area with which the vital interests of Poland and
Czechoslovakia are linked up.

2.  The purpose of the Confederation is to assure common
policy with regard to foreign affairs, defense, economic and financial matters, social questions, transport, posts and tele-
graphs.

3.  The Confederation will have a common general
staff, whose task it will be to assure the means of defense which
in the event of war a unified supreme command will be appointed.

4.  The Confederation will coordinate the policy of foreign trade and custom tariffs of the states forming the confederation with a view to the conclusion of a custom union.

5.  The Confederation will have an agreed monetary
policy.  Autonomous banks of issue of the states forming the
Confederation will be maintained.  It will be their task to assure
that the parity established between the various national cur-
rencies shall be permanently maintained.

6.  The Confederation will coordinate the financial
policy of the states forming the Confederation, especially with
regard to taxation.

7.  The development and administration of railway,
road, water and air transport as also the telecommunication
services will be carried out according to a common plan.  An
identical tariff for postal and telecommunication services will
be binding on all the territories of the Confederation.  The
states in possession of sea and inland harbors will take into
consideration the economic interests of the Confederation and
will mutually support the interests of sea and inland harbors
of the states forming the Confederation.

8. Coordination will also be applied in the realm of social policy of the various states of the Confederation.

9. The Confederation will assure cooperation among its members in educational and cultural matters.

10. Questions of nationality will remain within the competence of the individual states forming the Confederation. The passenger traffic between various states included in the Confederation will take place without any restrictions in particular without passports and visas. The question of free domicile and of the right to exercise any gainful occupation of the citizens of the individual states forming the Confederation over the whole territory of the Confederation will be regulated.

11. The question of the mutual recognition by the states forming the Confederation school and professional diplomas, of documents and sentences of court, as well as the question of mutual legal aid in particular in the execution of court sentences will be regulated.

12. The constitution of the individual states included in the Confederation will guarantee to the citizens of these states the following rights: freedom of conscience, personal freedom, freedom of learning, freedom of the spoken and written word, freedom of organization and association, equality of all citizens before the law, free admission of all citizens to the performance of all state functions, the independence of the courts of law, and control of government by the representative national bodies elected by means of free elections.

13. Both Governments have agreed that in order to ensure the common policy with regard to the above-mentioned spheres, the establishment of common organs of the Confederation will be necessary.

14. The states included in the Confederation will jointly defray the costs of its maintenance.

(Czechoslovak Sources and Documents: No. 2, Struggle for Freedom. New York, 1943; Wandycz, Piotr S., Czechoslovak-Polish Confederation and the Great Powers, 1940-43. Indiana Univ. Publ., 1956.)

TREATIES OF THE POLISH PEOPLE'S REPUBLIC,
1944-1960

17. Agreement between the USSR and the Polish Committee of
National Liberation of July 26, 1944

The Government of the Union of Soviet Socialist Republics and the Polish Committee of National Liberation, desiring
that relations between the Soviet Commander-in-Chief and the
Polish Administration on the territory of the Polish Republic
after the entry of Soviet troops to the territory of Poland be resolved in a spirit of friendship, have concluded the present
agreement to the following effect:

Article 1

In the zone of military operations on the territory of
Poland after the entry of Soviet troops, supreme power and the
responsibility in all affairs relating to the conduct of the war
for the time necessary for the execution of military operations
shall be concentrated in the hands of the Commander-in-Chief
of the Soviet troops.

Article 2

On Polish territory liberated from the enemy, the Polish Committee of National Liberation: (a) Sets up and directs
in conformity with the laws of the Polish Republic administrative organs which the latter establishes; (b) Carries out
measures for the further organization, formation, and replen-
ishment of the Polish Army; (c) Insures active assistance of
organs of the Polish Administration to the Soviet Commander-
in-Chief in the execution of military operations by the Red
Army and in meeting its requirements and needs during its
stay on Polish territory.

Article 3

Polish military units which are formed on the territory

179

of the U. S. S. R.  shall operate on the territory of Poland.

## Article 4

Contact between the Soviet Commander-in-Chief and the Polish Committee of National Liberation shall be maintained through the Polish Military Mission.

## Article 5

In the zone of direct military operations,  contact between Polish administrative organs and the Soviet Commander-in-Chief shall be maintained through the delegate of the Polish Committee of National Liberation.

## Article 6

As soon as any part of the liberated territory of Poland ceases to be a zone of direct military operations,  the Polish Committee of National Liberation shall fully assume the direction of all affairs of civil administration.

## Article 7

All personnel of Soviet troops on the territory of Poland shall be under the jurisdiction of the Soviet Commander-in-Chief.  All personnel of the Polish Armed Forces shall be subordinated to Polish military laws and regulations.  The civilian population on Polish territory shall also be under the latter jurisdiction,  even in cases of crimes committed against Soviet troops,  with the exception of crimes committed in the zone of military operations,  which shall be under the jurisdiction of the Soviet Commander-in-Chief.  In disputable cases the question of jurisdiction shall be decided by mutual agreement between the Soviet Commander-in-Chief and the delegate of the Polish Committee of National Liberation.

## Article 8

For the entire duration of joint military operations of Soviet troops and the Polish Armed Forces,  the latter shall be subordinated to the Supreme Command of the U. S. S. R.,  and in matters relating to organization and personnel to the

Chief Command of the Polish Armed Forces.

## Article 9

A special agreement shall be concluded as regards financial and economic problems relating to the stay of Soviet troops on the territory of Poland, also relating to Polish Armed Forces which are being formed on the territory of the U. S. S. R.

## Article 10

The present agreement takes effect immediately after it is signed. The agreement is made in two copies, each in the Russian and Polish languages. Both texts are equally valid.

(Signed)

On behalf of the Government of the Union of Soviet Socialist Republics                    MOLOTOV

On behalf of the Polish Committee of National Liberation.                    OSÓBKA-MORAWSKI

(Documents on American Foreign Relations, vol. 7, p. 854.)

18.  Treaty of Friendship between Poland and the Soviet Union of April 21, 1945

The Presidium of the Supreme Soviet of the Union of Soviet Socialist Republics and the President of the National Council of Polish Republics:

Filled with determination jointly to bring the war against the German invaders to complete and final victory;

Desiring to consummate the radical turn in the history of Soviet-Polish relations towards friendly, allied collaboration, which has arisen between the U. S. S. R. and Poland in the course of the joint struggle against German imperialism;

Confident that the further consolidation of relations of good neighbourliness and friendship between the Soviet Union and contiguous Poland meets the vital interests of the Soviet and Polish peoples;

Convinced that the maintenance of friendship and close collaboration between the Soviet and Polish peoples will serve

the cause of the successful economic development of both
countries both in time of war and after it;

Striving to support by every means the cause of the
peace and security of the nations after the war;

Have decided to conclude with this end in view the present treaty and appointed as their plenipotentiaries:

(Here follow the names)

Who, after exchange of their credentials found in due
form and in good order, agreed on the following:

## Article 1

The High Contracting Parties will continue jointly with
all the United Nations the struggle against Germany until final
victory.   The High Contracting Parties undertake to render
each other military and other assistance in this struggle by
every means at their disposal.

## Article 2

The High Contracting Parties, convinced that the interests of the security and prosperity of the Soviet and the Polish
peoples call for the preservation and strengthening of a stable
and permanent friendship in time of war and after the war, will
strengthen friendly collaboration between the two countries in
conformity with the principles of mutual respect for their independence and sovereignty as well as non-intervention in the
internal affairs of the other State.

## Article 3

The High Contracting Parties undertake also after the
termination of the present war with Germany to take jointly all
measures at their disposal in order to eliminate every threat
of a repitition of aggression on the part of Germany or any
other State which would unite with Germany directly or in any
other form.

To achieve this aim the High Contracting Parties will
participate in a spirit of most sincere collaboration, in all
international actions aimed at insuring the peace and security

of the nations, and will contribute their full share to the cause
of the materialization of these lofty aims.

The application of the present treaty by the High Contracting Parties will conform to international principles in the
adoption of which both contracting parties have participated.

## Article 4

In the event of one of the High Contracting Parties in the
post-war period finding itself involved in hostilities with Germany, the latter having resumed her aggressive policy, or with
some other State united with Germany directly or in any other
form in such a war, the other High Contracting Party will immediately render to the contracting party involved in hostilities
military or other assistance and support by every means at its
disposal.

## Article 5

The High Contracting Parties undertake not to conclude
without mutual consent an armistice or peace treaty either with
the Hitler Government or with any other authority in Germany
which encroaches or would encroach on the independence, territorial integrity or security of either of the High Contracting
Parties.

## Article 6

Each High Contracting Party undertakes not to conclude
any alliance and not to take part in any coalition directed against
the other High Contracting Party.

## Article 7

The High Contracting Parties will also after the termination of the present war collaborate in a spirit of friendship
with a view to further development and consolidation of economic
and cultural ties between the two countries, and assist each
other in the economic rehabilitation of both countries.

## Article 8

The present treaty comes into force from the moment

of its signing, and is subject to ratification within the shortest possible time. The exchange of ratification instruments shall be effected in Warsaw as soon as possible.

The present treaty shall remain in force for 20 years from the moment of its signing. If at the end of this twenty-year period either of the High Contracting Parties does not declare, 12 months prior to the expiration of the term, its desire to renounce the treaty, it shall remain in force for the next 5 years, and thus each time until either of the High Contracting Parties, 12 months prior to the expiration of the current five-year term, gives notice in writing about its intention to renounce the treaty.

In testimony whereof the plenipotentiaries signed the present treaty and affixed their seals to it.

Done in Moscow, April 21, 1945, in two copies, each in the Russian and Polish languages, both texts having equal force.

On Authorization of the Presidium of the Supreme Soviet of the U. S. S. R.:

J. STALIN

On Authorization of the President of the National Council of the Polish Republic:

OSÓBKA-MORAWSKI

(British and Foreign State Papers, vol. 145, p. 1166.)

19.  Treaty of Friendship between Poland and Yugoslavia of March 14, 1946

The President of the National Council of the Republic of Poland on the one part, and

The Presidium of the National Skupština of the Federative People's Republic of Yugoslavia on the other part,

Drawing conclusions from the experiences of the last war, which as the result of aggression by Germany and her allies wrought enormous destruction both in Poland and in Yugoslavia,

Desirous of tightening the bonds of secular friendship between the brother Slav nations of both countries, bonds which have been particularly strengthened and consolidated in the course of the joint struggle waged for liberty, independence, and democracy against Germany and her allies in the last war,

Believing that the strengthening and deepening of the friendship between Poland and Yugoslavia corresponds to the most vital interest of both countries and will most effectively serve the cause of the cultural and economic development of Poland and Yugoslavia,

Being desirous of consolidating the peace and security of Poland and Yugoslavia as well as world peace and security,

Have resolved to conclude a Treaty of Friendship and Mutual Assistance and for this purpose have appointed as their plenipotentiaries:

The President of the National Council of the Republic of Poland: Edward OSÓBKA-MORAWSKI, Prime Minister of the Government of National Unity of the Republic of Poland, and

The Presidium of the National Skupština of the Federative People's Republic of Yugoslavia: Joseph BROZ-TITO, Marshal of Yugoslavia and Prime Minister of the Government of the Federative People's Republic of Yugoslavia,

Who, after having exchanged their full powers, found in good and due form, have agreed on the following provisions:

## Article I

Each of the High Contracting Parties undertakes not to enter into any alliance or participate in any action directed against the other High Contracting Party.

## Article II

In the event of the peace and security of either country being threatened as well as in the more important matters affecting the interests of both countries the High Contracting Parties undertake to consult one another on their course of action.

## Article III

Should either of the High Contracting Parties, as a result of aggression, become involved in hostilities against Germany, or against a country which was an ally of Germany

8

directly or in any other way whatsoever had allied itself with
Germany, or with her allies in such aggression, the other
High Contracting Party shall afford such Party immediate military and other assistance and support by all means at its disposal.

### Article IV

The present Treaty shall not in any way prejudice the
engagements entered into by both High Contracting Parties with
third countries.

The High Contracting Parties shall execute the present
Treaty in conformity with the Charter of the United Nations
and shall support any steps taken to eliminate centers of aggression, as well as to consolidate peace and security throughout the world.

### Article V

The present Treaty shall come into force on the date
of  signature and shall be binding for twenty years.

Unless notice of intention to terminate the Treaty is
given by one of the High Contracting Parties at least one year
before the expiration of the period agreed upon, it shall be considered as having been renewed for a further period of five
years and similarly thereafter.

The Treaty is subject to ratification.  The exchange of
instruments of ratification shall take place at Belgrade at the
earliest possible date.

In faith whereof the above-mentioned Plenipotentiaries
have signed this Treaty and have thereto affixed their seals.

Done at Warsaw in two copies,  each in the Polish and
Serbo-Croat languages,  both of which are authentic, this 18th
day of March, 1946.

By authority of the President of the National Council of
the Republic of Poland:

(Signed)  Edward OSÓBKA-MORAWSKI

By authority of the Presidium of the National Skupština of the Federative Peoples Republic of Yugoslavia:

(Signed)   Joseph BROZ-TITO

(UNTS, 1946-47, vol. 1, No. 13, p. 53.)

## 20.  Treaty of Friendship between Poland and Czechoslovakia of March 10, 1947

The President of the Republic of Poland and

The President of the Czechoslovak Republic,

Being desirous of ensuring the peaceful development of both their Slav countries which, bordering directly upon Germany, have throughout their history been the object of German aggression which has repeatedly threatened their very existence,

Drawing appropriate conclusions from the experiences of the last war, which confronted both countries with deadly perils,

Realizing the vital interests of both countries in joint defense in the event of a renewal by Germany of her policy of aggression against their freedom, independence and territorial integrity,

Being convinced that joint defense against such a danger is in the interests of the maintenance of world peace and international security, the principal purpose of the United Nations, to which both States belong,

Recognizing that friendship and close co-operation between the Republic of Poland and the Czechoslovak Republic correspond with the most vital interests of both States and contribute to their cultural and economic development,

Have resolved to conclude a treaty of friendship and mutual aid and for this purpose have appointed as their Plenipotentiaries:

The President of the Republic of Poland:

Mr. Józef Cyrankiewicz, President of the Council of Ministers, and

Mr. Zygmunt Modzelewski, Minister of Foreign Affairs;

The President of the Czechoslovak Republic:

Mr. Klement Gottwald, President of the Council of Ministers, and

Mr. Jan Masaryk, Minister of Foreign Affairs,

Who, having exchanged their full powers, found in good and due form, have agreed on the following provisions:

## Article 1

The High Contracting Parties undertake to establish their mutual relations on a basis of firm friendship, to develop and strengthen them together with economic and cultural co-operation.

## Article 2

The High Contracting Parties undertake to carry out in mutual agreement all measures within the power to obviate any threat of further aggression by Germany or any other State associated with Germany for that purpose either directly or in any other way.

To this end, the High Contracting Parties will participate to the fullest extent in any international action aimed at ensuring international peace and security and will contribute fully to the realization of this aim.

In carrying out the present treaty, the High Contracting Parties will observe the obligations incumbent upon them as members of the United Nations.

## Article 3

Should either of the High Contracting Parties become involved in hostilities with Germany in consequence of her renewing her policy of aggression, or with any other State associated with Germany in such a policy, the other High Contracting Party shall without delay give the Party concerned military and all other assistance by every means at its disposal.

## Article 4

Each of the High Contracting Parties undertakes not to

enter into an alliance or take part in any coalition directed against the other High Contracting Power.

## Article 5

The present treaty shall remain in force for twenty years from the date of its entry into force. If neither High Contracting Party denounces the treaty twelve months before the expiration of the aforementioned twenty-year period, it shall remain in force for a further period of five years and thus for subsequent five-year periods, until such time as either High Contracting Party denounces it twelve months before the expiration of the current five-year period.

The present treaty, whereof the additional protocol constitutes an integral part, shall be ratified in the shortest possible time and the instruments of ratification shall be exchanged at Prague as soon as possible.

The treaty shall come into force on the date of signature.

## Article 6

The present treaty is drawn up in the Polish and Czech languages, both texts being equally authentic.

In faith whereof the plenipotentiaries have signed the present treaty and have affixed thereto their seals.

Done in duplicate, at Warsaw, on 10 March 1947.

For the President of the Republic of Poland:

(L. S.)  (Signed)  Józef CYRANKIEWICZ
         (Signed)  Zygmunt MODZELEWSKI

For the President of the Czechoslovak Republic:

(L. S.)  (Signed)  GOTTWALD
         (Signed)  Jan MASARYK

## ADDITIONAL PROTOCOL

To the Treaty of Friendship and Mutual Aid between the Republic of Poland and the Czechoslovak Republic

The High Contracting Parties
Being convinced that their firm friendship calls for the

settlement of all the questions outstanding between their two states, also agree:

To settle all territorial questions at present outstanding between the two States on a basis of mutual agreement not later than two years from the date of the signature of the treaty of friendship and mutual aid;

In view of the need for the earliest possible economic and cultural rehabilitation of both countries, to conclude agreements for this purpose as soon as possible;

To guarantee to Poles in Czechoslovakia and to Czechs and Slovaks in Poland, within the limits of law and on the basis of reciprocity, the possibility of national, political, cultural and economic development (schools, societies and co-operatives, on the basis of the unity of co-operative organizations in Poland and in Czechoslovakia).

Done at Warsaw, on 10 March 1947.

> (Signed)    Józef CYRANKIEWICZ
> (Signed)    Zygmunt MODZELEWSKI
> (Signed)    GOTTWALD
> (Signed)    Jan MASARYK

(UNTS, vol. 25, No. 365, p. 231.)

21.  Treaty of Friendship between Poland and Bulgaria of May 29, 1948

The President of the Polish Republic and the Presidium of the Supreme National Assembly of the People's Republic of Bulgaria,

Desirous of expressing the will of their two peoples to consolidate friendly relations and close co-operation between Poland and Bulgaria,

Fully realizing that the experiences of the Second World War constrain both countries to join in resisting threats to their security and independence,

Being deeply convinced that a lasting rapprochement between these two Slav countries is in conformity with their vital interests and will serve the cause of peace and international security, in accordance with the spirit of the Charter of the United Nations,

Have resolved to conclude a treaty of friendship, co-operation and mutual assistance, and for that purpose have appointed as their plenipotentiaries:

The President of the Polish Republic:

Mr. Józef CYRANKIEWICZ, President of the Council of Ministers of the Polish Republic, and

Mr. Zygmunt MODZELEWSKI, Minister for Foreign Affairs of the Polish Republic;

The Presidium of the Supreme National Assembly of the People's Republic of Bulgaria:

Mr. Georgi DIMITROV, President of the Council of Ministers of the People's Republic of Bulgaria, and

Mr. Vasil KOLAROV, Vice-Premier and Minister for Foreign Affairs of the National People's Republic of Bulgaria,

Who, having exchanged their full powers, found in good and due form, have agreed upon the following provisions:

## Article 1

The High Contracting Parties agree to take all action in their power to prevent further aggression by Germany or any other State which might be associated with Germany directly or in any other way.

The High Contracting Parties will, in a spirit of sincerest co-operation, participate in all international action for maintaining international peace and security and will contribute to the realization of these lofty aims.

## Article 2

Should either of the high Contracting Parties be subjected to aggression by Germany or any other State which might be associated with Germany directly or indirectly or in any other way, the other High Contracting Party shall immediately afford it military and other assistance and support with all the means at its disposal.

## Article 3

The High Contracting Parties agree respectively not to enter into any alliance or take part in any action directed against the other High Contracting Party.

## Article 4

The High Contracting Parties will consult together on all the more important international problems affecting the interests of their two countries, more especially their security and territorial integrity or the interests of peace and international co-operation.

## Article 5

The High Contracting Parties will develop and strengthen their economic and cultural relations with one another in the interests of the multilateral development of their two countries.

## Article 6

The provisions of the present treaty will in no contravene obligations previously undertaken by either of the High Contracting Parties towards other States and will be implemented in accordance with the Charter of the United Nations.

## Article 7

The present treaty shall come into force on the date of the exchange of the instruments of ratification and shall remain in force for a period of twenty years.

The exchange of ratifications shall take place at Sofia. Unless the present Treaty is denounced by one of the High Contracting Parties twelve months before the expiration of the said period of twenty years, it shall remain in force for five years, and for similar periods thereafter, until one of the High Contracting Parties denounces it twelve months before the expiration of the current five-year period.

The present treaty is done in duplicate, in the Bulgarian and Polish languages, both texts being equally authentic.

In faith whereof the aforesaid plenipotentiaries have signed the present treaty and have affixed thereto their seals.

Warsaw, 29 May 1948

For the President of the Polish Republic:

> (L. S.) (Signed)  J. CYRANKIEWICZ
> (Signed)  Z. MODZELEWSKI

For the Presidium of the Supreme National Assembly of the People's Republic of Bulgaria:

> (L. S.) (Signed)  G. DIMITROV
> (Signed)  V. KOLAROV

(UNTS, 1949, vol. 26, no. 389, p. 213.)

## 22.  Treaty of Friendship between Poland and Hungary of June 18, 1948

The President of the Republic of Poland and

The President of the Republic of Hungary,

Basing themselves upon the age-long tradition of friendship between the two peoples,

Considering that the strengthening and deepening of mutual friendship and co-operation corresponds to the wishes and interests of the Polish and Hungarian peoples and will contribute to the economic development of both countries,

Declaring their firm determination to strengthen universal peace and security in accordance with the purposes and principles of the United Nations,

Having resolved to conclude a treaty of friendship, co-operation and mutual aid for this purpose have appointed as their plenipotentiaries:

The President of the Republic of Poland:

> Mr. Józef Cyrankiewicz, President of the Council of Ministers, and

> Mr. Zygmunt Modelewski, Minister of Foreign Affairs;

The President of the Republic of Hungary:

> Mr. Lajos Dinnyés, President of the Council of Ministers, and

Mr. Erik Molnár, Minister for Foreign Affairs;

Who, after having exchanged their full powers, found in good and due form, have agreed on the following provisions:

## Article 1

The High Contracting Parties will participate to the fullest extent in all international actions aimed at ensuring international peace and security and will fully contribute to the realization of these lofty aims.

The High Contracting Parties undertake all joint measures within their power to obviate any threat of further aggression by Germany or any other Power associated with her either directly or in any other way.

## Article 2

Should either of the High Contracting Parties become involved in hostilities with Germany in consequence of her attempting to renew her policy of aggression, or with any other State associated with Germany in a policy of aggression, the other High Contracting Party shall give him immediate military and all other assistance by every means at his disposal.

## Article 3

Each High Contracting Party undertakes not to enter into any alliance or participate in any coalition, action or activity directed against the other High Contracting Party.

## Article 4

The High Contracting Parties undertake to consult one another in any important international questions affecting the interests of both countries or those of international peace and co-operation.

## Article 5

The High Contracting Parties will continue to develop and strengthen their mutual economic and cultural relations in the spirit of sincere friendship and close co-operation.

## Article 6

The High Contracting Parties will carry out the present treaty in conformity with the Charter of the United Nations.

## Article 7

The present treaty shall come into force on the date of the exchange of the instruments of ratification and shall remain in force for a period of twenty years.

The exchange of the instruments of ratification shall take place at Budapest.

Should the treaty not be denounced by one of the High Contracting Parties at least one year before the expiration of the twenty-year period agreed upon, it shall remain in force for a further five years. The same shall apply for subsequent periods until either of the High Contracting Parties gives notice in writing one year before the expiration of the current five-year period of his intention to terminate the treaty.

Done in duplicate, in Polish and Hungarian, both texts being equally authentic.

In faith whereof the plenipotentiaries have signed the present treaty and affixed their seals thereto.

Warsaw, the 18th day of June, 1948.

For the President of the Republic of Poland:

(L. S.)  (Signed)  J.  Cyrankiewicz
         (Signed)  Z.  Modzelewski

For the President of the Republic of Hungary:

(L. S.)  (Signed)  L.  Dinnyés
         (Signed)  E.  Molnár

(UNTS, 1949, vol. 25, No. 370, p. 219.)

23.  Treaty of Friendship between Poland and Rumania of January 26, 1949

The President of the Polish Republic and the Presidium of the Great National Assembly of the People's Republic of Rumania,

Desirous of consolidating friendly relations and close co-operation between the Polish Republic and the People's Republic of Rumania,

Bearing in mind the experiences of Hitlerite aggression and the Second World War,

Desirous of maintaining and strengthening universal peace in accordance with the purposes and principles of the United Nations,

Have resolved to conclude a treaty of friendship, cooperation and mutual assistance, and for this purpose have appointed as their plenipotentiaries:

The President of the Polish Republic:

Mr. Józef Cyrankiewicz, President of the Council of Ministers, and

Mr. Zygmunt Modzelewski, Minister of Foreign Affairs;

The Presidium of the Great National Assembly of the People's Republic of Rumania:

Dr. Petru Groza, President of the Council of Ministers, and Mrs. Ana Pauker, Minister of Foreign Affairs,

Who, having exchanged their full powers, found in good and due form, have agreed upon the following provisions:

Article 1

The High Contracting Parties undertake to carry out all joint measures within their power to obviate any threat of further aggression by Germany or any other State associated with Germany either directly or in any other way.

The High Contracting Parties declare that they will participate in any international action aimed at ensuring international peace and security and will contribute fully to the realization of these lofty aims.

Article 2

Should either of the High Contracting Parties become involved in hostilities with Germany in consequence of her renewing her policy of aggression or with any other State as-

sociated with Germany in its own policy of aggression either
directly or in any other way, the other High Contracting Party
shall immediately give the Party involved in hostilities military and all other assistance by every means at its disposal.

The present Treaty will be carried out in conformity
with the principles of the United Nations Charter.

## Article 3

Each of the High Contracting Parties undertakes not to
enter into any alliance or take part in any action directed
against the other High Contracting Party.

## Article 4

The High Contracting Parties will consult together on
all important international questions involving the interests of
both countries.

## Article 5

The High Contracting Parties shall take, in conformity
with the agreements concluded between the Polish Republic and
the People's Republic of Rumania, all the necessary steps to
develop and strengthen the economic and cultural ties between
the two States in a spirit of friendship and co-operation.

## Article 6

The present Treaty shall come into force on the date
of the exchange of the instruments of ratification and shall remain in force for a period of twenty years from the date of
entry into force.

The exchange of the instruments of ratification shall
take place at Warsaw.

If neither High Contracting Party gives notice in writing
one year before the expiration of the aforementioned twenty-
year period that it wishes to denounce the Treaty, it shall remain in force for a further period of five years and thus for
subsequent five-year periods, until such time as either High
Contracting Party gives notice in writing, one year before

the expiration of the current five-year period, of its intention to terminate the Treaty.

The present Treaty is done in duplicate, in the Polish and Rumanian languages, both texts being equally authentic.

In faith whereof the plenipotentiaries have signed the present Treaty and attached their seals thereto.

Done at Bucharest, on 26 January 1949.

By authorization of the President of the Polish Republic:

(Signed)  J. Cyrankiewicz
(Signed)  Z. Modzelewski

By authorization of the Presidium of the Great National Assembly of the People's Republic of Rumania:

(Signed)  Petru Groza
(Signed)  A. Pauker

(UNTS, 1951, vol. 85, no. 1143, p. 21.)


24. Agreement between Poland and the German Democratic Republic of July 6, 1950

The President of the Polish Republic and the President of the German Democratic Republic,

Desiring to give expression to their will for the strengthening of universal peace and wishing to made a contribution to the noble cause of harmonious co-operation between peace-loving peoples,

Having regard to the fact that such co-operation between the German and Polish peoples has become possible thanks to the total defeat of German Fascism by the USSR and to the progressive development of the democratic forces in Germany, and

Desirous of establishing, after the tragic experiences of Hitlerism, indestructible foundations upon which the two peoples may live together in peace and as good neighbors,

Wishing to stabilize and strengthen mutual relations on the basis of the Potsdam Agreement, which established the frontier on the Oder and Western Neisse,

In pursuance of the provisions of the Warsaw Declaration of the Government of the Polish Republic and the Dele-

gation of the Provisional Government of the German Democratic
Republic dated 6 June 1950,

Recognizing the established and existing frontier as an
inviolable frontier of peace and friendship which does not divide
but unites the two peoples,

Have resolved to conclude this Agreement and have appointed as their plenipotentiaries:

The President of the Polish Republic:

> Mr. Józef CYRANKIEWICZ, President of the Council of
> Ministers,

> Mr. Stefan WIERBLOWSKI, Chief of the Ministry of
> Foreign Affairs;

The President of the German Democratic Republic:

> Mr. Otto GROTEWOHL, Prime Minister,
> Mr. Georg DERTINGER, Minister of Foreign Affairs,

Who, having exchanged their full powers, found in good
and due form, have agreed as follows:

## Article 1

The High Contracting Parties concur in confirming that
the established and existing frontier, running from the Baltic
Sea along a line to the west of the inhabited locality of Swin-
oujscie and thence along the Oder River to the confluence of the
Western Neisse to the Czechoslovak frontier, is the State frontier between Poland and Germany.

## Article 2

The Polish-German State frontier as demarcated in
accordance with this Agreement shall also delimit vertically
the air space, the sea and the subsoil.

## Article 3

For the purpose of demarcating on the ground the Polish-
German State frontier referred to in Article 1, the High Contracting Parties shall establish a Mixed Polish-German commission having its headquarters at Warsaw.

The Commission shall comprise eight members, four of whom shall be appointed by the Government of the Polish Republic and four by the Provisional Government of the German Democratic Republic.

## Article 4

The Mixed Polish-German Commission shall meet not later than 31 August 1950 to begin the work referred to in Article 3.

## Article 5

After the demarcation of the State frontier on the ground, the High Contracting Parties shall draw up an instrument confirming the demarcation of the State frontier between Poland and Germany.

## Article 6

In carrying out the demarcation of the Polish-German State frontier, the High Contracting Parties shall conclude agreements relating to frontier crossing points, local frontier traffic and navigation on frontier waterways.

Such agreements shall be concluded within one month after the entry into force of the instrument mentioned in Article 5 confirming the demarcation of the State frontier between Poland and Germany.

## Article 7

This agreement shall be subject to ratification, which shall take place as soon as possible. The Agreement shall come into force on the exchange of the instruments of ratification, which shall take place in Berlin.

In witness whereof the plenipotentiaries have signed this Agreement and have thereto affixed their seals.

## Article 8

Done at Zgorzelec on 6 July 1950 in duplicate, in the Polish and German languages, both texts being equally authentic.

For the President of the Polish Republic:

(L. S.)  J. CYRANKIEWICZ
Stefan WIERBLOWSKI

For the President of the German Democratic Republic:

(L. S.)  O. GROTEWOHL
G. DERTINGER

(UNTS, 1959, vol. 319, no. 4631, p. 93.)

25.  Treaty of Warsaw of May 14, 1955

The Contracting Parties,

Reaffirming their desire for the establishment of a system of European collective security based on the participation of all European states irrespective of their social and political systems, which would make it possible to unite their efforts in safeguarding the peace of Europe;

Mindful, at the same time, of the situation created in Europe by the ratification of the Paris agreements, which envisage the formation of a new military alignment in the shape of "Western European Union," with the participation of a re-militarized Western Germany and the integration of the latter in the North Atlantic bloc, which increases the danger of another war and constitutes a threat to the national security of the peaceful states;

Being persuaded that in these circumstances the peaceable European states must take the necessary measures to safeguard their security and in the interests of preserving peace in Europe;

Guided by the objects and principles of the Charter of the United Nations Organization;

Being desirous of further promoting and developing friendship, cooperation and mutual assistance in accordance with the principles of respect for the independence and sovereignty of states and of non-interference in their internal affairs,

Have decided to conclude the present Treaty of Friendship, Cooperation and Mutual Assistance and have for that purpose appointed as their plenipotentiaries:

The Presidium of the People's Assembly of the People's Republic of Albania:

Mehmet Shehu, Chairman of the Council of Ministers of the People's Republic of Albania;

The Presidium of the People's Assembly of the People's Republic of Bulgaria:

Vylko Chervenkov, Chairman of the Council of Ministers of the People's Republic of Bulgaria;

The Presidium of the Hungarian People's Republic:

Andras Hegedus, Chairman of the Council of Ministers of the Hungarian People's Republic;

The President of the German Democratic Republic:

Otto Grotewohl, Prime Minister of the German Democratic Republic;

The State Council of the Polish People's Republic:

Józef Cyrankiewicz, Chairman of the Council of Ministers of the Polish People's Republic;

The Presidium of the Grand National Assembly of the Rumanian People's Republic:

Gheorhe Gheorghiu-Dej, Chairman of the Council of Ministers of the Rumanian People's Republic;

The Presidium of the Supreme Soviet of the Union of Soviet Socialist Republics:

Nikolai Alexandrovish Bulganin, Chairman of the Council of Ministers of the U.S.S.R.;

The President of the Czechoslovak Republic:

Viliam Siroky, Prime Minister of the Czechoslovak Republic,

Who, having presented their full powers, found in good and due form, have agreed as follows:

## Article 1

The Contracting Parties undertake, in accordance with the Charter of the United Nations organization, to refrain in their international relations from the threat or use of force, and to settle their international disputes peacefully and in such manner as will not jeopardize international peace and security.

## Article 2

The Contracting Parties declare their readiness to participate in a spirit of sincere cooperation in all international actions designed to safeguard international peace and security, and will fully devote their energies to the attainment of this end.

The Contracting Parties will furthermore strive for the adoption, in agreement with other states which may desire to cooperate in this, of effective measures for universal reduction of armaments and prohibition of atomic, hydrogen and other weapons of mass destruction.

## Article 3

The Contracting Parties shall consult with one another on all important international issues affecting their common interest, guided by the desire to strengthen international peace and security.

They shall immediately consult with one another whenever, in the opinion of any one of them, a threat of armed attack on one or more of the parties of the Treaty has arisen, in order to ensure joint defense and the maintenance of peace and security.

## Article 4

In the event of armed attack in Europe on one or more of the Parties to the Treaty by any state or group of states, each of the Parties to the Treaty, in the exercise of its right to individual or collective self-defense in accordance with Article 51 of the Charter of the United Nations Organization, shall immediately, either individually or in agreement with other Parties to the Treaty, come to the assistance of the state or states attacked with all such means as it deems necessary, including armed force. The Parties to the Treaty shall immediately consult concerning the necessary measures to be taken by them jointly in order to restore and maintain international peace and security.

Measures taken on the basis of this Article shall be reported to the Security Council in conformity with the provisions of the Charter of the United Nations Organization. These measures shall be discontinued immediately after the Security Council adopts the necessary measures to restore and maintain international peace and security.

## Article 5

The Contracting Parties have agreed to establish a Joint Command of the armed forces that by agreement among the Parties shall be assigned to the Command, which shall function on the basis of jointly established principles. They shall likewise adopt other agreed measures necessary to strengthen their defensive power, in order to protect the peaceful labours of their peoples, guarantee the inviolability of their frontiers and territories, and provide defense against possible aggression.

## Article 6

For the purpose of the consultations among the Parties envisaged in the present Treaty, and also for the purpose of examining questions which may arise in the operation of the Treaty, a Political Consultative Committee shall be set up, in which each of the Parties to the Treaty shall be represented by a member of its Government or by another specifically appointed representative.

The Committee may set up such auxiliary bodies as may prove necessary.

## Article 7

The Contracting Parties undertake not to participate in any coalitions or alliances and not to conclude any agreements whose objects conflict with the objects of the present Treaty.

The Contracting Parties declare that their commitments under existing international treaties do not conflict with the provisions of the present Treaty.

## Article 8

The Contracting Parties declare that they will act in a

spirit of friendship and cooperation with a view to further developing and fostering economic and cultural intercourse with one another, each adhering to the principle of respect for the independence and sovereignty of the others and noninterference in their internal affairs.

## Article 9

The present Treaty is open to the accession of other states, irrespective of their social and political systems, which express their readiness by participation in the present Treaty to assist in uniting the efforts of the peaceable states in safeguarding the peace and security of the peoples. Such accession shall enter into force with the agreement of the Parties to the Treaty after the declaration of accession has been deposited with the Government of the Polish People's Republic.

## Article 10

The present Treaty is subject to ratification, and the instruments of ratification shall be deposited with the Government of the Polish People's Republic.

The Treaty shall enter into force on the day the last instrument of ratification has been deposited. The Government of the Polish People's Republic shall notify the other Parties to the Treaty as each instrument of ratification is deposited.

## Article 11

The present Treaty shall remain in force for twenty years. For such Contracting Parties as do not at least one year before the expiration of this period present to the Government of the Polish People's Republic a statement of denunciation of the Treaty, it shall remain in force for the next ten years.

Should a system of collective security be established in Europe, and a General European Treaty of Collective Security concluded for this purpose, for which the Contracting Parties will unswervingly strive, the present Treaty shall cease to be operative from the day the General European Treaty enters into force.

Done in Warsaw on May 14, 1955, in one copy each in the Russian, Polish, Czech and German languages, all texts being equally authentic. Certified copies of the present Treaty shall be sent by the Government of the Polish People's Republic to all the Parties of the Treaty.

In witness whereof the plenipotentiaries have signed the present Treaty and affixed their seals.

For the Presidium of the People's Assembly of the People's Republic of Albania:

Mehmet Shehu

For the Presidium of the People's Assembly of the People's Republic of Bulgaria:

Vylko Chervenkov

For the Presidium of the Hungarian People's Republic:

Andras Hegedus

For the President of the German Democratic Republic:

Otto Grotewohl

For the State Council of the Polish People's Republic:

Józef Cyrankiewicz

For the Presidium of the Grand National Assembly of the Rumanian People's Republic:

Gheorghe Gheorghiu-Dej

For the Presidium of the Supreme Soviet of the Union of Soviet Socialist Republics:

Nikolai Alexandrovich Bulganin

For the President of the Czechoslovak Republic

Viliam Siroky

## ESTABLISHMENT OF A JOINT COMMAND

of the Armed Forces of the Signatories to the Treaty of Friendship, Cooperation and Mutual Assistance

In pursuance of the Treaty of Friendship, Cooperation and Mutual Assistance between the People's Republic of Albania, the People's Republic of Bulgaria, the Hungarian People's Republic, the German Democratic Republic, the Polish People's Republic, the Rumanian People's Republic, the Union of Soviet Socialist Republics and the Czechoslovak Republic, the signatory states have decided to establish a Joint Command of their armed forces.

The decision provides that general questions relating to the strengthening of the defensive power and the organization of the Joint Armed Forces of the signatory states shall be subject to examination by the Political Consultative Committee, which shall adopt the necessary decisions.

Marshal of the Soviet Union, I. S. Konev, has been appointed Commander-in-Chief of the Joint Armed Forces to be assigned by the signatory states.

The Ministers of Defense or other military leaders of the signatory states are to serve as Deputy Commanders-in-Chief of the Joint Armed Forces, and shall command the armed forces assigned by their respective states to the Joint Armed Forces.

The question of the participation of the German Democratic Republic in measures concerning the armed forces of the Joint Command will be examined at a later date.

A Staff of the Joint Armed Forces of the Signatory states will be set up under the Commander-in-Chief of the Joint Armed Forces, and will include permanent representatives of the General Staffs of the signatory states.

The Staff will have its headquarters in Moscow.

The disposition of the Joint Armed Forces in the territories of the signatory states will be effected, by agreement among the states, in accordance with the requirements of their mutual defense.

(American J. Suppl., vol. 49 (1955) p. 194-99.)

# Part III

# SELECTED TEXTS OF DOCUMENTS

# DOCUMENTS ISSUED, 1914-1923

## 1. Manifesto of the Austro-Hungarian Supreme Command

Following the outbreak of World War I, the Supreme command of the Austro-Hungarian armies, hoping to attract the active support ot the Polish people, issued its first manifesto:

> To the Polish people! With blessings from the Almighty who guides the fate of nations and under the command of their respective monarchs, the allied Austro-Hungarian and German armies are crossing the borders, thus bringing you, Poles, liberation from the Muscovite yoke.
>
> Greet our banners with trust, for they are ensuring you justice.
>
> These banners are not alien to you nor to your countrymen. To be sure, for a century and a half your fellow countrymen have experienced constant development under the rule of Austria-Hungary and Germany; and certain traditional glories of your past, since the time Jan Sobieski brought his decisive assistance to the beseiged Hapsburg dynasty, are closely related to the traditions of your Western neighbors.
>
> We know well and acknowledge both the chivalry and the eminent qualities of the Polish people. We want to remove the obstacles which make it difficult for you to have closer relationships with the life of the West; we wish to open the way toward spiritual and economic acquisitions. This is the important task which is an integral part of our whole campaign.
>
> We did not instigate the war with Russia. For a long time Russia applied defamation and various other provocations as means of struggle,

211

and at last did not hesitate to side openly with those
who endeavored to wipe out the traces of abomin-
able crimes directed against the Austro-Hungarian
dynasty, and took advantage of this situation to
attack that monarchy and her ally, Germany. This
compelled our eminent ruler, to whom Europe had
attributed peace for decades, to resort to arms.

All those living in Russia whom the victory
of our allied armies shall place under our protection can expect from us, the victors, justice
and humanity.

Poles, trust our protection willingly and
with full confidence and support us and our struggle wholeheartedly. Trust our rulers' sense of
justice and humanity, fulfill your duties, fulfill
your obligations by holding the land of your ancestors, fulfill those obligations which were placed
upon you in this hour of peril by the will of God
Almighty.

Supreme Command of the Austro-Hungarian Armies

(August 10, 1914)

(Jaworski, K. and K. Blaszczyński. Zmartwychstanie Polski
w świetle dokumentów. Poznań, 1928, p. 6.)

2.  Proclamation of the Russian Commander-in-Chief

Four days later, on August 14, 1914, the Russian Commander-in-Chief, the Grand Duke Nicholas, issued the following
proclamation to the Polish nation in order to equalize the German and Austro-Hungarian initiative toward ensuring Polish
support and sympathy:

Poles! The time has come when the dream
of your fathers and forefathers will at length be
realized. A century and a half ago the living body
of Poland was torn into pieces, but her soul has
not perished. She lives in the hope that the time
will come for the resurrection of the Polish nation and its fraternal union with all Russia. The
Russian armies bring you glad tidings of this
union. May the frontiers which have divided the

Polish people be united under the scepter of the
Russian Emperor. Under this scepter Poland will
come together, free in faith, in language, and in
self-government. From you Russia expects an
equal consideration of the rights of those nations
with which history has linked you. With open heart
and with hand fraternally outstretched, great Russia comes to you. She believes that the sword has
not rusted which overthrew the foe at Tannenberg.
From the shores of the Pacific Ocean to the Polar
Sea the Russian War-hosts are in motion. The
morning star of a new life is rising for Poland.
May there shine resplendent in the dawn the sign
of the Cross, the symbol of the passion and the
resurrection of nations.

    Commander-in-Chief General Adjutant

                Nicholas

August 14, 1914

(Gazeta Warszawska, August 16, 1914; Jaworski, op.
cit., pp. 6-7.)

3. Reply of the Polish Political Parties

    The representatives of the undersigned
political parties, assembled in Warsaw on August
16, 1914, welcome the Proclamation, issued to
the Poles by His Imperial Highness, the Commander-in-Chief of the Russian forces, as an
act of foremost historical importance, and im-
plicitly believe that, upon the termination of the
War, the promises uttered in that proclamation
will be formally fulfilled, that the dreams of
their fathers and forefathers will be realized,
that Poland's flesh, torn asunder a century and
a half ago, will once again be made whole, and
that the frontiers severing the Polish Nation will
vanish.

    The blood of Poland's sons, shed in united
combat against the Germans, will serve as a sacrifice, offered upon the altar of her resurrection.

                              The Democratic National Party
                              The Polish Progressive Party
                              The Realist Party
                              The Polish Progressive Union

(Gazeta Warszawska, August 17, 1914.)

4.  Pilsudski's First Statement

    On the day the Polish armies marched out of Kraków,
i. e. , on August 6, 1914, Józef Pilsudski issued the following
statement:

        The National Government.

            The hour of decision has struck! Poland
        has ceased to be slavish; she alone wants to de-
        cide her fate and to build her future, throwing
        into struggle her own strength of arms.  The Po-
        lish army cadres entered the land of the Polish
        Kingdom; they occupied that land for its true and
        only owner, the Polish people, who have popu-
        lated and enriched it.  The land is occupied in the
        name of the Supreme National Government.  We
        carry unfettered by chains to the whole nation
        and by the same token conditions for normal de-
        velopment.

            From this day on the whole nation should
        gather into a single camp under the leadership
        of the National Government.  Outside this camp
        will remain the undesirable whom we can disre-
        gard.

        Commander of the Polish Army, Józef Pilsudski

                          (August 6, 1914)

(Jaworski, op. cit. , p. 8.)

5.  Declaration of the Polish Faction of the Austrian Parliament

        Poles:

            The hour for which three generations of our
        people have anxiously awaited in unbearable and
        hopeless struggle against the Muscovites, the

hour for which our whole nation has been praying, the great hour, has struck.

The whole of Europe is on the threshold of war.

The length and breadth of the Polish land is covered with bloody ray of war, the most devastating war ever. Austria, in order to protect the liberty of her people, is sending considerable armies to the Polish lands to oppose the Russian oppression.

In this dangerous but decisive hour, the Polish faction, being aware of its responsibilities, considers it its holy obligation to guide the national thoughts and deeds in order to prepare for a better future and a fuller understanding.

Being aware of this great task, the Polish faction, which has the support of every member of the Parliament in this decisive hour, is calling all Poles to action, to decision, to single-mindedness, and to the greatest degree of exertion.

By ensuring against a possible Russian victory in this age of bloody changes in Europe, we can gain a great deal. But we must also sacrifice a great deal. He who waits cautiously for the game to end does not win.

The noble Monarch, under whose just and wise rule the glory of our people has been blossoming and our national fortunes and mighty armies have been developing for more than half a century, is looking upon the Polish people as on ardent defenders of those ideals which can be fulfilled in this unprecedented opportunity.

In this hour the people must be aware that they are alive and want to live and that they long for and are able to retain their God-given place.

In order to gather the Polish national strength into armed legions, the Polish faction, together with all sections of Poland, unanimously decided to create a single, open organization.

Under the Polish command, but closely
linked to the Austro-Hungarian armies, the legions
will go into battle in order to be part of the praise-
worthy deed in this most intensive war. It is
bound to guarantee us a better future.

Fellow Poles! With trust and unbending
faith, submit to the commands of the Polish Faction and to the national organization appointed by
it.

Fellow Poles! Unite with an unbreakable
will to attain a better future, and with an unbending faith in that future! Stand in defense of our
freedom and of our ancestors' faith! Cast aside
your doubts and become strong by uniting; be
proud of the tasks dedicated to your country's
life and name.

The Polish Parliamentary Faction

(August 16, 1914)

(Dziennik Poznański, 1914, No. 190; Jaworski, op. cit., pp.
8-9.)

6. Manifesto of the Polish National Council

The newly-formed Polish National Council issued in
Warsaw on November 25, 1914, the following Manifesto addressed to the Poles in all three Empires:

Countrymen!

When the present War broke out, our nation
instantly became aware that an important page of
her history was being turned and that her future
hung in the balance.

Poland's most dread foe, Germany, had
vowed our complete annihilation and with approved
cunning had, through wide-spread influence, armed
all forces against us. Suddenly Germany stood
forth as the enemy of ourselves and of almost the
whole of Europe. And we, who hitherto along in
desperate daily strife had defended against this

enemy the domains of our fathers, saw lifted
against her the arms of the world's great powers:
Russia, France, England.

We had always understood on which side our
place would be. This was now indicated without
hesitation by the thought of all sections of the community and by the healthy instinct of the people
themselves.

Germany's defeat in this struggle means
victory for us.

Our attitude was responded to by Russia in
the proclamation of the Commander-in-Chief of
the Army, a proclamation announcing the fulfillment of our most sacred desires -- the joining
together of the dismembered body of the Nation
and the protection of her freedom of being and of
growth. This proclamation found an echo among
Russia's western allies: the restoration of Poland was seen to be one of the great tasks of this
bloody war, a task crying for accomplishment.
And our Nation itself received the proclamation
with increased ardor. The purpose, which a new
dawn had illumined for us at the very outbreak of
war, stood clearly expressed before the world.

Because of the efforts and sacrifices necessary for the realization of this purpose, all the
conflicts and tortures of yesterday faded into the
past. One object alone confronts the Nation: the
overthrow of Germany's sinister power, the unification of Poland under the scepter of the Russian
Monarch.

Our Nation concentrated upon this object
and turned all its endeavours towards this goal.

From the very first the majority recognized
that, if singleness of purpose were to find expression in unity of action, it must first find leadership. We understand that the historic magnitude
of this moment thrusts aside all the programs
for which we have been combating and that in
time of war parties must cease to speak. The

Nation, acting as a whole, was bound to produce
our national organization competent to give expression to the manifest will of the immense majority.
The creation of this organization, of this unifying
body, had to be undertaken by those who above all
were responsible for the country's politics. The
undersigned, deputies from the Kingdom of Poland
to both legislative bodies of the Empire, former
deputies, and leaders of social work in this country,
have united with the object of drawing together
around the common cause all our countrymen irrespective of views or convictions, unanimous only
in the possession of one purpose, and herein expressing today the clear will of the Nation. Not
being able, owing to present conditions, to assem-
ble all those whom they would desire to see in
their midst and proposing to fill out the frame
according to the measure of their work's progress,
they realize that further delay in setting about that
work would hinder the cause. Therefore, the
undersigned this day unite to form a Polish National Council, thus laying the foundation of Poland's
political organization, giving expression to her
leading tendencies, making her one in purpose
and in deed.

        The Nation is at this moment with the whole
of her strength helping to secure victory over the
Germans. Our youth has rushed with ardor into
the ranks of that Russian army in which the sons
of our land are fighting in hundreds of thousands
for the great cause. The Polish civil population
has zealously cooperated with that army, doing
all in its power to assist in the struggle against
our mighty foe; and whereas war has carried to
our territory devastation, ruin, and destruction,
we are bearing the calamity with calm, confident
in a luminous tomorrow for the land of our fathers.
The foe did not terrify us by his strength, even
when he appeared at the gates of our capital, nor
did he deceive us by his promises. The mass
of the people preserved an unmoved composure
in the presence of danger and replied to his pro-

testations by contempt.

This unshaken attitude was maintained not
only in those parts of the country which the enemy
did not actually invade, but also there where he
took possession, proclaiming his occupation as
definite.

The enemy's expectations were equally disap-
pointed in the case of the Polish detachments formed
in Austria, to which a certain portion of our ignor-
ant youth was drawn, beguiled by patriotic watch-
words.   These detachments, destined to decoy the
population of the Kingdom into an alliance with
Austria and Germany, met with ill will and opposition in all levels of a society, possessing clear
knowledge of its aims in this portentous hour.

The skillful intrigues of the Austrian Government, which sought for a while by deceptive ap-
pearances to prove that this armed movement had
the support of all the political elements of Galicia,
were to no avail.   Clearly today the detachments
of sharpshooters have against them not merely
the judgment of the Kingdom and of Prussian Poland, but also of the majority of our fellow-
countrymen in the Austrian provinces.

Even to the least enlightened minds it became  evident that the few whose hopes were
fixed on Austria, as the only State in which our
national  rights had met with a measure of recognition, overrated her independence, not having
yet discovered that she had become the  mere
compliant tool of Prussian policy.

Today, in face of the manifest will of the
Polish Nation, which has with all the strength of
its soul come forward against Germany, in face
moreover of  the fact that Germany alone is the
opposing force, independent, conscious of her
aims-- whereas those who fight with her are sim-
ply the instruments of her schemes-- in face of
all this, any help willfully given by Poles to Germany or her allies must be looked upon as a

transgression against Poland.

The Russian army has, in Austria, already
set foot upon earth Polish in pith and marrow,
and we are now expecting its advance into those
immemorial fastnesses of our Nation which Prussia possesses.

In this grave moment there lies before our
fellow-countrymen in those parts the solemn duty
of affirming that in thought and deed they are one
with the rest of Poland.  It behooves them to protect themselves in such a manner that the enemy
shall not impose upon them even the semblance of
an act contrary to the purposes of our Nation.
Such would be accounted any opposition whatsoever of the population against the Russian Army,
an opposition which Germany will invariably
attempt to rouse in many places.

Countrymen!  For one hundred years, boundaries, which the circle of events have left un-
touched , have divided us; today, the sons of our
soil are being forced to spill the blood of brothers,
fighting in the ranks of their own enemies.  This
war, great, epoch-making, abolishes those boundaries and opens a radiant morrow of reunion for
our nation, which in spirit never suffered itself
to be divided.  This our unity we today irrefutably
confirm, for the national attitude bears testimony
to the fact that in all parts of the great land of our
fathers, we Poles have one idea, one purpose --
the unification of Poland and the laying of foundations for the free development of the Nation.

Warsaw, November 25, 1914

The Polish National Council

Zygumnt Balicki          Stanislaw Leśniowski
Stefan Badzyński         Zdzislaw Lubomirski
Stanislaw Czekanowski    Maryan Lutostawski
Seweryn Czetwertyński    Józef Nekonieczny
Henryk Dembiński         Franciszek Nowodworski
Roman Dmowski            Konstanty Plater

| Marceli Godlewski | Maciej Radziwil |
|---|---|
| Jerzy Gościcki | Jan Rudnicki |
| Wladyslaw Grabski | Jan Stecki |
| Jan Harusewicz | Ignacy Szebeko |
| Wiktor Jaroński | Zygmunt Wielopski |
| Walenty Kamocki | Józef Wielowieyski |
| Czeslaw Karpiński | Stanislaw Wojciechowski |

Maurycy Zamoyski

(Jaworski, op. cit., pp. 12-13)

7.  Independence Proclamation --Polish Kingdom of November 5, 1916.

Inspired by firm confidence in a final victory of their arms and prompted by a desire to
lead the Polish territories, wrested by their armies under heavy sacrifices from Russian domin-
ation, toward a happy future, His Majesty the
German Emperor and His Imperial Majesty the
Emperor of Austria and Apostolic King of Hungary
have resolved to form of these territories an independent State with a hereditary monarchy and
a constitutional government. The exact frontiers
of the Kingdom of Poland will be outlined later.
The new Kingdom will receive the guarantees
needed for the free development of its own forces
by a union with the two allied Powers. The glor-
ious tradition of the Polish armies of the past and
the memory of the brave Polish comrades in arms
in the great war of our days shall continue to live
in your own national army. The organization,
instruction, and command of this army will be
arranged by common agreement.

Taking due consideration of the general
political conditions prevailing in Europe and of
the welfare and the safety of their own countries
and nations, the Allied monarchs express the
confident hope that Polish wishes for the evolu-
tion of a Polish state and for the national development of a Polish Kingdom will now be fulfilled.

The great realm which the western neigh-

bors of the Kingdom of Poland will have on their
eastern frontier will be a free and happy State,
enjoying its own national life; and they will welcome with joy the birth and prosperous development of this State.

(November 5, 1916)

(Lewinski - Corwin, Edward H.  The Political History of Poland.
New York, 1917, p. 603; Kumaniecki, Wl. Odbudowa państwo-
wości polskiej, p. 48.)

8.  President Wilson's Fourteenth Point:

An independent Polish State should be erected
which should include the territories inhabited by
indisputably Polish populations, which should be
assured a free and secure access to the sea, and
whose political and economic independence and
territorial integrity should be guaranteed by
international covenant.

(January, 1917)

9.  Proclamation of the Russian Provisional Government

(Excerpts)

... The Russian Provisional Government
considers that the creation of an indepent Polish
State from all territories where the Polish people
constitute a majority of the population is a certain guarantee of durable peace in a future unified Europe.  United to Russia by a free military
alliance, the Polish State will become a strong
bulwark against the pressure of the Central
Powers against Slavism....

Russia believes that the nationalities attached to Poland by the secular bonds of common
life will obtain guarantees of their civic and
national existence. ... it will be for the Russian
Constituent Assembly finally to ratify the new
brotherly alliance and give its consent to the
changes of the Russian State territory, which

will be required for the constitution of an independent Poland from all her three parts, now divided.
...May the union of our feelings and hearts prepare the future alliance of our states.

(March 29, 1917)

(Komarnicki, Titus Rebirth of the Polish Republic; A Study in
the Diplomatic History of Europe 1914-1920.  London, 1957,
p. 156.)

10.  Declaration by Clemenceau, Lloyd George, and Orlando

The creation of a united and independent
Polish State, with free access to the sea, con-
tinues to be one of the conditions for a just and
durable peace and of the rule of right in Europe.

(June 3, 1918)

(Komarnicki, op. cit., p. 141.)

11.  Annulment of the So-called "Partition-Treaties" by the
Soviet Government

Art. 3.  All agreements and acts concluded by
the Government of the former Russian Empire
with the Government of the Kingdom of Prussia
and the Austro-Hungarian Empire referring to
the partitions of Poland are irrevocably annuled
by the present decree, since they are contrary
to the principle of the self-determination of peoples and to the revolutionary legal conceptions
of the Russian people, which recognizes the
inalienable right of the Polish nation to independence and unity...

Signed:  Chairman of the Council of People's
Commissars:

V. Ulianov-Lenin

Deputy People's Commissar for Foreign Affairs:

L. Karakhan

Executive Secretary of the Council of People's

Commissars:

Vlad. Bonch-Bruevich

(Moscow, August 29, 1918)

(Sobr. zak. i rasp. R.-K. Pravitelstva RSFSR, 1917-18, No.
64; Degras, I, 98; Documents on Polish-Soviet Relations, v. I,
p. 1.)

## 12. Announcement by the National Government

    The evident step toward self-government was the decision
of the Regency Council on October 23, whereby the government
of Józef Świeżyński was formed without an understanding with
or the approval of the occupational powers. On November 3,
that government made an announcement which threatened to up-
set the order of the Regency Council and at the same time to re-
vive the past political and unitary conditions of Poland. The
text was as follows:

    Fellow Poles! In the face of the gravest tasks
which the prevailing conditions could place upon the
Polish people, with due regard for responsibility
toward the people and history, the present Polish
government is aware of the gigantic wishes of the
whole nation and is building the foundations for a
united and free Polish nation, guarding the national freedom and boundaries, protecting the
population from famine, and creating assurance
of Polish rights in regard to relations with other
nations.

    The Polish people must give their unquali-
fied support to the government, which is both a
faithful and a strong expression of the whole national will. With full realization local interests
should be placed on a level secondary to national
interests as a whole. The present government
has initiated the creation of the National Government to govern the local areas, this being done
with the approval of political parties which represent the working people of Poland.

    The National Government, in view of the
fact that it consists of the working masses,

should emerge without opposition.  Remaining on guard until such time as the National Government will be formed to govern and until the law-making Senate is summoned, we are asking the whole nation to co-operate in this, today's most important task of constructing a Polish Republic.

Signed: Świeżński, Chrzanowski, Englich, Głąbiński, Grabski, Higersberger, Mińkiewicz, Paszkowski Ponikowski, Wierzbicki, Wolczyński.

(October 23, 1918)

(Dziennik Poznanski, 1918, No. 255.)

13.  Manifesto of the Provisional People's Government

(This provisional government, which included representatives of the left factions in Poland, was headed by Ignacy Daszyński).

To the Polish people!  Polish workers, peasants and soldiers!  Over blood-drenched, tortured humanity rises the dawn of peace and freedom. . . .

By order of the People's and Socialist Parties' former Congress Kingdom and of Galicia, we proclaim ourselves the Provisional People's Government of Poland; and, until the convening of the Constitutional Sejm, we take over complete and full authority, pledging ourselves to exercise it justly for the good and benefit of the Polish people and state, not shrinking, however, from the severe and absolute punishment of those who will not recognize in Poland the authority of Polish democracy.  As the provisional People's Government we decree and proclaim the following laws binding on the whole Polish nation from the moment of issuance of the present decree:

The Polish state, embracing all lands inhabited by the Polish people, with the seacoast of its own, is to constitute for all times a Polish People's Republic whose first President will be elected by the Constitutional Sejm.

The Constitutional <u>Sejm</u> shall be convoked by us during the current year on the basis of general, equal, direct, secret, and proportional suffrage for both sexes. Electoral regulations will be announced within the next few days. Every citizen who has reached twenty-one years of age will have the right to vote or to be elected.

From this we proclaim in Poland full equality of political and civic rights for all citizens, irrespective of origin, faith and nationality, freedom of conscience, press, speech, assembly, procession, association, trade-unionization and freedom to strike.

All donations and great landed properties in Poland are hereby declared state property. Special prescriptions will be issued to counteract land speculation.

All private as well as former government forests are declared state property; the sale and cutting of forests without special permission is prohibited from the time of the publication of the present decree.

In industry, handicrafts, and commerce we hereby introduce an eight-hour working day.

After we have finally constitutionalized ourselves, we shall at once proceed to the reorganization of community councils, county assemblies, and municipal local government, as well as the organization in towns and villages of a people's militia which will insure to the population order and safety, obedience to and execution of the orders of our legislative organs, and the proper settling of the problems of food supply for the population.

At the Constitutional <u>Sejm</u> we shall propose the following social reforms:

.          Forceful expropriation and abolition of big- and medium-sized landed property and its trans-

ference to the working people under state supervision;

Nationalization of mines, salt mines, the
oil industry, roads of communication, and other
branches of industry where this can be done at
once;

Protection of labor, unemployment, sickness
and old-age insurance;

Confiscation of capital accumulated during
the War through criminal speculation with articles
of primary necessity and supplies for the army;

Introduction of universal, obligatory, and
free lay-school education.

We shall call upon the Poles living in the
lands of the former Grand Duchy of Lithuania to
strive in brotherly harmony with the Lithuanian
and Belorussian nations for the reconstruction
of the Lithuanian state on its old historical boundaries, and upon the Poles in Eastern Galicia and
in the Ukraine to settle peacefully all controversial questions with the Ukrainian nation until they
are ultimately regulated by competent agents of
both nations. . . .

We consider it to be most important and
most urgent to organize a regular people's army.
We trust that the peasant and working youth will
gladly join the ranks of the revolutionary Polish
Army, emanating from the people, defending the
political and social rights of the working people,
faithfully and completely devoted to the People's
Government, subject only to its orders.

Polish people! The hour of your action has
struck. Take into your worn, powerful hands the
great task of liberating your land, which is soaked
with the sweat and blood of your fathers and forefathers, and bequeath to subsequent generations
a great and free united homeland. Rise united to
action, do not spare wealth or sacrifice or life
for the great task of Poland's and Polish workers'

liberation.

We call upon you, brotherly Lithuanian, Belorussian, Ukrainian, Czech, and Slovak nations, to live in harmony with us and to support each other mutually in the great work of creating an association of free and equal nations.

> The Provisional People's
> Government of the Polish
> Republic
>
> Lublin-Krakow, November 7, 1918

(Kridl, Manfred et al., For Your Freedom and Ours. New York, 1943, pp. 219-221.)

## 14. Decree Issued by Pilsudski and Moraczewski

On November 14, appeared a decree from Józef Pilsudski, as the tentative Head of State. Together with the Moraczewski Government decree it resembles a republican form. Both decrees propose:

> Upon my release from the German prison, I was confronted with the most chaotic internal and external conditions in Poland's efforts to free herself from beneath the yoke. The Polish people alone must show their organizational ability, for no external aid can help them in their restoration. I consider it my obligation to set the pattern for over-all organization, and have decided to consider and include local considerations which would characterize the new government.
>
> In the course of my conversations with the various representatives of local areas, my thoughts were, to my pleasure, met with approval. A considerable majority of them advised the formation of a government not only on a democratic basis, but also including in it representatives from village and city populace. In view of these predominant trends in both Eastern and Western Europe, I decided to nominate Ignacy Daszyński as President of the Cabinet. His patriotic and cooperative

work in the past assures me that his work will be
of considerable assistance in bringing Poland up
from ruins.

The difficult conditions of our people did
not permit him to take advantage of the experience
which our country needs at this time; I requested
the President of Ministers to consider this and to
make assignments on the basis of past experience
and without regard to political affiliations.

In view of the prevailing conditions in Poland,
the nature of our government does not permit us
to make any substantial changes until the law-
making Senate is summoned, for only the Senate
can approve such changes. I am convinced that
only the Senate can be the rightful maker of laws
in the course of its session.

Considering the legal circumstances under
which the Polish people are, I requested the President of Ministers to report on the highest representatives of the Polish Republic until such time as
the law-making Senate is summoned to rule over
all three parts.

All considerations and programs which
were placed in my hands I surrender to the present government of the Republic.

War saw                          November 14, 1918

Józef Pilsudski

(Dziennik Praw Państwa Polskiego, No. 17, Pos. 40,
1918; Jaworski, op. cit., pp. 32-33.)

15.  Decree on the Highest Representation of the Polish Republic

On the basis of a decree issued on November
14, the President of Ministers proposed a project
for the establishment of the highest representative
body of the Polish Republic. It was approved by
the Tentative People's Government of the Polish
Republic.

Approving the proposed project, I bring to

your attention the following:

**Article 1:** As the Tentative Head of the Nation, I will lead the Highest Government of the Polish Republic and will guide it until the law-making Senate is summoned.

**Article 2:** The Government of the Polish Republic shall consist of the President of Ministers and Ministers nominated and responsible to me until the Senate is summoned.

**Article 3:** The laws which are approved by the Ministerial Assembly are subject to my approval and become binding, unless there are laws to the contrary, from the time of their publication in the Daily of National Laws of Poland; they shall lose their binding effect if they are not presented to the law-making Senate for its approval during its first session.

**Article 4:** All governmental acts shall be counter-signed by the President of Ministers.

**Article 5:** The Court decisions are in the name of the Polish Republic.

**Article 6:** All officials of the Polish Nation shall take an oath to serve the Polish Republic faithfully and according to the rules of the Ministerial Assembly.

**Article 7:** The appointment of higher national officials shall be in accordance with the tentative rules set forth by me, as the Head of the Nation, and upon the proposal of the President of Ministers and the individual ministers concerned.

**Article 8:** The budget of the Polish Republic shall be approved by the Government and then presented to me for approval.

| Warsaw | President of Ministers |
|---|---|
| November 22, 1918 | Moraczewski |

Józef Pilsudski

(Dziennik Praw Państwa Polskiego, No. 17, Pos. 41, 1918;
Jaworski, op. cit., p. 33.)

## 16. Pilsudski's Declaration on Wilno

On April 21, 1919, Wilno was occupied and a day later
the following Declaration from Józef Pilsudski:

Being forcefully suppressed by (tsarist)
Russia, by Germany, and finally by the Bolsheviks,
for more than a century your Nation has not en-
joyed any noteworthy degree of freedom.

This state of continuous suppression, so
well known to us and born on this unfortunate land,
must be removed at last; and this land, as if for-
saken by God, must be ruled by freedom and
self-rule. It must fulfill the wishes and satisfy
the needs of its rightful owners.

The Polish Army, which I brought with me
to remove chaos and suppression and to install a
government chosen by the will of the people, is
bringing you freedom and independence. I wish
to give you an opportunity to settle your national
and internal affairs in any manner you may wish
and without intervention or pressure of any kind
on the part of Poland. Therefore, in spite of the
fact that on your land a war is still being waged
and blood is being spilled, we will not introduce
military rule, but will form a civil government
consisting of local people, the sons of this land.

The task of this civil government shall be:
(1) To arrange for the needs of the people and
to prepare for the future through freely elected
representatives. The elections shall be conducted on the basis of secret, universal, and
unhindered voting.

(2) To assist the populace in attaining means
of livelihood, to assist the creative activities,
to assure peace and order, to protect the welfare of all, and not to discriminate on the basis
of faith or nationality.

To head the government I have appointed
Jerzy Osmolowski. Refer to him, or to the people
whom he will appoint, with confidence and without
hesitation, in all matters which concern or which
are unjust to you.

Wilno

April 22, 1919              Pilsudski

(Monitor Polski, April 28, 1919, No. 95.)

## 17. Declaration by the Allied and Associated Powers

Even prior to this the Western Powers acknowledged
Polish national sovereignty in the agreements of 1919. The
Treaty between the Allied and Associated Powers, on the one
hand, and Poland, on the other (known as the "Treaty of Minorities," June 28, 1919), made the following declarations:

In view of this, the Allied and Associated
Powers, by employing force, returned to the
Polish people that independence of which they
were unjustly deprived.

In view of this, the Russian Government,
by its declaration of March 30, 1917, agreed to
reestablish an independent Polish State.

That the Polish State which at the present
time exercises control over areas which were
formerly parts of tsarist Russia but which are
inhabited by Poles are declared by the Great
Powers to be independent and self-governed.

In view of this, on the basis of the Peace
Treaty signed with Germany through the Allied
and Associated Powers and also signed by Poland,
certain designated areas which were formerly
under the German Kingdom shall be included in
the Polish territory.

According to the Peace Treaty mentioned
above, the Polish boundaries which were not
established by the said Treaty shall be designated at some future date and through the Allied
and Associated Powers.

The United States of America, Great Britain,
France, Italy, and Japan on their part, by their
recognition of the Polish State in the boundaries
described above, accept her as a member of the
family of independent and supreme nations. ...

June 28, 1919

(Dziennik Ustaw Rzecz. Polskiej, 1919, No. 110, Pos. 728.)

18.  Treaty of St. Germain-en-Laye

Article 89

Austria hereby recognizes and accepts the
frontiers of Bulgaria, Greece, Hungary, Poland,
Rumania, the Serb-Croat-Slovene State and the
Czecho-Slovak State as these frontiers may be
determined by the Principal Allied and Associated
Powers.

September 10, 1919

(The Treaty of St. Germain-en-laye; A Documentary History of
its Territorial and Political Clauses.  ed, Almond, Nina; Ox-
ford University Press, 1935, p. 150.)

19.  Appeal to the Ukrainians

An appeal to Ukrainians in connection with the movement
of the Polish and Ukrainian armies toward the Great Ukraine
after signing the Military Convention between Poland and the
Ukraine (Symon Petliura).

To all inhabitants of the Ukraine!

On my command, the armies of the Polish
Republic began to move forward and entered deep
into the Ukrainian land.

The inhabitants are aware of the fact that
the Polish armies will remove the various plun-
derers against whom the Ukrainian people have
risen with arms in order to protect their belong-
ings against chaos, robbery, and banditry.

The Polish armies will remain only so

long as it will be necessary for the rightful
Ukrainian government to take over.

From the time the National Government of
the Ukrainian Republic is able to function, when
the Ukrainian armies are in their full strength and
are able to defend that country against new inva-
sions and when the people are able to decide on
their own future, the Polish soldier will return
to the Polish Republic being certain that he has
fulfilled his vital task of defending the people's
freedom. Together with the Polish armies, many
of the faithful sons of the Ukraine will return to
that land under the leadership of their Ataman Symon
Petliura, who found both protection and assistance in the Polish Republic during the most try-
ing days of the Ukrainian people.

I believe that the Ukrainian people will extent their efforts to the utmost in order to help
the Polish Republic to gain its freedom and to
assure the inhabitants of their lands both of hap-
piness and of welfare, for which they will be
thankful after returning to peace and work.

To all inhabitants of the Ukraine, without
regard to origin or faith, the armies of the Polish Republic assure protection and security.

I am calling the Ukrainian people and all
inhabitants of that land to assist the Polish army
to the utmost of their ability in their bloody struggle for their own life and freedom.

                         Józef Pilsudski

                         Head Commander of the
                         Polish Armies Head-
                         quarters, April 26, 1920

(Monitor Polski, 1920, No. 97.)

In the same issue of the Polish Monitor:

The Ministry of Foreign Affairs communicates:

"The Polish Government, affirming the right
of the Ukraine to independent national existence,

recognized the Directorate of the independent
Ukrainian People's Republic, with <u>Ataman</u> Symon
Petliura as the Head of the Government of the
Ukrainian People's Republic. "

20. <u>Protocol</u> of <u>Spa</u>

Protocol of the Spa Conference of July 10, 1920.

"Poland will honor the Supreme Council
decisions regarding the Lithuanian frontier, the
future of Eastern Galicia, the Teschen problem,
and the Poland-Danzig Treaty."

At the Spa Conference President Grabski
was able to gain four points which were threatened
at first. They were: (1) Wilno will be placed not
under Russian but under Lithuanian tentative occupation; its future is to be decided upon at a conference in London. The present Polish Government did not renounce its rights to Wilno. (2)
The Eastern boundary shall be determined by the
areas which the Polish and Russian armies are
occupying at the time when the treaty is signed
and not on the line as it was decided on December
18, 1919. (3) Between the Polish and the Soviet
line will be established a neutral belt, 50 kilometres in width. (4) The representatives of
Eastern Galicia shall be admitted to London, not
as equals to the other delegates, but as consultants. The conditions proposed by the President
of Ministers were approved by the Ministry of
National Defense.

(Blociszewski, Joseph, <u>La Restauration</u> de la <u>Pologne</u> et de la
diplomatie <u>europeene</u>, Paris, 1927; <u>Monitor Polski</u>, 1920, No.
164.)

21. <u>Decision Regarding the Partition of Upper Silesia</u>

The Plebiscite in Upper Silesia was held on March 20,
1921. When a month later a rumor was spread that Poland
would acquire only the Pszczyńsk and Rybnik areas, the Poles
of Upper Silesia reached for armaments for the third time in

order to bring the unification with the rest of Poland.  This up-
rising in Upper Silesia had a decisive effect on the final decisions regarding the partition of this area which was undertaken
in the Conference of Ambassadors on October 20, 1921.

In certain cases, the decisions were as
follows:

The British Empire, France, Italy, and
Japan, who, together with the United States of
North America made up the Allied and Associated
Powers, signed the Treaty of Warsaw.

Taking into consideration the last condition
of Article 88 of the Treaty of Warsaw, it was their
responsibility to draw the border line between Germany and Poland in Upper Silesia, it agrees to
the plebiscite and to abide by its decision;

Considering that on March 20, 1921, a vote
was taken under the conditions specified by the
article mentioned above;

Considering the results of local voting, together with geographic location and economic
conditions, the questions of territorial transfers
must be settled.

After gathering the necessary facts, the
League of Nations decided:

(1)  (arrangements on and description of boundaries)
(2)  The governments of Poland and Germany, on
the basis of Article 92 of the Peace Treaty, will
hold a conference in the shortest possible time in
order to sanction the arrangements.

The Treaty concerning protection for the
national minorities, which was signed on June 28,
1919, between the United States, the British Empire, France, Italy, and Japan, on the one hand,
and Poland, on the other, brought that part of
Upper Silesia to which it pertained under Polish
domain.  Justice, as well as the difficult economic conditions in Upper Silesia, demands that
the Government of Germany be responsible, for
no less than the next fifteen years, for putting the

following articles into effect, beginning with the
final settlement of territorial claims: 1, 2, 7, 8,
and 9 (sections 1 and 2), 10, 11, and 12, concerning
Upper Silesia, thus, bringing it into the German
sphere.

The agreements which will be made between
the governments of Poland and Germany in order
to put the above-mentioned proposals into practice
will oblige Poland and Germany to consider them
as having international significance and will be
placed under the care of the League of Nations in
the same manner as the proposals of the Treaty
of June 28, 1919.

All petitions from individuals and/or col-
lected on the part of the inhabitants of Upper
Silesia to the Assembly of the League of Nations,
regarding these proposals or fulfillments of proposals of the Treaty of June 28, 1919, if such
proposals pertain to individuals belonging to racial, religious, or linquistic minorities, shall be
directed to the government under whose jurisdiction the petitioners are living permanently.
That government shall be under obligation to
send such petitions, with or without comments,
to the League of Nations for investigation.

The following shall be established to insure
that the proposals are carried out:

(1)  Upper Silesian Mixed Commission, consisting
of two Germans and two Poles originally from Upper Silesia, together with a representative from
another nationality appointed through the League
of Nations.

(2)  A legal system which would settle all private
disputes arising from the above-mentioned commission.  This system should consist of one arbitrator appointed by the German government and
one arbitrator appointed by the government of Poland.  The League of Nations will be requested to
appoint a presiding official of this tribunal.

All disputes pertaining to the fulfillment
and the interpretation of the present agreement
shall be settled in accordance with the present

agreements.

(3)  The rules of convention, as specified by
Article II at this time, will be put into effect by
one German official and one Polish official, under
the supervision of an individual appointed by the
League of Nations and authorized to break a tie
in case of dispute.

(This agreement was signed on May 22, 1922,
in Geneva.  Part of Upper Silesia was granted to
Poland, and part of Teschen Silesia entered into
the Republic as an autonomous area of Silesia for
which the organic status was approved in the Senate of July 15, 1920.)

May 22, 1922

(Dziennik Ustaw Rzecz. Polskiej, 1922, No. 44, Pos. 369.)

22.  Decision of the Conference of Ambassadors, March 15, 1923

(Excerpts)

The British Empire, France, Italy and Japan,
signatories with the United States of America as
the principal Allied and Associated Powers of the
Peace Treaty of Versailles,

Whereas under Article 87, paragraph 3 of
the same Treaty it is for them to fix frontiers of
Poland not specified in that Treaty;

Whereas the Polish Government submitted
to the Conference of Ambassadors on February
15, 1923 a request that the Powers represented
thereon should make use of the rights conferred
upon them by the said article;

And the Lithuanian Government for its part
had previously expressed in its Note dated November 18, 1922 its desire that the said Powers should
make use of the said rights;

Whereas, under Article 91 of the Peace
Treaty of St. Germain-en-Laye, Austria renounced
in favour of the principal Allied and Associated
Powers all its rights and titles to the territories

formerly belonging to the Austro-Hungarian Monarchy, which, being situated without the new frontiers of Austria as described in Article 27 of that
Treaty, have not yet been assigned to any other
state;

Whereas it is recognized by Poland that ethno-
graphical conditions necessitate an autonomous regime in the Eastern part of Galicia;

Whereas the Treaty concluded between the
principal Allied and Associated Powers and Poland
on June 28, 1919 provides in respect of all territories placed under Polish sovereignty special
guarantees for racial, linquistic or religious minorities;

Whereas as regards her common frontier
with Russia, Poland has entered into direct negotiations with that State with a view to determing
the line of that frontier;

And whereas, as regards the frontier between
Poland and Lithuania, account must be taken of the
de facto situation by the Resolution of the Council of
the League of Nations dated February 3, 1923,

Have entrusted the Conference of Ambassadors with the settlement of this question.

The Conference of Ambassadors therefore:
I. Decides to recognize as the Polish frontier:
(1)  With Russia:
A line drawn and delimited by agreement
between the two States and on their responsibility
on November 23, 1922.
(2)  With Lithuania:
A line described below (according to the
German map on the scale of 1/100, 000):

. . . .

The demarcation of this line on the ground
is entrusted to the Governments concerned, which
shall have absolute discretion to carry out, by
common agreement, such rectifications of detail
as they may consider indispensable after visiting
the spot.

II.   Decides to assign to Poland, who accept the decision, all rights of sovereignty over the territories situated within the frontiers defined above, and the other frontiers of Polish territory,   subject to the provisions of the Treaty of Peace of St. Germain-en-Laye regarding the duties and obligations incumbent on the States to which any territory of the former Austro-Hungarian Monarchy is transferred.

Done at Paris, on the fifteenth day of March, nineteen hundred and twenty-three.

> Eric PHIPPS.
> Romano AVEZZANA.
> Romano POINCARE
> M. MATSUDA.

The undersigned, being duly authorized declares, in the name of the Polish Government that he accepts the above provisions.

> Paris
> March 15, 1923
> Maurice ZAMOYSKI

(LNTS, vol. 15, p. 260.)

23. Decision of the Crimea Conference, February 12, 1945

(Excerpts)

"A new situation has been created in Poland as a result of her complete liberation by the Red Army. This calls for the establishment of a Polish provisional government which can be more broadly based than was possible before the recent liberation of western Poland. The provisional government which is now functioning in Poland should, therefore, be reorganized on a broader democratic basis with the inclusion of democratic leaders from Poland itself and from Poles abroad. This new government should then be called the Polish Provisional Government of National Unity.

"Mr. Molotov, Mr. Harriman, and Sir A. Clark Kerr are authorized as a commission to consult in the first instance in Moscow with members of the present Provisional Government and with other Polish democratic leaders from within Poland and from abroad, with a view to the reorganization of the present government along the above lines. This Polish Provisional Government of National Unity shall be pledged to the holding of free and unfettered elections as soon as possible on the basis of universal suffrage and secret ballot. In these elections all democratic and anti-Nazi parties shall have the right to take part and to put forward candidates.

"When a Polish Provisional Government of National Unity has been properly formed in conformity with the above, the Government of the USSR, which now maintains diplomatic relations with the present Provisional Government of Poland, and the Government of the United Kingdom and the Government of the United States of America will establish diplomatic relations with the

241

new Polish Government of National Unity and will
exchange ambassadors, by whose reports the respective governments will be kept informed about
the situation in Poland.

"The three heads of government consider
that the eastern frontier of Poland shall follow
the Curzon line with digressions from it in some
regions of five to eight kilometers in favor of
Poland. They recognize that Poland must receive
substantial accessions of territory in the north
and west. They feel that the opinion of the new
Polish Provisional Government of National Unity
should be sought in due course on the extent of
these accessions and that the final delimitation
of the western frontier of Poland should thereafter await the peace conference."

February 12, 1945

(Konovalov, S., Russo-Polish Relations; An Historical Survey,
Princeton University Press, 1945, pp. 101-102; Dept. of State
Bulletin, vol. 12, No. 295, February 18, 1945; Shotwell, James
T., Poland and Russia, 1919-1945, New York, 1945, pp. 108-
109.)

24. Report of the Tripartite Conference of Berlin, August 2,
1945

(Excerpts)

VIII. Poland.

The Conference considered questions relating to the Polish Provisional Government and
the western boundary of Poland.

On the Polish Provisional Government of
National Unity they defined their attitute in the
following statement:

A. We have taken note with pleasure of the agreement reached among representative Poles from
Poland and abroad which made possible the formation, in accordance with the decisions reached
at the Crimea Conference, of a Polish Provisional Government of National Unity recognized by
the three Powers. The establishment of the
British and United States governments of diplo-

matic relations with the Polish Provisional Government has resulted in the withdrawal of their recognition from the former Polish Government in London, which no longer exists. The British and
United States governments have taken measures
to protect the interest of the Polish Provisional
Government as the recognized Government of the
Polish State, in the property belonging to the Polish State located in their territories and under
their control, whatever the form of this property
may be. They have further taken measures to
prevent alienation to third parties of such property. All proper facilities will be given to the
Polish Provisional Government for the exercise
of the ordinary legal remedies for the recovery
of any property belonging to the Polish State which
may have been wrongfully alienated.

The three Powers are anxious to assist the
Polish Provisional Government in facilitating the
return to Poland as soon as practicable of all
Poles abroad who wish to go, including members
of the Polish armed forces and the merchant
marine. They expect that those Poles who return home shall be accorded personal and property rights on the same basis as all Polish citizens.

The three Powers note that the Polish provisional Government, in accordance with the decisions of the Crimea Conference, has agreed to
the holding of free and unfettered elections as
soon as possible on the basis of universal suffrage and secret ballot in which all democratic
and anti-Nazi parties shall have the right to take
part and to put forward candidates, and that
representatives of the Allied press shall enjoy
full freedom to report to the world the develop-
ments in Poland before and during the elections.

B. The following agreement was reached on the
Western Frontier of Poland:

In conformity with the agreement on Poland,
reached at the Crimea Conference, the three heads

of Government have sought the opinion of the Polish Provisional Government of National Unity in
regard to the accession of territory in the north
and west which Poland should receive. The President of the National Council of Poland and members of the Polish Provisional Government of
National Unity have been received at the Conference and have fully presented their views. The
three heads of Government reaffirm their opinion
that the final delimitation of the western frontier
of Poland should await the peace settlement.

The three heads of Government agree that,
pending the final determination of Poland's western
frontier, the former German territories east of a
line running from the Baltic Sea immediately west
of Sinnemuende, and thence along the Oder River
to the confluence of the western Neisse River and
along the Western Neisse River to the Czechoslovak frontier, including that portion of East Prussia
not placed under the administration of the Union
of Soviet Socialist Republics in accordance with
the understanding reached at this Conference and
including the area of the former free city of Danzig shall be under the administration of the Polish
State and for such purposes should not be considered as part of the Soviet zone of occupation
in Germany.

XII.   Orderly Transfer of German Population.

The three Governments, having considered
the question in all its aspects, recognize that the
transfer to Germany of German populations, or
elements thereof, remaining in Poland, Czechoslovakia, and Hungary, will have to be undertaken. They agree that any transfers that take
place should be effected in an orderly and humane
manner.

Since the influx of a large number of Germans into Germany would increase the burden
already resting on the occupying authorities,
they consider that the Control Council in Germany should, in the first instance, examine the

problem, with special regard to the question of the equitable distribution of these Germans among the several zones of occupation. They are accordingly instructing their respective representatives on the Control Council to report to their Governments as soon as possible, the extent to which such persons have already entered Germany from Poland, Czechoslovakia and Hungary, and to submit an estimate of the time and rate at which further transfers could be carried out having regard to the present situation in Germany.

The Czechoslovak Government, the Polish Provisional Government, and the Control Council in Hungary are at the same time being informed of the above and are being requested meanwhile to suspend further explusions pending an examination by the Governments concerned of the report from their representatives on the Control Council.

April 2, 1945

(British and Foreign State Papers, vol. 145, pp. 864-68.)

## 25. De Jure Recognition of Poland

| | |
|---|---|
| Russia: | On March 30, 1917, by the Russian Provisional Government; October 28, 1917, by the Decree of RNK of the RSFSR |
| France: | February 24, 1919 |
| Great Britain: | February 25, 1919 |
| Italy: | February 27, 1919 |
| USA: | January 30, 1919 |
| Germany: | November 21, 1918, de facto; May 18, 1919, de jure |
| Belgium: | March 6, 1919 |
| Japan: | March 22, 1919 |
| Brazil: | April 15, 1919 |
| Czechoslovakia: | May 28, 1919 |

| | |
|---|---|
| Spain: | May 30, 1919 |
| Sweden: | June 3, 1919 |
| Rumania: | June 21, 1919 |
| Argentina: | July 7, 1919 |
| Chile: | August 28, 1919 |
| Paraguay: | September 1, 1919 |

# INDEX BY COUNTRIES

247